# No Ordinary Dog

# No Ordinary Dog

My Partner from the SEAL Teams
to the Bin Laden Raid

## Will Chesney

with Joe Layden

St. Martin's Press
New York

First published in the United States by St. Martin's Press, an imprint of St. Martin's Publishing Group

NO ORDINARY DOG. Copyright © 2020 by Willard Chesney. All rights reserved. Printed in the United States of America. For information, address St. Martin's Publishing Group, 120 Broadway, New York, NY 10271.

www.stmartins.com

Designed by Omar Chapa

The Library of Congress Cataloging-in-Publication Data is available upon request.

ISBN 978-1-250-17695-0 (hardcover)
ISBN 978-1-250-17696-7 (ebook)

Our books may be purchased in bulk for promotional, educational, or business use. Please contact your local bookseller or the Macmillan Corporate and Premium Sales Department at 1-800-221-7945, extension 5442, or by email at MacmillanSpecialMarkets@macmillan.com.

First Edition: April 2020

10  9  8  7  6  5  4  3  2  1

FOR CAIRO

# Acknowledgments

I want to thank everyone who came together to make this book possible. It has been a pleasure working with my editor, Marc Resnick, assistant editor, Hannah O'Grady, and the entire team at St. Martin's Press who worked so hard to put this project together. It's been a long road!

My co-writer, Joe Layden, has made the difficult process of telling Cairo's story much easier and even enjoyable at times. As much as I miss Cairo, it has been rewarding to have an opportunity to share memories of our time together.

Special thanks to producers Mark Semos and Jay Pollak from The Reserve Label and Cairo Holdings, and a big thank-you to Producer Alan Rautbort. And thanks also to our literary agent, Frank Weimann.

I would like to thank the U.S. Navy and the SEAL teams for allowing me to serve my country and giving me the opportunity to participate in countless great events. I want to thank my teammates for always being there and their families for allowing them to be. I would like to acknowledge everyone who served or who is currently serving in any capacity, to keep this country safe. Most notably, I want to recognize my fallen brothers in the military who have made the ultimate sacrifice.

I would also like to thank everyone who has helped me get through the difficult times transitioning out of the Navy, both on a personal and medical side. Natalie Kelley was there for me (and Cairo) when I needed a lot of support, and I will always be grateful. There were many doctors and support personnel at various treatment centers I attended: your kindness and expertise meant the world to me and helped me on the path to recovery. Among this group I would like to specifically recognize Kara Williams and the staff of the Brain Treatment Foundation for all their hard work on behalf of veterans. There are many other friends and teammates who helped on a personal level, too many to name individually here, and I don't want to leave anyone out. You know who you are!

I would like to thank my mother and father for providing me with a loving home and family and for supporting my decision to enter the Navy and chase my dream of becoming a SEAL. Thanks for always being there for me.

Finally, I would like to thank God for watching over me through times good and bad.

# Introduction

This may not be quite the story you are expecting. I might as well make that clear from the outset.

I served thirteen years in the U.S. Navy, including eleven as a SEAL, participating in countless operations and missions as part of the post-9/11 war on terrorism. As a member of SEAL team ████████ I was on the ground in Pakistan in the spring of 2011, when the highest of high-value targets, Osama bin Laden, was shot and killed. So it's fair to say that I have seen some shit. But that is only part of the story here, and not the most important part.

You see, while I have had the privilege of serving alongside some of the bravest and best men you could ever hope to meet, I also had the distinct honor of working and living with an unusual and unsung hero whose role in modern warfare—specifically counterterrorism—is hard to comprehend. Unless, of course, you served with him or one of his fellow four-legged warriors.

I grew up with dogs, had always been a dog lover, but I had no idea of the extent to which canines had been incorporated into the military until I became a SEAL and began to hear the stories. I remember walking into a training room once, early in my tenure, and hearing the following directive:

"Raise your hand if your life has ever been saved by a dog."

Without hesitation, roughly 90 percent of the men in the room lifted their arms. They did not laugh. They did not smile. This was serious, earnest business.

A dog can save your life? It sure as hell can. In my case, many times over. Both on and off the battlefield.

This is my story, but it is also the story of one of those military working dogs, or MWDs (more accurately, he was part of a particularly advanced subset of MWDs known as *combat assault dogs*, or CADs; and he was the most famous of them all, thanks to his participation in the raid on bin Laden's compound), a canine SEAL named Cairo, a seventy-pound Belgian Malinois who jumped out of planes, fast-roped out of helicopters, traversed streams and rivers, sniffed out roadside IEDs, and disarmed—literally, in some cases—insurgents. In short, he did everything expected of his human counterparts, and he did it with unblinking loyalty and unwavering courage. I would have taken a bullet for him, and he did in fact take one for me. So this is his book as much as it is mine. Maybe more.

I first met Cairo in the summer of 2008. I'd been in the navy for six years by that time, almost all of it as a SEAL, and had been through multiple deployments, most recently to Iraq. I was stationed in Virginia, satisfied with my work, and not really looking for any big changes. But when I was introduced to the canine program, it immediately caught my interest. I had rottweilers and pit bulls as a kid, but had never bothered to do any training with them. They were pets and companions, not working dogs. Fortunately, in those early days of MWDs being incorporated into Special Operations, experience was not a hard-core prerequisite for becoming a dog handler; all you had to do was express an interest in the job, and suddenly there you were, attached 24-7 to a magnificent Malinois (German shepherds, Dutch shepherds, and Labrador retrievers have also been used as MWDs, but the Malinois—basically a smaller, leaner, more agile version of the shepherd—is the ideal combat assault dog).

Not everyone is a dog person—I think sometimes you are either born with that trait or you are not—and not every SEAL wants to babysit an animal both at home and on deployment. My fellow SEALs were all happy to have Cairo out in front of us when we approached a quiet compound in the middle of the night, unsure of whether the perimeter was lined with explosives or how many people were lying in wait. And when not on the job, he was the sort of dog—friendly, playful—that encouraged human interaction; simply put, just about everyone on the team loved him.

But to take on the burden of being a dog's handler? That was left to someone who really wanted the job. Someone who understood and embraced the designation.

That was me. Cairo was my dog. And I was his dad. I don't use that term euphemistically. The relationship between a handler and a canine SEAL is profound and intimate. It goes well beyond friendship and the usual ties that bind man to dog. The training is experiential and all-encompassing, a round-the-clock immersion designed to foster not just expertise but an attachment of uncommon depth and complexity.

Anyone who has ever shared his life with a dog understands the symbiotic nature of the relationship—how a dog relies on his master for sustenance and shelter, and responds with love and loyalty so unconditional that it can take your breath away. Well, take that relationship and multiply it tenfold, and then factor in the almost incomprehensible bond that is forged when a dog puts his life on the line for you and your brothers, every single day, and you get an idea of what it was like for Cairo and me—and indeed for almost anyone who is fortunate enough to be the handler of a canine SEAL.

So, yeah, in a very real sense, I *was* Cairo's dad, as close to him as a father is to a son.

He was three years old when I met him, having already graduated from a class of potential military candidates and emerged as a one percenter—a dog with not only freakish athletic ability and sensory gifts but a tireless work ethic, as well. In short, a dog who might become a SEAL. But there was something else about Cairo that made him special: an affectionate and laid-back demeanor that in other dogs might be grounds for dismissal. A military working dog, after all, must be a fighter, first and foremost, and in many cases, that trait is not easily juxtaposed with gentle companionship.

Cairo was different. He had the ability to throw a switch. When it was time to go to work, he would work. And his work was exhausting, dangerous, and sometimes bloody. Cairo was exceptional—the product of centuries of natural evolution, impeccable breeding, rigorous training, and, let's be honest, a winning ticket in the genetic lottery. But there was something else that made him special, a ferocious drive to hunt and perform and to serve; as with his human counterparts in Special Operations, Cairo seemed fearless and indefatigable.

That isn't quite true, of course. Everyone who has walked into battle understands what it is like to experience fear; certainly, I felt it. Just as we all experienced pain and injury and exhaustion. Dogs are animals, driven by nothing so much as instinct—it is their natural inclination to withdraw from danger and to rest when weary. They are not so different from humans in that regard. So it shouldn't come as much of a surprise to learn that on the way to becoming MWDs in Special Operations, dogs must pass through a funnel every bit as narrow as the one that culls roughly 80 percent of the men who enter the navy's SEAL program. And for those who make it further, the selection process is even more rigorous.

It isn't for everyone; nor should it be. Let's face it—most people don't want to enlist in the navy. And most people in the navy have enough self-awareness and good sense to know that they don't want to endure the agony of SEAL training. Of those who do take the plunge, most quickly discover they are in over their heads. It's a self-selecting program, with the overwhelming majority of men who enter the infamous thirty-week training program known as *Basic Underwater Demolition/Seal* (*BUD/S*) weeded out not through injury or expulsion but through the simple act of surrender.

In a word, quitting.

That's the whole point of BUD/S—not just to teach the basics of naval Special Operations and to produce skilled military tacticians but to find through natural selection the true warriors, men who will not quit under any circumstances.

The same basic tenets apply when it comes to developing military working dogs. Physical attributes are essential, but all the speed and strength in the world is useless if a dog freezes at the sound of a rocket-propelled grenade exploding into a hillside, or if instinct wins out and he withers in the face of enemy gunfire, or refuses to enter a darkened room because the last time he did this, a bad guy stabbed or shot him.

It is a fact of life that military dogs are at enormous risk for sustaining injury, as they are often the first members of a SEAL unit on the ground and thus first in harm's way. Even armed with the most advanced technology, human soldiers are no match for canines when it comes to detecting explosive devices and ferreting out bad guys in hiding. It was part of Cairo's job to search the perimeter before we advanced on a building or compound. Similarly, he often was the first member of the troop to enter a dark and dangerous building. He did this repeatedly and with unwavering reliability; he did it fearlessly.

Like I said, humans aren't supposed to do this sort of thing; nor are dogs. It's not natural. It's not . . . *normal*. But some of them do. Cairo was one of them. He could sniff out an IED and in the process save dozens of lives. He could, and would, venture into a compound fairly buzzing with bad guys and yank some heavily armed asshole out of a closet before the guy could get off a shot. Did Cairo realize he was risking his life for the sake of his human counterparts? Probably not. But he knew that his work was dangerous; I don't doubt that for a second. He did it, anyway, and he did it with not just skill and professionalism but with little regard for his own safety.

In the mountains of Afghanistan, on mission after mission, Cairo was a fighting machine—a military asset every bit as valuable as an AK-47 or night-vision goggles. But when it was time to go home and hang out with Dad, he could do that, as well. We'd sit on the couch and watch movies together. He'd eat steak right next to me. He would sleep in my bed. He could be trusted with strangers and kids; this was especially true after he retired. He was, in my estimation, a damn-near perfect dog.

If I do my job right, this book will be a tribute to Cairo, a story that captures not just the extraordinary work he did in support of the U.S. military and the enormous time and effort that goes into the making of a great military dog but what he did for me personally. He was, in many ways, my closest friend. I lost him for a while when our careers went in different directions, and then I got him back long enough to care for him when his health failed. In turn, he cared for me when I needed him most, when the emotional and physical scars of battle, including a traumatic brain injury, took a toll so heavy that I wasn't sure I could handle it.

My hope is that this will not be quite like anything you've

read before. Although there will be battlefield scenes and blood-shed, it will not be as violent as some of the books that have come before it. I want to focus on the exhaustive and intricate training that went into making Cairo the extraordinary sol-dier he was; and what he meant to his fellow fighters, and to me personally; and why I went to such enormous lengths to cut through the bureaucracy that nearly kept us apart in his waning years.

There is a code of quiet selflessness among SEALs, an acknowledgment that while the work we do is serious and important, we are not, individually, *special.* We are a team united in purpose, none of us more vital than the next. I am proud of my military service and of my work as a Navy SEAL, but I am keenly aware of the fact that there are men who did much more . . . who sacrificed more. I share this story not because I seek the spotlight—indeed, I have always withdrawn from its glare—but to honor my fellow soldiers, including a mul-tipurpose canine military dog named Cairo, who was in many ways just as human as the rest of us.

We fought together, lived together, bled together. Cairo was right by my side when we flew through Pakistani airspace that night in 2011. He was an integral part of the most famous mis-sion in SEAL history. After nearly a decade of pursuit, he helped us get the ultimate bad guy, and he was no more or less vital than anyone else on the mission.

But the story doesn't end there, and it doesn't end on a high note. It never does with dogs, right? Someone once said that buying a dog is like buying a small tragedy. You know on the very first day how it all will turn out. But that's not the point, is it? It's the journey that counts, what you give the dog and what you get in return; Cairo gave me more than I ever imagined, probably more than I deserved.

This is for you, buddy.

# No
# Ordinary
# Dog

# Chapter 1

Five feet ten inches tall. One hundred seventy-five pounds.

That's the average size of a U.S. Navy SEAL. Not exactly superhero proportions. I'm not here to dispel myths, but the truth is, SEALs for the most part look like ordinary guys. Fit as hell, sure, especially by the end of BUD/S, but not in a larger-than-life way, which I guess only goes to show that the old adage is true: you can't judge a book by its cover.

There is no "typical" SEAL. We come from all walks of life and from all parts of the country. I knew guys who struggled to get through high school. I knew others who were straight-A college graduates. Most of us were in our late teens or early twenties, full of adolescent energy; others were a decade older, already settled into an adult life that I could barely comprehend. I got to know guys who had been exceptional athletes and who had physiques that appeared to have been chiseled from granite. Most of them didn't make the cut. I also knew guys who were physically unimpressive and had little in the way of formal athletic training. Most of them fell by the wayside, too. That's the nature of the SEAL program—doesn't matter where you are from or what you have accomplished or failed to accomplish before you hit the beach in Coronado, California, for the start of BUD/S. You're going to get your ass kicked; in all likelihood, you'll find the experience so miserable that you'll give up.

That is precisely the way it's supposed to be. It's not that the navy wouldn't like more SEALs—it's just that process is so relentlessly awful that only 20 percent succeed. The failure rate has remained consistent almost since the program began in the early 1960s, although modern-day SEALs can actually trace their lineage to the underwater demolition teams of World War II and the Korean War. This is by design. The point of BUD/S is not simply to torture the poor souls who are accepted into the training program but to ensure that only the strongest reach the finish line.

There is a method to the madness, and it is simply this: war is hell, and SEALs will venture into the fire in a uniquely dangerous and clandestine manner. They are expected to be physically fit, mentally strong, psychologically resilient, smart, and ferociously devoted to the cause. It's not about blind patriotism, although SEALs are some of the most patriotic people I have ever known; nor is it about recklessly engaging in combat. Special Operations work is far more technical and precise than that; it requires discipline and diligence as much as it does courage or bloodlust. Indeed, to see a frequently outnumbered SEAL unit moving methodically and efficiently through a darkened building, eliminating one armed combatant after another in search of a high-value target, is to see a team working with machinelike precision. There is no room for the cowboy or the rogue warrior in this scenario. There is only professionalism and 100 percent commitment to the mission.

It's not mindless execution, either, since the SEAL frequently encounters situations that vary dramatically from what he'd anticipated. You learn to think on your feet and to respond accordingly. It's a brutal and often bloody job, one with extraordinarily high stakes, and no one pretends otherwise, so it makes sense that BUD/S is designed to eliminate all but the best candidates for this type of service.

There have been only minor changes made to the program over the years, and most of those, in the form of oversight and better medical care, have been instilled primarily for safety reasons. The beatdown is as relentless as it has ever been. Whatever growth there has been in the United States Navy's Sea, Air, and Land (SEAL) program, it is not a result of BUD/S softening; it is just a function of more people entering the program. In the end, the result is always the same.

Twenty percent graduate.

Eighty percent fail.

What made me arrogant (or stupid) enough to think I'd be one of the 20 percent? I don't have a good answer for that. Thinking about it now, as a thirty-four-year-old veteran with the wisdom of hindsight, it seems almost crazy. I enlisted in the navy, entered the SEAL program, and . . . well, I just kept putting one foot in front of the other. There was nothing special about my background. I was an ordinary kid from nowhere, Texas (actually a little town called Lumberton, located about fifteen miles north of Beaumont and a hundred miles east of Houston). But I wouldn't quit. I knew what I wanted, and what I wanted was to be a Navy SEAL.

I couldn't have been much more than twelve or thirteen years old when I started thinking about joining the military. And not just any branch of the service—I wanted to be a SEAL. I can't really explain why I felt this way. A lot of people end up in the military because of lineage—they have close family members who served with distinction—and those that are drawn to Special Operations often have a background in sports or outdoor activities, such as hunting or fishing.

None of this really applied to me. I had a grandfather who

had served in the navy and an uncle who had been in the army, but their service did not have a deep or persistent impact on my life; although I spent a fair amount of time with them, it wasn't like I grew up hearing war stories at the dinner table. Despite being reared in East Texas, I wasn't much of an outdoorsman, either. I did a little fishing as a kid, but I did not own a rifle and wasn't an avid hunter. I wasn't involved with the Cub Scouts or the Boy Scouts. I did some hiking and camping, and I liked being outdoors, but I was hardly an expert on wilderness survival. In middle school, if you'd thrown me down in a remote area, I likely would have sat there crying until someone came to my rescue. I wouldn't have known how to forage for edible plants or find my way home.

This didn't change much in high school, either. Although I played some football—because, after all, it was Texas—I wasn't exceptionally talented. By tenth grade, I'd reached the conclusion that certain things in life were more important than others; at the top of the list, not surprisingly, were girls. If you wanted to have access to girls, you really needed a car. And if you wanted a car, then you needed money to buy the car. I suppose in some families, Mom or Dad provided the car and cash, but that wasn't the case for me, nor for most of my friends.

I grew up in a trailer park, which might sound worse than it was. It was kind of a nice trailer park, and though my parents split up while I was in school, we all got along reasonably well, and I spent time at both homes. I never thought of myself as poor, but I was certainly aware of the fact that I had less than many other kids at school. It didn't particularly bother me, and I never felt sorry for myself. It was just the way things were. Both my parents worked, and at the end of the day, there just wasn't a lot of money left over. I was an only child, so I spent a lot of time by myself, trying to figure things out. For better or worse, I was a bit of a loner. But I was also a self-sufficient kid.

I don't remember talking to my mother or father about wanting a set of wheels. There was no point. I knew what the answer would be. So instead, I slowly gave up sports and other extracurricular activities in exchange for a job at a local restaurant. And by restaurant, I mean a fried fish place that specialized in catfish—see, southeastern Texas bleeds into western Louisiana; Lumberton is only about an hour from Lake Charles, so I grew up with a bit of bayou culture, as well. Working at a catfish restaurant isn't the most glamorous job in the world, but I didn't mind. I'd wash dishes, clean the floors, bus tables . . . and generally do whatever was asked. I was one of the youngest kids in my peer group to have a job; far from being angry or embarrassed about it, I was proud to be out making my own money so that I didn't have to ask my parents for things they couldn't afford.

A lot of people look back on their first job and cringe at the memory. Not me. There was something appealing about showing up for work, being assigned a task, executing it to the best of my ability, and then going home at the end of the shift, knowing I was fifty or sixty bucks closer to buying a car, and proud that I hadn't screwed anything up along the way. Whatever I was asked to do, I did. And I did it to the best of my ability and without bitching about it. I learned to keep pushing the proverbial mop until the job was done, and I kept my mouth shut—skills that would prove invaluable when I was getting my nuts punched 24-7 during Hell Week at BUD/S, and during much of my time in the navy, for that matter.

I did all right in school, and I had some street smarts, but I wasn't exactly blessed with great intellect. Similarly, I wasn't the most athletic kid. But I learned early on that I was a lot more resilient than most people. I could get my ass kicked and come back for more. I could go to a shitty job, day after day, and come home smelling like catfish and grease, night after night, and not whine about how much it sucked.

Well, most of the time, anyway.

By the time I was a junior in high school, I had opted for a work-study program that got me out of the classroom half the day so that I could work more hours and earn more money. I learned a hard lesson when I got fired for not putting in enough effort at one of my jobs, working as a landscaper for the local school district. Totally my fault. I tried to learn from that mistake. When you have a job, you do it. You don't complain about it, and you don't ask someone else to do it for you. Try to figure out what you want, and then go after it. If you want something badly enough, you devote every ounce of energy and focus to making it happen. No bullshit. No excuses.

Eventually, when I was close to graduating, I went to work for a company that specialized in the construction and service of cell towers and other high-rise structures. This provided an opportunity to work alongside my father, who also worked for the company, and who got me the job. On the plus side, it was real money—significantly more than I had earned mowing lawns or washing dishes. On the negative side, my father was my boss, which I think is tough for any kid.

I love my dad; we have a close relationship. Still, working for him was not the best experience of my life. But I didn't let it affect my performance on the job. He was my boss, and you don't always agree with your boss. That's another lesson that served me well. Here's the other thing about that job that proved invaluable: to do it well—or do it all—I had to conquer a significant level of fear. See, I'm terrified of heights. Or, at least, I used to be. Weird, right, considering that SEALs routinely parachute from planes or fast-rope out of a helicopter? Or, as I would discover, spend an inordinate amount of time hiking across the jagged ridgeline of a mountain in some remote Afghanistan province.

For some reason, though, none of those SEAL-related tasks

affected me quite as acutely as working on a tower, a hundred feet in the open air and broad daylight. With skydiving, the ride up is the worst part. Once you reach a certain altitude, it's no big deal: you just step out into the sky and let your gear do its job. There is no time to think or fret about the multiple ways in which things can go wrong. It's almost surreal. One minute you're sitting in the back of a plane, the next you are, quite literally, flying. In Special Operations, more often than not, you jump at night, anyway. But even in the daytime, skydiving is far less intimidating (to me, anyway) than a simple climbing exercise. From ten thousand feet, the earth doesn't even look real. It's just an enormous tapestry laid out before you, waiting to reach up and cradle you as you float gently to the ground.

But climbing? Hand over fist, for long stretches of time, with a hard and real view of the ground right there in front of you?

That will mess with your head in a whole different way.

Again, this is another of those things that makes it so hard to predict who is cut out for BUD/S and who isn't. Just as you never know how someone will react to battle until the first shots are fired, it's virtually impossible to know who will wilt under the relentless pressure of and exhaustion of BUD/S and who will find the inner strength to endure. The loudest and most arrogant guys are often the first to call it quits—not a surprise, because all that bluster just masks a lot of insecurity. Conversely, some of the quietest guys find a way to keep going, without complaint.

A lot of people who are afraid of heights wouldn't even think about becoming a SEAL. An innate sense of self-preservation, combined with a desire to avoid embarrassment at all costs, would squash that dream before it even started. I figured it was an obstacle to overcome, but one that was hardly insurmountable. Every day, I showed up to work with my father and scaled up the bones of a tower or derrick, butterflies rumbling in my stomach. For the better part of eight hours, percolating in the South Texas heat and humidity, I'd push through my fear and anxiety. I wouldn't say I ever got comfortable in that environment, but after a while I did become somewhat desensitized. By simply adhering to the routine and facing my fears every single day, I was able to cope with something I found extremely discomforting. I hated the job and the anxiety it provoked, but I liked the money, and I knew on some level that the experience would prove beneficial if I ever got a chance to enter the SEAL training program.

Most of this happened on a subconscious level. I was only seventeen years old and just trying to save some money before getting out of town. Looking back now, though, I can see how much I learned from that job and how it helped me to prepare for the challenges that lay ahead.

I graduated from high school in the spring of 2002. By that time, I had already enlisted in the U.S. Navy. Although I was a senior in high school on September 11, 2001, and thus a prime candidate to be instantly provoked into service by the sight of the Twin Towers crumbling to the ground, that wasn't really the case. Don't get me wrong—I was filled with anger and sadness by what happened on 9/11, and it contributed to my wanting to get out there and help find the people responsible for the attack and contribute in any way possible to making sure that it never happened again. It's just that I had already decided that I was not only going to enter the military, I would also become a Navy SEAL. I knew that if I hung around my little town, and especially my neighborhood, I'd likely not amount to much. There was a significant drug scene among the kids in our trailer park, and it would have been easy to get sucked into it if I had stuck around. I had no interest in college, so my options were limited.

I also had no burning desire to simply serve in the navy. I want to be honest about that. There is nothing wrong with traditional military service. It's vital to the American way of life and the freedom we value. But for me, as a seventeen-year-old kid itching to leave Texas and do something special with my life, and no real plan for making it happen?

For me, it was the SEALs or nothing.

The thing is, to become a SEAL, you have to start by enlisting in the navy. I did that many months before graduating from high school, with grudging cooperation from my parents. See, you can't enlist in the military at the age of seventeen unless your parents sign the appropriate consent forms. My mom naturally had some reservations, if only because she questioned whether I knew what I was getting myself into, and because, after all, our country had just been attacked by terrorists, and at that time, no one had any idea what the ensuing military response entailed. My father, however, was into it; he was proud as hell that I wanted to be a SEAL. That's the way I presented it to my parents. Not, "I want to enlist in the navy," but rather, "I'm going to be a SEAL." Not because it sounded better but because it was what I believed.

To my father, this represented a goal, and a noble one at that. I'm sure he was happy to see that I had found some purpose in life. I hadn't been a problematic kid growing up. I managed to mostly avoid trouble through sports and school when I was younger and by working a lot of hours when I was older. Still, I had some friends who liked to raise a bit of hell, and I had a couple of little run-ins with the law when I was in high school. Very minor stuff related to underage drinking, but still, it was the kind of thing that a parent might find troublesome. My father was happy to see that I had some ambition, and I think he liked the idea of his son becoming a part of Special Operations at a time when the country was in the early stages of a sweeping wave of patriotism. Whether he thought I had any chance at achieving this goal is another matter. He certainly never conveyed any doubt to me. Not that it would have mattered. I believed with every fiber of my being that I was going to succeed. I attribute that primarily to being young and naïve. I'd read all the books about SEAL training. I'd seen the movies and documentaries. I knew, on some level, what was involved—the level of pain and degradation.

But like any epic journey, you have to see it—and live it—to believe it.

My mother was far less enthusiastic, or even accepting, than my father. Not a big surprise, I guess. Forget about the SEALs—she could not see past the inherent risk of enlisting in any branch of the military during such a volatile period in history. She was simply a mother worried about harm coming to her son. Practically speaking, though, there wasn't much she could do to stop me. If she wouldn't sign the forms when I was seventeen, then I would have just waited until after graduation when I turned eighteen and enlisted, anyway. Any opposition my parents might have presented was pointless, and they knew it.

At the end of the summer, I left for basic training in Chicago. It was the first time I had traveled any great distance on my own, so a bit of homesickness might have been expected. But I really wasn't homesick. Some guys sign up for the military with a couple of buddies. Not me. I went entirely on my own, and as I flew out of Houston, I mainly just felt excitement about starting a new life. But it didn't take long for my plans to go off course. In fact, it happened almost as soon as I arrived at boot camp, when I was pulled aside by an instructor who had reviewed my enlistment credentials and seemed surprised by my intention to enter SEAL training.

"You're supposed to be going to submarine school," he said.

"That's right, Chief," I responded. "And then I'm going to BUD/S."

He shook his head. "Well, that's not going to happen."

Here's the thing about the enlistment process: it is conducted by recruiters who are shrewd and experienced. Navy recruiters—and, I presume, recruiters from every branch of the armed services—are adept at telling young men and women exactly what they want to hear at a stage in their lives when they are both immature and easily influenced. In every sense of the word, the meeting between adolescent recruit and adult recruiter is a mismatch. Which is fine. Navy recruiters have a job to do, and that job entails filling the ranks with eager young bodies. It's not like it took a lot of convincing to get me to sign on the dotted line. I walked into the recruiting office ready to sign up and fight for my country. I just wanted someone to point me in the right direction. There was, however, one stipulation: I wanted to be a SEAL. If that path wasn't an option, I would have walked right back out the door.

The recruiter had assured me that I would get a shot at my dream. More than that, he could not promise.

As part of the recruiting process, I had to choose what technical training school, known as *Class A school*, I wanted to attend after basic training. Typically, a new sailor goes from boot camp to A school, and then on to another school for more specialized training that will prepare him for the job he is expected to do. I had made it clear from the outset that I wanted to be a SEAL, so, if all worked out, my path would be different. After graduating from A school, I'd be able to apply for BUD/S. That's the way it worked. The recruiter explained the various A school options. I didn't feel strongly about any of the schools; I was totally focused on the step *after* A school: BUD/S. (This, in fact, is true of a lot of recruits, regardless of whether they have any interest in BUD/S—they simply choose the shortest A school to get it over with as quickly as possible.) When the re-cruiter suggested submarine school, which came with a $5,000 signing bonus, and assured me this would not interfere with my plans to become a SEAL, I shrugged and said, "Sure, why not? I could use the money."

Imagine my surprise when I got to boot camp and discov-ered that this was not the case. Now, I don't want to accuse any-one of lying or even misrepresenting the facts. I was seventeen years old and perhaps not the most patient or discerning young man. Maybe I should have done more due diligence. Then again, you hear about this sort of thing happening in all branches of the military—recruiters shading the truth a bit to fill classes and steer recruits to where they are needed the most. Regardless, there I was, at the Recruit Training Command, Great Lakes on the western shore of Lake Michigan, just outside of Chicago, a newly minted recruit who viewed basic training as just a stop-over on the way to becoming a SEAL.

And suddenly I was informed that I had fucked up and my dream was dead.

"I don't know what you were told," the instructor explained. "But submarine school is not preparation for BUD/S. It's a com-pletely different school, and it's long and involved. But it's a good job, and it's important."

I didn't doubt that it was important. I also didn't care. I had only agreed to submarine school because it had been suggested to me and came with a nice bonus. But if going to submarine school meant I couldn't be a SEAL, then I wanted no part of it. I tried to explain this to the instructor, but it turned out he was an old submariner himself, and he not only valued the pro-gram enormously, he didn't like the idea of some kid trying to get out of it. Maybe he was just wielding his authority. Maybe he thought I was spoiled or immature. Either way, he told me I was stuck.

"This is what you signed up for," he said. "It'll be good for you."

And with that, he laid out the course of my life. I would go to A school to study information technology, and then on to submarine school. I'd spend the next four years quietly traveling around the world on a submarine, armed with apocalyptic weaponry, including nuclear missiles, which I guess might appeal to some people but did nothing for me. I could hardly believe that I'd gotten myself into this predicament, and I figured I might as well do my best to rectify the situation immediately. So that's what I did: I began my navy career by refusing to do what I was told.

"Sir, with all due respect, I have no interest in serving on a submarine," I said. "I signed up to be a SEAL. That's all I'm interested in. I'm only here because I want to go to BUD/S, and if that's not going to happen, you might as well just send me home right now."

I sure didn't plan to start my navy career as a malcontent, and I understood the risks of insubordination. Fortunately, the instructor wasn't quite as much of a hard-ass as he appeared to be. He took my request under consideration, and in reasonably short order, I was reclassified and assigned to Machinist's Mate Class A school—surface division, as opposed to submarine division.

"Of course, you're going to lose that signing bonus," I was told.

"Of course," I responded.

I could not have cared less about the money. My dream of becoming a SEAL was still alive, and it was worth a lot more than $5,000.

# Chapter 2

I had done my homework, so I had a pretty good idea of what to expect from BUD/S—although experiencing it is certainly different from reading about it or watching movies or videos. I also knew a little bit about the SEAL physical screening test (PST) test that would quickly and mercilessly separate the wannabes from the serious candidates, and I had spent a big chunk of the summer trying to prepare appropriately. In addition to working long hours in construction, I trained relentlessly. I was in great shape by the time I left for basic training and figured I'd have no trouble passing the PST.

There was just one problem: because I was so focused on becoming a SEAL, I hadn't put a lot of time or effort into examining the day-to-day routine of boot camp, which was not at all what I had anticipated. I figured boot camp would be demanding—hour after hour of marching and training and psychological pressure. If there was one thing I knew, it was this: at the very least, boot camp would allow me to sustain, if not advance, my current level of conditioning, thus ensuring that I'd be fit as hell by the time I entered BUD/S.

I was mistaken.

Here's what happened in boot camp: I got fat. I was five foot nine, 175 pounds when I showed up (pretty close to the average for a SEAL, as noted); within a few weeks, I was closer to 185. Despite everything I'd heard about the rigors of basic training, navy boot camp turned out to be mostly an exercise in boredom. We spent a lot of time in classrooms or marching to and from classrooms. Slowly . . . without breaking a sweat. We spent endless hours studying and absorbing navy customs and culture. Important stuff, to be sure, especially for anyone who would be spending the next four years serving in the "regular" navy. But for those of us who aspired to become SEALs, it was almost detrimental. When we weren't marching or studying, we were eating. Big, starchy, fat-laden meals. It was like breakfast at Cracker Barrel, all day, every day. Within two weeks, I'd gotten soft. By three weeks, I was almost doughy. I started to get anxious.

What if I wasn't fit enough to pass the PST?

Fortunately, the recruits who had expressed an interest in the SEAL program were allowed two days of physical training per week. It wasn't much, but it was better than nothing. And the physical training was directed by a pair of men who represented my introduction to the world of Navy SEALs. One guy was in his early thirties and incredibly fit; the other guy was probably in his fifties and also in great shape. He was a little more old-school, as you might expect, but both of these guys were impressive in both demeanor and physicality. They pushed us hard in training, but they were also supportive; it seemed like they wanted us to believe that we could one day join their ranks.

The SEAL PST is rigorous and includes five exercises—or *evolutions*, as I would come to know them in BUD/S—each of which must be completed in a certain timeframe. The minimum standard is as follows:

> **500-yard swim (12 minutes, 30 seconds)**
> **42 push-ups (2 minutes)**
> **50 sit-ups (2 minutes)**
> **8 pull-ups (no time limit)**
> **1.5-mile run (11 minutes)**

The five exercises are completed consecutively, so it's more like a pentathlon than a series of individual tests. Rest time is minimal: ten minutes after the swim, then two minutes after the push-ups and sit-ups, followed by another ten-minute rest before the final event, the 1.5-mile run. It should also be noted that the standards listed above are merely that: minimum qualifying standards. If you hit those numbers, you are allowed to enter BUD/S, where you will almost certainly be among the very first to drop out. BUD/S is challenging enough for the fittest and strongest of candidates. For those who enter the program having met only the minimum standards, it's basically an exercise in futility, with a failure rate that hovers around 97 percent. To increase the odds of success, the navy recommends training for and achieving "competitive" scores on the PST. For example: 10:30 on the swim, and 10:20 on the run, as well as seventy-nine push-ups and sit-ups, and eleven pull-ups.

These are not subtle variations; they are significant. Most of the candidates who are serious about becoming SEALs shoot for the higher numbers and hit at least a few of them.

I was confident that I would easily meet the minimum standards, and I had been training diligently for months prior to basic training. I wasn't even worried about the 500-yard swim, which, believe it or not, is a common barrier for many aspiring SEALs. A lot of people come to BUD/S with a strong background in swimming. Some were competitive swimmers in high school or college. Some played water polo. Others had extensive lifeguard training. One guy was even a former college diver.

But not everyone fits this profile, and even those who do are often shocked to discover that the "wet" portion of BUD/S is about much more than swimming. When it comes to water, it's about survival and strength, and overcoming the natural fear of drowning. A great many exceptionally strong and otherwise capable candidates drop out of BUD/S during water training; and some of them are quite adept at swimming.

I loved the water—it was one of the reasons I was drawn to the SEAL program—but I was not a trained or competitive swimmer. My high school did not have a swimming team, and my family wasn't exactly the country club type, so I didn't spend a lot of time swimming laps when I was growing up. But I liked water: rivers, lakes, the ocean. Didn't matter. I was a self-taught swimmer who never had any issues taking care of himself in a water environment. I knew that if I were out on a lake or an ocean bay somewhere, and the boat capsized, I could get to shore. What more did I need to know?

A lot, as it turned out.

For one thing, I was a technically inefficient swimmer, most often utilizing what could best be described as a modified crawl. This was perfectly fine if you were just messing around with your buddies on a summer afternoon but not the most effective strategy for a timed 500-yard 1.5-mile swim. Further complicating matters was a little rule I discovered only after arriving at basic training and beginning preparation for the PST: the swim would be conducted in the safety and calm of a pool, but the distance covered had to be executed using a combination of the breaststroke and sidestroke, neither of which I had ever been taught.

So I learned. Before long, I became reasonably proficient; I wouldn't have won any medals as a competitive swimmer, but I developed a level of comfort and efficiency that helped me prepare for the PST. The truth is, like everyone else, once I got into the PST, I relied heavily on the sidestroke, since the breast-stroke is both technically difficult and exhausting.

In the end, I was one of only a few guys from my boot camp class who qualified for BUD/S. It did, however, take me more than one attempt. This is not unusual. A lot of guys fail to meet the standard on one or more of the events and therefore retake the entire PST. With the help of the SEAL trainers, and a lot of practice time in the pool, I passed on the second try.

I trained mostly with Jacob, an older guy from Arizona. Jacob was in his midthirties, which made him one of the oldest in boot camp. He was an amazing athlete, lean and muscular, with an easy and graceful way of moving. Jacob sailed through boot camp and easily qualified for BUD/S. I found it kind of inspiring to be around a guy like that. Here he was, nearly twice my age, and he could kick my ass in most of the physical events. I'm in my midthirties now, and frankly, I can't imagine going through BUD/S at this age. So, yeah, Jacob was unique.

Unfortunately, he didn't last long. Like a lot of guys, Jacob succumbed to the mental strain of BUD/S. He struggled with one of the many water evolutions in which candidates come perilously close to experiencing the feeling of drowning. It's a horrifying sensation, one that routinely triggers withdrawal from the program for candidates who previously had appeared exceptionally qualified. Certainly, that was the case with Jacob, who, both on paper and in person, looked like an ideal SEAL candidate, age notwithstanding.

You just never know.

I arrived at Naval Base Coronado in March 2003, having completed basic training and A school, and spent some time just waiting for a spot to open up in BUD/S while I was at Great Lakes. A sprawling complex in a resort community on San Diego Bay, Coronado is home to, among other things, the Naval Special Warfare Training Center, where the six-month BUD/S course is held. I actually volunteered to go to Coronado nearly a month early to help out with training exercises for one of the earlier BUD/S classes, which was both exciting and intimidating.

BUD/S typically begins with a five-week conditioning and training program known as *Indoctrination*. But I got a sneak preview of a later phase of the program when I was sent out to an offshore training facility. Here, the members of SEAL Class 243 were in the final portion of the program, three and a half weeks of intense training handling live explosives and ammunition, along with rigorous physical training. To me, it seemed almost harsh beyond description, but also thrilling. I could only imagine what these guys had endured in the preceding six months. I mean, I had an image in my head of what it must have been like, but to see the survivors here now, roughly fifty badass Special Operations warriors, each of them sunbaked and lean, so close to their goal . . . well, it was inspiring.

And a little scary.

One day, my job was to stand in the back of a box truck and hand out ammo to the candidates as they went through various evolutions. One of the guys—an older student, probably close to thirty—took a moment to make small talk.

"How old are you?" he asked.

"Eighteen," I said.

The guy smiled. "You'll quit," he said dryly.

I didn't know what to say, and I figured saying nothing was probably the right response, anyway. So I just looked at him.

"Yeah," he said, nodding. And then, just in case I hadn't heard him the first time, he repeated himself. "You'll quit. But don't worry about it. You can always try again later."

He walked away, and I went back to work, trying not to let his assessment, which apparently was based entirely on my age and youthful appearance, get into my head.

There are several BUD/S classes each year, with overlapping schedules. So while BUD/S class 243 was completing Third Phase of training, Classes 244 and 245 were already under way and at various points along the timeline. It is not unusual for a member of one class to end up graduating with a later class due to injury or illness or failure to meet a standard in one of the required exercises. For example, let's say a candidate fails to complete the ocean swim that is a requirement in Third Phase. Assuming he does not quit—and quitting is relatively rare in Third Phase—the candidate will get another opportunity, although often he will "roll back" to join the next class to complete his training. Similarly, if someone is injured or sick and must take time off from the program but is otherwise progressing well and does not want to quit, he is given the opportunity to roll back and finish with a later class.

I entered SEAL training as part of BUD/S class 246. There were 168 men in our class; of that number, only 22 would reach the finish line. And yet, several others from previous classes would graduate with us as part of Class 246.

In that sense, BUD/S is not entirely unforgiving. In just about every other way, however, it is an utterly merciless, non-stop, six-month beatdown.

Did I say six months? If you include the indoctrination phase, which isn't nearly as gentle or encouraging as the name might imply, it's more like seven months and change. BUD/S was simultaneously one of the best and worst experiences of my life—I would guess this is a sentiment shared by every SEAL who successfully completes the program—and I wouldn't trade it for anything. It was horrible and exhausting; it was, at times, darkly and weirdly funny. The purpose of BUD/S is to determine not just who wants to be a SEAL but who is really equipped for the job. When I arrived in Coronado, I knew I was part of the first camp; I didn't know yet whether I'd be part of the second.

To its credit, the navy understands that neither boot camp nor A school does much to prepare a recruit for the physical and emotional demands of BUD/S. In my best guess, diving right into First Phase would result in a success rate of somewhere around 0 percent. To level the playing field, students new to BUD/S enter a pre-indoctrination stage known as *Physical Training, Rest, and Recuperation (PTRR)*. Here the emphasis is on preparation and fitness, along with medical screening to ensure that candidates are up to the challenge of BUD/S. Candidates from previous classes who have been rolled back due to illness or injury all end up in PTRR, where they train and recuperate and generally bide their time while awaiting assignment to another class when that class reaches the same point at which the candidate was rolled back. For these students, PTRR can be a long and frustrating experience.

When numbers are sufficient, an entire class moves on to Indoctrination. Although technically BUD/S is a three-stage training program, Indoc is much more than just a warm-up. Ask anyone who has been through it: Indoc is where BUD/S begins in earnest. It's five weeks of intense physical training and conditioning and mental strain, designed not only to prepare the class for the rigors of BUD/S but to introduce the customs and traditions that are part and parcel of the entire experience. Indoc is a total and instantaneous immersion into the world of BUD/S. For twelve hours a day, you swim, run, climb ropes, traverse obstacle courses, carry inflatable boats, and generally experience exhaustion on a level you couldn't imagine. You also spend time in classrooms, absorbing lessons on the SEAL ethos, with a heavy emphasis on ethical and honorable behavior.

It is during Indoctrination that a SEAL candidate becomes acquainted with degradation and exhaustion doled out with great passion by instructors whose job is to not merely train but to push students to the breaking point through physical and verbal means. I'd been through boot camp, so I knew what it was like to have a recruit division commander (basically a drill instructor) tell me what a worthless pile of shit I was. But that was amateur hour compared to the abuse meted out by SEAL instructors during BUD/S. These guys were tireless and inventive; they were, quite often, funny. And while they didn't always scream in your face—they were more likely to just shake their heads and call you a fucking idiot—they did sometimes appear to be truly malevolent bastards who took joy in witnessing the pain and suffering of their recruits.

In truth, BUD/S instructors are performing a vital service. Their job is to train young men for one of the most demanding positions in the military, and they do this, in part, by weeding out everyone who isn't 100 percent committed to the cause, and both temperamentally and physically up to the challenge. I learned on the first day of Indoc that everyone screws up; that indeed a student is a worthless ball of slime who can do nothing right, and so you might as well just own up to your mistakes and make no excuses. If you were ordered to do ten push-ups, an instructor would stand over you counting; he would give you credit only for the push-ups that were done perfectly. And, of course, there is no such thing as "perfect."

Every inspection or interrogation resulted in some type of beatdown. Make the slightest mistake and you'd find yourself running to the surf for a quick submersion in sixty-degree water. The water off the coast of Southern California is surprisingly cold, especially when you never get a chance to dry off. The dunking was typically followed by a roll in the sand, until your entire body was covered with sticky, hard granules. This was known as the *sugar cookie*, and if it sounds relatively harmless, well, let's just say the result was far less appetizing than the name might indicate. And if you half-assed the sugar cookie by rolling in the sand with a lack of enthusiasm, rest assured—you would be sent right back to the beach to do it all over again. This was the endless, persistent refrain of BUD/S: do it right the first time, or you will do it again.

It's funny—you go to BUD/S worrying about whether you might drown, or how well you will hold up while running end-less miles in the sand while wearing heavy boots—or, in my case, whether your fear of heights will prove to be an imped-iment as you try to climb a twenty-foot rope wall during the obstacle course. You fear withering in the face of a ceaseless barrage of torment from a seemingly sadistic instructor. In the end, though, it's the more mundane stuff that drives you crazy: the sleeplessness, the bone-chilling cold that comes with being wet all the time; and the skin rubbed raw by wet clothes and sugar cookies. Everyone at BUD/S suffered from jock itch so horrific that they learned to run bowlegged. We all experienced the sublime pleasure of bleeding nipples.

Indoctrination was a giant mind fuck—a glimpse into the mental and physical challenges that would escalate during First Phase of BUD/S. In a very real sense, the purpose of Indoc was to scare the living crap out of everyone, to chase off the pretenders before the real work began.

*If I can't handle this, how the hell am I going to survive the next six months?*

It was a brutal but effective training strategy. The seeds of self-doubt were planted on day one, and by the end of Indoc, a typical class had been substantially pared. We lost roughly thirty guys from Class 246 before First Phase even began.

That's nearly 20 percent who decided that maybe being a SEAL wasn't such a great thing after all.

And so they rang the bell.

Oh, yeah. The bell. There was no quiet or dignified exit from BUD/S. Although students were actively encouraged to quit, often in a condescending or sarcastic manner, and some-times in an almost sympathetic manner ("Hey, it's okay, most people aren't meant to be SEALs; no shame in dropping out, son"), the act of quitting was, by its very nature, a public admis-sion of failure. You could quit at any time. All you had to do was ring the drop-on-request (DOR) bell that hung prominently near the grinder (the asphalt area where candidates did endless cal-isthenics: push-ups, sit-ups, pull-ups, etc.). Just walk over to the bell, grab the long, thick braided rope that dangled temptingly from its opening, and give it three quick tugs.

*Clang! Clang! Clang!*

Relief was instantaneous.

So was shame. And, often, regret.

It shouldn't be this way. Washing out of BUD/S is hardly embarrassing. Hell, most people don't want any part of the SEALs, and fewer still ever qualify for BUD/S. And eight out of ten students fail to complete the program. Ringing the bell, therefore, was hardly an unusual act; most people did it. Then they moved on to some other type of job in the navy. What's the big deal?

In your weaker moments—and there are many of them dur-ing BUD/S—this is what you tell yourself. It is the lie that seeps into your sleep-deprived brain and tempts you with the promise of rest and recovery. Then you hear the bell ringing out across the base, and you know what it means: that someone has quit; he has surrendered. You instantly picture that person changing into dry clothes and eating a warm meal and then collapsing into a comfortable bed. And for just a moment, maybe you're a little bit envious; you want to run to the bell yourself and end the suffering. Some people do just that; I get it. But not me. I heard the bell, and no matter how shitty I felt, no matter how much my knees hurt or how chafed I was from being covered with sand and salt; no matter how badly I wanted to quit . . . the sound of the bell always signaled to me that I was one step closer to the finish line.

*I will not quit. You'll have to kill me first!*

One of the more intimidating and ruthlessly effective evolutions in BUD/S was something called *drownproofing*. It's an interesting choice of names, since the test actually makes you feel like you're drowning, as opposed to making you feel impervious to the possibility. In reality, it is a test designed to teach that candidate that there are ways to prevent drowning under even the most adverse conditions; it's also a great way to cull the class—to shake out a few more pretenders—before Hell Week even kicks in.

In drownproofing, candidates entered the deep end of a pool with ankles tied together and hands bound behind their backs. It was a simple and, to some, terrifying exercise, designed to test not only a student's stamina but his ability to remain calm under pressure. If you didn't panic, drownproofing was a manageable exercise. You took a deep breath and sank to the bottom of the pool; then you kicked off the bottom and surfaced, took another deep breath, and repeated the cycle.

Over and over.

And that was just the beginning.

After repeating the bobbing exercise twenty times, at the end of which exhaustion was guaranteed, we had to float for five minutes, then swim to the shallow end of the pool (using a dolphin kick, since our legs and hands were bound), turn around without touching the bottom, and swim back to the deep end.

And still the test wasn't over. We were expected to execute

a forward and backward somersault underwater, and then dive to the bottom and retrieve a face mask. How did we do this with our hands tied behind our backs? Well, by using our teeth, of course.

Drownproofing could go wrong in so many ways. In the bobbing portion, some guys would stay too long on the bottom or not grab enough air when they broke the surface, which of course put them in oxygen debt and set them up for failure. Pacing was crucial, as was the ability to remain calm. I didn't have any problem with drownproofing, simply because it was less about being a strong swimmer than remaining focused and relaxed in the water. But some guys panicked and quit or had to repeat the test one or more times. It wasn't unusual for someone to nearly pass out during drownproofing and have to be pulled quickly from the water.

There have been fatalities in BUD/S, but it is an exceptionally rare occurrence. The young men are strong and athletic and fit, and the navy goes to great lengths to ensure their safety, even as they endure training that is always rigorous and sometimes downright dangerous. Medical personnel constantly monitor candidates for signs of hypothermia or illness or injury. Meals are huge and frequent to ensure that students have the necessary fuel. BUD/S is not inhumane. It is not torture, although it does sometimes feel that way.

My modest swimming skills became something of a factor a few times during BUD/S. Not necessarily during drownproofing, because, name notwithstanding, drownproofing was less about swimming than it was about self-control. But sometimes being a strong and experienced swimmer was an asset during the hundred-meter underwater pool swim or during something known as the *water rescue test*. If that sounds fairly simple, well, it wasn't nearly as tame as the kind you might encounter in your basic lifeguard course, where the person being saved basically floats peacefully while being pulled to safety.

In real life, it's more common for someone who is thrashing about in the water, struggling to stay afloat, to be completely panic-stricken. You try to rescue someone in that state of agitation and you're liable to be dragged right down beside him. If you don't know what you're doing, you'll both drown. Naturally, BUD/S rescue training presents to the rescuer the most distressing scenario possible: a drowning victim (played by an instructor), with weights in his pockets to pull him under and make the whole package even heavier, who kicks and screams and punches and claws. In short, he makes the job insanely difficult. Some instructors embrace the role more eagerly than others; I happened to get one of those guys, and his enthusiasm, coupled with the fact that I wasn't the strongest swimmer, really messed me up.

It was a challenging test even under the best of circumstances, and these were not the best. I jumped into the pool wearing full camouflage and boots and immediately felt the weight of my clothing slowing me down. Then I swam to my target—and I swear I could see him smiling—and immediately became entangled in a knot of thrashing arms and legs. The instructor, an expert at this drill, as well as a very good swimmer and a very big guy, put me in a headlock and used his legs to tackle me beneath the water. I quickly became exhausted, prompting the instructor to calmly tap me on the shoulder and proclaim, "You're done." Beaten and barely able to breathe, I swam slowly to the side of the pool, leaving my "victim" in the water.

Failure.

Fortunately, on the second try, I caught a break in the form of a victim who was more open to the idea of being rescued. This instructor made me work to save him, but at least he gave me a fair shot. Eventually, I was able to hook my arm under his shoulder and drag him to the side of the pool. I was exhausted, but I had passed.

In a word . . . BUD/S sucks. From start to finish, it is relentlessly awful. And the awfulness reaches a peak near the end of First Phase, with the appropriately named Hell Week.

It's weird—I remember BUD/S as a communal experience, like the ultimate team-building exercise. But the truth is that the early stages of BUD/S are about survival and suffering, and much of the pain is experienced on a private and personal level.

"You know, you didn't talk to me very much before Hell Week," one of my best friends and classmates said to me after we graduated from BUD/S. "I thought you didn't like me or something."

The truth is, I didn't have an opinion one way or the other. On a subconscious level, I think I tried to avoid getting too close to anyone during Indoc or First Phase. I'd look around and think, *Most of these guys are not going to make it.* A fun and healthy sense of competition permeated the proceedings; it wasn't like I rooted for anyone else to fail. Oh, sure, there were a handful of arrogant shitbags whose quick departure was not seen as any great loss, but in general, I liked most of the guys in my BUD/S class, and the training encouraged both competition and a sense of camaraderie. Misery loves company, after all, and we were pretty damn miserable. Still, we all knew the numbers, and with that knowledge came a certain reluctance to forge close relationships.

First Phase was a lot like Indoc, with an emphasis on physical training, only much more intense and demanding. There were endless beatdowns on the grinder, miles of running in heavy sand, hours of frigid surf torture. Some of the worst evolutions involved the rubber rafts commonly used by SEALs during various water operations. Known as an *IBS* (*Inflatable Boat—Small*), the rafts appear to be fairly light and flexible. In truth, they weigh approximately 185 pounds and are incredibly unwieldy. The first time I lifted an IBS, I couldn't believe how heavy it was; with the boat resting awkwardly on my skull, I could feel my head collapsing into my shoulders. Early in First Phase, we would be divided into crews of eight and instructed to hoist the IBS over our heads. Each team would hold the boat with arms extended for fifteen-minute intervals. The first team to collapse would endure a punishment of one type or another.

There were land races with the IBS, known as *elephant runs*, with the winning team often getting extra time to rest or eat. There were sea exercises, including treacherous and exhaustive landings on the rocky shoreline. The IBS is a fundamental part of SEAL training and invaluable in practical application. But, man, I came to hate it. We all did. Exercises involving the IBS were frequently responsible for guys dropping out. The exhaustion would seep into the deepest part of your body. Additionally, accidents and injuries were common during IBS exercises. Eight exhausted men dragging a nearly two-hundred-pound boat across slippery rocks sometimes lost their footing. Broken bones and wounds were not unusual. I also heard about a couple of guys who suffered neck injuries simply from the repeated strain of hoisting and carrying the IBS.

And then there were the logs. Jesus . . . the fucking logs. This was old-school physical training, supposedly dating back to British commandos in World War II. Like IBS training, log training is about team building as much as it is about pain and suffering. It sounds like such a simple and innocuous exercise— *log PT*—when in fact it is often remembered by SEALs as one of the worst evolutions in BUD/S. Picture seven men, already wet and tired, hoisting an eight-foot-long, 250-pound log over their heads. And holding it in place until further instruction.

We did team squats with the log. We did jumping jacks and crunches with the log. We lay on our backs and rolled it up a sand berm with our feet, pushing until our legs burned and we collapsed. We raced across the beach and tossed the log at the finish line. Then rested for a few seconds, picked it up, and ran back the other way. Sometimes a team would screw up and be assigned as punishment a famously large and awful log known as *Old Misery*.

Let's just say it was an appropriate nickname.

Log PT tested not just your personal resolve but your commitment to the team, for if one person weakened or quit, the remaining members of the team were, in a word, screwed. Losing a team member did not relieve your team of the burden of log PT; it just meant increased suffering for those left behind. The log felt bigger, heavier, more cumbersome. It was interesting to see the way different teams handled the stress and pain. Some fought and bitched at each other. Others worked together and encouraged each other. Still, it was a war of attrition, and log PT claimed a lot of casualties. We lost another forty guys in the first four weeks of First Phase.

And Hell Week was still to come.

# Chapter 3

The anticipation—that sense of impending doom—might have been the worst part.

It was another example of how BUD/S was a test of mental strength as much as anything else. The reality is this: by the time we got to Hell Week, we had experienced just about every soul-sucking evolution that BUD/S had to offer. We knew what it was like to be exhausted and cold and wet; to be screamed at and told we were worthless pieces of shit from sunup until sundown. There were few surprises left. The first month of First Phase had been all about acclimating to the physical and mental strain, and to understanding what was expected of us. Hell Week would just be more of the same.

Only worse.

If you looked at it that way, the beast didn't seem so fearsome. Everything about First Phase had sucked. Hell Week would just suck a little bit more. I'd be a little bit colder, a little bit tireder, a little more disoriented. I could handle that. Or so I told myself, anyway.

Other people weren't so sure. They talked themselves into expecting the very worst and in the process laid the groundwork for failure. The minute doubt seeps into your mind, the moment you start thinking about how great it would be to walk out of the water and get into some warm, dry clothes, you are done. If you believe Hell Week will be the shittiest experience of your life, then that's exactly what it will be. I mean, it is absolutely horrible, but the whole point is to instill a sense of invincibility: *If I can get through this, I can get through anything.*

I can honestly say I never thought about quitting. Not for one second. I knew there was a chance I could fail to meet the standards required on certain tests and evolutions. I might get sick or injured. But quit? No way. You'd have to kill me first. I don't mean for that to sound arrogant or cocky. I didn't think I was in any way superior to the other members of my class, and I have never felt like I was anything special when compared to the men with whom I served throughout my career. This was just something I felt in my heart.

It's a gift, I guess, just like any other attribute that determines success or failure in BUD/S. Some guys are blessed with speed or strength or size. I was mediocre in all of those categories, but I was not a quitter. I was resilient. And the awareness of that fact—an understanding of my own personality—allowed me to enter Hell Week with a sense of calm. I wouldn't go so far as to say I was looking forward to the madness, but neither was I filled with dread. Indeed, on Sunday evening, as we moved from our bunks to a bunch of tents that had been set up on the beach, I felt almost giddy with anticipation. I was anxious, nervous, curious. But not scared. Whatever Hell Week dished out, I figured, perhaps naïvely, that I could handle it. I wasn't going to die, and I wasn't going to quit. Whatever else happened was entirely out of my hands. And I was okay with that.

Most people aren't built that way. A lot of guys who enter BUD/S are type A personalities: focused, driven, hypercompetitive. They are also control freaks. During Hell Week, you learn very quickly that you are in control of almost nothing except your own emotions. You can succumb to the fear and pain, or you can find a way to endure it.

The folks at Naval Special Warfare Command understand all of this. There is a reason SEAL training hasn't evolved much over the years: it's highly effective exactly as it is. The SEALs want not just warriors but men who can follow orders while also thinking on their feet; men who will not panic in the heat of battle, and who will not quit under stress; men who will die for their brothers. The making of a SEAL occurs during BUD/S and further training, but some of it is simply ingrained. There is a subtle difference between toughness and strength. The first is often superficial and fleeting. The second is bone-deep and permanent.

You need strength to get through Hell Week.

It was shortly before midnight Sunday when the insanity began—instructors bursting into our tents and screaming at the top of their lungs, firing blanks from machine guns and tossing smoke grenades. Outside, more instructors unleashed a hellstorm of machine-gun fire and flash grenades, lighting up the night sky with fireworks. The noise was deafening; and yet, through the explosions and the screaming, I could hear music. Yeah, music, for Christ's sake. The unmistakable sound of Guns N' Roses' "Welcome to the Jungle" crackling through the sound system. The volume had been turned up so loud that distortion and scratching accompanied every note, which I suppose was part of the desired effect: to create a sense of utter anarchy and confusion. Lights flashed like strobes; explosions echoed above the beach, while Axl Rose screeched in the background, providing a weirdly appropriate soundtrack to the proceedings.

"Welcome to the Jungle!"

*No shit.*

The first few hours of Hell Week is known as *Breakout.* It

marks the line of demarcation from the awful but orderly first month of First Phase and the seemingly random wretchedness of Hell Week. Of course, the reality is that there is nothing random or unpredictable about it. The seeds of self-doubt are planted in the hours leading up to Breakout and take root firmly as you scramble about in the darkness, searching for your teammates (we were all divided into groups for the upcoming evolutions), trying not to get lost.

Breakout is intended to simulate the confusion and chaos of battle. Since none of us had ever been in combat, we had nothing to compare it to, but it sure felt like the real thing at the time. Throughout Indoctrination and First Phase, we had been taught the importance of relying on your teammates, of working together and fighting the urge to fend only for yourself when things get hard. This is of the utmost importance in battle, and Breakout was designed to test our resolve and aptitude in this regard.

For the most part, we failed. Which was exactly the expected outcome. The instructors made it impossible to stay with your teammates during Breakout. The sky was filled with smoke and fire. Fire trucks were lined up near the grinder, hoses spraying water into the air. The sound of artillery rounds rattled the ground like thunder. And in the midst of the craziness, instructors ran around and shouted orders, all the while imploring us to stay with our teammates.

"Where are your guys?" one of the instructors yelled at me, his face so close to mine that I could almost feel him spitting into my ear.

"I don't know," I replied, my voice not quite as confident as I would have liked.

"Well, fucking find them!"

But I couldn't find them. Not right away. The goal of Breakout, from the instructors' point of view, was to instill a sense of complete and utter panic in the mind of an already frazzled and frightened trainee.

"Find your guys! Find your guys!" they repeatedly screamed, but they had made it virtually impossible to stay together. It's well known that the stress and confusion of Breakout, combined with the anxiety that precedes it, sometimes causes trainees to quit on the spot. Not that you'd be able to tell, since no one could hear the ringing of the DOR bell in that environment. I know we lost some guys during the first night. I found that somewhat surprising. They had already withstood four weeks of First Phase; the real pain of Hell Week hadn't yet begun. So why quit? The answer, I guess, is that they were overwhelmed by dread and fear. That's another mind trick that BUD/S so brilliantly applies: the idea that weakness can be exploited through simple anticipation. It wasn't Breakout that made people quit— it was the *idea* of Breakout and what it represented: impending doom and anguish so horrific that it could make almost anyone say, "Fuck this shit. I'm done."

The first thing we did when we came out of our tents was make our way to the grinder, where we were doused with water from the fire hoses and ordered to do push-ups and sit-ups and jumping jacks, all against a backdrop of gunfire and whistles and sirens and explosions. Moments later, we were sent into the ocean in full camouflage uniforms and boots for the first of many sessions of surf torture. We were ordered back into the ditch, where we all had just pissed, and instructed to roll around in the dirt. A nice little urine-soaked sugar cookie to start things off on the right foot.

We were all completely shell-shocked and disoriented. Fewer than fifteen minutes had passed, and already I was shivering and sore. I wasn't scared, but I did find myself thinking, *How the hell I am going to do this for the next five days?*

There was no answer. For me, the ideal strategy for surviving Hell Week was to think of it as a series of small challenges, rather than one gigantic test. Just try to make it from one meal to the next. I'm not a real mystical guy or anything, but I learned very quickly the value of taking a meditative approach to some of the harsher aspects of Hell Week. Silly as it might sound, if we were instructed to lie down in the surf and let the cool water roll up over our faces, I would just close my eyes and go to my happy place. I'd imagine I was somewhere warm and calming, and pretty soon the worst of it was over and it was time to move on to the next awful exercise. I have no explanation as to why this worked for me. Everyone had their own way of coping with the pain. Look at photos of trainees during Hell Week, and you'll see a row of guys on their backs in the surf, arms locked, bodies rigid. Some of them will be bug-eyed with fear. Others have their faces contorted in pain. And some will appear to be almost asleep, as if they are oddly at peace with their surroundings.

That was me. I was one of the lucky ones.

Not that it wasn't terrible. It was. Every second of Hell Week sucked. For some reason, though, I found a way through the relentless agony by taking the smallest of bites and reminding myself that eventually I'd be able to swallow it and move on. I guess you could say I was temperamentally suited to BUD/S, in general, and to Hell Week, in particular.

I remember one day sitting in the elephant cages (where the inflatable boats were stored), savoring an MRE (*meals ready to eat*). One of the few good things about Hell Week is that we ate almost constantly. Massive meals three times a day, along with MREs and power bars to ensure we had enough calories to fuel the endless evolutions. For me, sitting quietly and savoring an MRE was a calming and restorative experience. Yes, I was cold and wet. Yes, I was so exhausted I thought I might fall asleep on

the spot. But at least I wasn't in the water. At least I wasn't holding a log over my head or cranking out hundreds of push-ups or
sit-ups. No one was in my face, calling me a motherfucker or a
pussy.

It was, for a few moments, peaceful.

Therefore, I simply could not fathom the sound I heard off
in the distance.

*Clang! Clang! Clang!*

And then, a few minutes later, it happened again.

*Clang! Clang! Clang!*

I looked at one of my buddies. He shrugged wearily. By now,
the sound of our classmates ringing the DOR bell had become
so routine that it was usually met with utter indifference. *Another one bites the dust. What are you going to do?* For some
reason, though, this one baffled me. I simply could not understand why anyone would quit during one of the few times in the
day when pain was replaced by pleasure.

Another time, I walked through the chow hall, carrying a
big plate of food. I was feeling pretty good about having a few
minutes of free time and plenty to eat, while all around me guys
were nodding off in mid-bite. This actually happened: you'd see
someone shovel a spoonful of food into his mouth, and as he
was chewing, his eyelids would drop, and he'd sort of list to the
side. You'd have to give him a little shove to prevent him from
choking. Once I saw an instructor walk by a sleeping student
in the middle of the chow hall. The instructor stopped, picked
up a lemon from a table, and squirted juice into the student's
eyes. He woke up rather quickly. But none of this was unusual;
in fact, guys fell asleep everywhere during Hell Week: in the
chow hall, the latrine and porta-potties, the barracks, even on
the beach.

Anyway, as I walked past the instructors' table, I heard
someone yell, "What the hell are you smiling about?"

Smiling? I was smiling? I hadn't even realized it, but yeah, I guess I might have been.

"I asked you a question!" the instructor barked.

I kind of shrugged and nodded. "Just happy to be here, sir."

The instructor shook his head and went back to his meal. He must have thought I was either too stupid to realize what was happening or suffering from some sort of dementia. The truth was, in that moment, Hell Week didn't seem all that bad.

But that, I would later discover, is part of the genius of Hell Week. You can almost grow accustomed to the ceaseless hurt. It becomes normal to the point that you forget how it feels to be warm and dry and comfortable. Then, suddenly, you get a taste of it—when you switch into fresh clothes, or at the chow hall, or even just nibbling an MRE—and the brief encounter with normalcy sparks a moment of weakness.

*I have had enough of this shit.*

And you quit.

In fact, this was quite common—guys were just as likely, if not more likely, to quit during a lull in the torture as they were to quit after twenty minutes of lying in the frigid surf, waiting for hypothermia to set in.

Oh, and here's another awesome thing about the DOR process—another example of the devious mind games they played on all of us. When someone quit, he was not treated like a pariah by the instructors. There was no tongue-lashing or walk of shame—beyond ringing the bell, of course. In fact, typically, when someone quit, he would be met by the instructors with a smile and a warm blanket.

"It's okay, son. No shame in this at all."

The disgraced student would nod. The instructor might even hand him a cup of coffee and something to eat. They'd commiserate together, right there in front of the entire class, which had the effect of minimizing the whole experience, allowing doubt to seep into the minds of anyone who might be on the fence.

*Shit . . . that looks like a pretty good deal. Maybe I should quit, too.*

In fact, quitting, especially during Hell Week, was rarely an isolated incident. Rather, it came in waves. One guy would stand up and walk out of the water. His surrender paved the way for others, until soon there were three or four guys huddled together in front of the class, all wrapped in blankets, warm and comfortable.

But their dream was over. For the rest of us, it lived on.

The first twenty-four hours of Hell Week were the worst. Between the dread and anxiety that filled the hours before Breakout, and the shock and chaos of the actual experience, I think it took at least a full day to adjust to the madness. I wouldn't say there was any sort of rhythm or routine to it—it was just ceaseless, random evolutions. But at least I'd expected this and figured that if I could get through the first twenty-four hours, I'd be okay.

A little luck is involved. I had gotten sick early in First Phase, which made things even more challenging for a while, but by the time Hell Week rolled around, I had kicked the bug out of my system and felt reasonably strong. Unfortunately, I had passed the virus on to my roommate, who first started feeling shitty just a couple of days before Hell Week commenced. I felt terrible for him, as I knew the odds were now stacked against him. When he dropped out midweek, I felt somewhat responsible. He was a good guy, and if not for being compromised by illness, I think he probably would have made it. But it could just as easily have been me or anyone else. They did give my roommate the option of taking some time to recover and then rolling back with Class 247. He declined the offer.

One of the first things we did after Breakout was an elephant run from Coronado to Imperial Beach—a nearly ten-
kilometer test of strength and endurance in which teams of six
men awkwardly transported inflatable boats on their heads and
shoulders. I remember hearing the bell ring just a few minutes
into the elephant run and picturing that unfortunate team trying to shoulder the added weight when down a man for most
of the entire six miles. Trust me—when you're in that position,
you don't feel empathy for the guy who dropped out; you're just
pissed that he's made your job harder.

We had done elephant runs previously, but during Hell
Week, they were longer and more frequent, and often complicated by the sudden disappearance of a teammate or two. Carrying an IBS was challenging not just because of the weight but
because of the boat's flexibility and ungainly shape. It was like
trying to carry a giant, 185-pound water balloon. Inevitably, as
your arms grew weary, the IBS slowly dropped, until eventually
there was no space between the top of your head and the surface of the boat.

To ease the burning in your arms, you'd let the boat rest
almost entirely on the top of your head. It was, for a little while,
anyway, the lesser of two evils. While your aching biceps and
triceps recovered, your upper body bore the brunt of the work-
load. Unfortunately, this could lead to an assortment of problems, ranging from the merely annoying or humorous (like the
bald spot I developed on the top of my head, where the hair
was burned off from miles of chafing), to the potentially catastrophic (migraines, back and neck injuries that could neces-
sitate medical withdrawal from the program). But in the middle
of a six-mile elephant run, you do whatever it takes to get to the
finish line. You don't worry about the consequences.

The beatdown of Hell Week was relentless, but medical personnel were always nearby to ensure the safety of

participants—in a sense, to protect us from ourselves. There was a formula that was used to minimize the risk of hypothermia: the colder the water, the briefer the episodes of surf torture. But the envelope was routinely pushed. It always felt like surf torture ended just as you thought you couldn't last another second. Once in a while, there would be a brief period of recovery—a few minutes of resting on the berm, letting the sun warm your face and body. This was especially true if you were fortunate enough to win one of the many team competitions.

"Pays to be a winner!" was a refrain often echoed by the instructors.

Damn straight. I remember one race in which we had to carry inflatable boats in one direction and then return with logs. It was almost indescribably painful. But our team won, and our reward was a solid twenty minutes of rest—or even sleep!—on the berm, under a warm and sunny sky.

But every interlude was followed by another beatdown. A whistle would sound, and we'd be ordered to walk back into the water for another round of surf torture.

Sometimes we did "surf laundry." This was another of those exercises that was exponentially worse than it sounds. March into the water. Take a seat. Remove your clothes—right down to your underwear. Rinse the sand from your clothes. Fold your clothes neatly and place them in a pile on the beach. Do all of this while sitting in waist-deep, sixty-degree water, your fingers so numb they barely function. Finally, when everyone in the entire class finishes their "laundry," everyone is allowed out of the water. The prize for completing the task: getting dressed in the same cold, soaking wet clothes we had just removed.

Then more elephant runs, often followed by dangerous and exhausting portage exercises, in which teams carried their boats over wet and craggy and sometimes steep boulders on the shoreline. This was followed by more log PT . . . more sit-ups, push-ups, and surf torture—in full clothes or half-naked. Time in the water was almost always followed by a sugar cookie or a crawl through the mudflats, to ensure maximum chafing. By the end of the second day, some guys discovered that their scrotums had swollen to nearly twice the normal size. By the end of the week, they had doubled in size again and resembled raw hamburger.

But at least I wasn't alone. We all suffered the same maladies and indignity, and we did it with as much humor as we could muster. I was lucky. Class 246 had its share of not only outstanding SEAL candidates but some world-class ballbusters, as well. We made fun of each other, and we supported each other. As Hell Week wore on and our numbers dwindled, the jokes became darker, funnier, and more frequent. It was a way to fight off not just the pain but the ever-present threat of humiliation and failure. During Hell Week, the DOR bell was rarely out of view. It would follow us in the back of a pickup truck, from evolution to evolution, from the beach to the grinder to the streets where we suffered through elephant runs. If you started to weaken, you could count on a sympathetic instructor getting in your ear and whispering, "Just ring the bell. It's right there. Give it a pull and this will all be over."

But, like I said, DORs were most common not in the midst of the agony but during the rare instances of rest and recuperation—immediately after meals, for example, or following a warm decontamination shower and a subsequent medical evaluation. For some guys, the slightest respite was an invitation to quit. And the longest break was, for nearly everyone, the greatest temptation of all.

It came after more than two days of nonstop insanity. We were all giddy with exhaustion and sleep deprivation. It isn't possible to go five days without sleep and still meet the brutal physical demands of Hell Week; a bare minimum of rest is required, and the bare minimum is what we got: a grand total of four hours, divided into two-hour increments. We were allowed to shower, eat, and change into dry clothes. Then we slogged into our tents and passed out on the ground. Some of us slid into sleeping bags. I don't remember falling asleep. I think I was out before I hit the ground.

Then, in what felt like a matter of seconds, we were roused rather gently from our nap. Unlike Breakout, when we woke to the heart-stopping thunder of machine-gun fire and explosions, the midweek nap ended with instructors walking through the tents and softly urging us to "rise and shine." It seemed out of character; almost like they felt bad for us and wanted us to enjoy every possible second of sleep.

In fact, that is exactly what they were doing.

We were coaxed from the tent in the early evening hours. No one said much of anything as we walked to the top of the berm and stood in a long, woozy line, watching the sun slowly set beyond the Pacific. I remember thinking, as I looked out at the glorious red sunset and the shimmering sea, that it was absolutely gorgeous. It would have been ever better with a beer in my hand and a cookout on the sand, and a pretty girl as company.

But such thoughts are dangerous when your world is about to be rocked. See, that's exactly the kind of warm daydream they expected us to conjure. It was evil, it was sadistic, and it was absolutely brilliant. I would have to say that waking from that first nap was one of the hardest parts of Hell Week for a lot of people. Personally, I didn't consider quitting, but when the bell rang a few minutes later, just as we were ordered to hit the surf, signaling the withdrawal of yet another classmate, and the dashing of another dream, I understood exactly why it had happened.

We all walked toward the water, arms interlocked, and

stood in the crashing surf. As one of the instructors shouted, "Take seats!" we all just stood there. This was the only time during Hell Week when we hesitated to follow an order. The idea of sitting in the cold water, just moments after a nap, was almost too much to bear.

"*Take seats!*" the instructor shouted again, this time louder and more emphatically. Slowly, we sank to the beach and leaned back into the sand, letting the Pacific roll up over our bodies. The chill was stark and immediate, rendering the nap a distant memory.

By the halfway mark, I felt confident that I would not succumb to the doubt and fatigue that causes so many candidates to DOR. I was much less certain of whether I would be able to meet all the physical demands.

Throughout First Phase, including Hell Week, the obstacle course was my biggest concern, as it had been since the day I arrived in Coronado. The O Course was the biggest ballbuster of BUD/S. Imagine the worst CrossFit workout you've ever seen, and you get some idea of the intensity of the BUD/S obstacle course.

It starts off with an arm walk through a set of parallel bars, followed immediately by a sprint through a set of tires (with hands clasped behind your head), and a climb over a seven-and-a-half-foot "low wall" that is preceded by jumping off two short tree stumps, which aids in momentum but can of course compromise balance. Then a short sprint across the sand to a higher wall (eleven feet six inches) that is scaled with the aid of ropes, followed by a nasty low crawl under a set of logs encircled with barbed wire (with only three inches of clearance at the lowest point), another sprint across the sand to a daunting fifty-foot-high rope wall (or *cargo net*, as it is commonly known), another exhausted sprint across sand and a series of balance logs, and a stationary rope climb.

This is not even the halfway mark of the O Course, but by this point, your lungs are on fire and your legs are aching. And it is here that you encounter the single-most problematic barrier on the course: the Dirty Name. It's basically two consecutive hurdles, one five feet tall, the other ten feet tall, separated by a distance of maybe four or five feet. The idea is to jump to the first barrier, landing on your arms, and pull yourself up quickly. Then climb to your feet and leap immediately to the second. It looks simple enough when done well by an experienced SEAL, and preferably one who is either very tall or blessed with great leaping ability. But for many people, the first few attempts at the Dirty Name result in mistimed collisions with the hurdles, bruised or busted ribs, and nasty falls to the sand. Even a reasonably well-executed attempt at the Dirty Name could result in getting the wind knocked out of you.

While still reeling from the Dirty Name, the obstacle course runner quickly encounters something known as *the Weaver*, which looks sort of like a V-shaped ladder and must be traversed by going first over one rung and then under the next. By the time you get through the Weaver, with nearly half the course ahead of you, the possibility of passing out is not only real but welcome; at least the pain would end.

The second half of the course is comprised of more tires, more ropes, more walls, more climbing and running, and, near the end, something known as *the Slide for Life*, which is more like the Slide for Death. It is not the most tiring event in the obstacle course; it is the most dangerous. Basically, to complete the Slide for Life, you climb a forty-foot platform and affix yourself to a stationary rope that angles toward the ground, over a distance of one hundred feet. With hands and feet wrapped around the rope, you "slide for life." Make a mistake on this one, and you could be seriously injured; you'll almost certainly find yourself medically disqualified or rolled back.

The first time I saw the obstacle course, I thought to myself, *This is going to be a problem.*

It was.

Like I said, I am not a gifted athlete, so I expected certain parts of it to be challenging—specifically, the Dirty Name. There are time standards that must be met in BUD/S, and the standards become more difficult with each phase. I had spent a lot of time practicing during Indoc, so eventually I gained enough technical proficiency to meet the requirements. But every time I ran the obstacle course—and we did it repeatedly—it took a little piece of my soul.

In case you couldn't tell, I hated the O Course, and I *really* hated it during Hell Week, when we would do it in teams while carrying inflatable boats. This is hard to envision and even harder to execute. The first time I heard we were going to carry boats through the obstacle course, I almost thought it was a joke. It wasn't, of course. I mean, we didn't do the entire course, obviously—there is no way to haul a 180-pound boat over a fifty-foot rope wall, or carry it while on the Slide for Life. But just about everything else? Yeah. It was almost comically awful, and it beat us to shreds.

Much of Hell Week was spent either on our backs or stomachs. We constantly were told to hit the ground and crawl toward the sound of a whistle. Sometimes this would take us through water or over sand. Sometimes we crawled over concrete and asphalt, or through mudflats or culverts. Whatever we were instructed to do, we did it. Without hesitation.

"March to the surf!"

We marched to the surf.

"Sit down in the water!"

We sat in the water.

"Roll in the sand!"

We rolled in the sand.

If you screwed up, an instructor would instantly get in your face and pepper you with insults and expletives. The SEALs want men who can not only handle adversity but who will not let their emotions get in the way of completing a job. When you're wet and cold and practically falling asleep on your feet, and someone starts screaming in your ear and telling you what a worthless pile of garbage you are, it's very tempting to go off on the guy. Indeed, that is exactly the response is intended to provoke. So while you might think that the ideal Navy SEAL candidate is someone who is basically a live wire—intense, focused, ready to spark at any moment—the opposite is actually true. The best candidates are ambitious and indefatigable, sure. But they also are surprisingly low-key and unflappable.

I learned to respond with either silence or an enthusiastic "Hoo-yah, instructor!" (basically, the SEALs' response to virtually everything).

Again, I think this is a gift, something you are either born with or not. Shit always ran off my back when I was a kid. I didn't let much get to me. My parents divorced, we lived in a trailer park, and I worked hard for everything I had, but I never felt angry or resentful about any of it. It was just the way things were. I learned early on that there are things you can't control in life—a lot of things—so you find a way to deal with them. Eventually, even the worst shit passes. This attitude, more than anything else, helped me get through BUD/S, and Hell Week in particular.

In the last couple of days of Hell Week, there was a perceptible shift in attitude among both the instructors and students. The physical toll was no less demanding; if anything, it was compounded by mounting sleep deprivation. But the majority of people who quit during Hell Week did so in the first two or three days, urged on by instructors whose primary job was to separate the weak from the strong. If you made it to

Wednesday, it was presumed you had the ability to get through Hell Week. And if you could get through Hell Week, the odds of getting through BUD/S tilted in your favor. So in the final forty-eight hours, the instructors were a bit less vicious and sadistic, more likely to encourage than discourage.

As for the students of Class 246, we could finally see the finish line drawing near.

The final evolution of Hell Week, on Friday morning, was known as *So Sorry Day*, a combat-simulation exercise featuring an obstacle course through mudflats and culverts and barbed wire, among other things. The mudflats of Hell Week are legendary, as they are not merely muddy but sometimes tainted with sewage and other untreated waste that spills from the Tijuana River into the Pacific Ocean. And in this putrid swamp, we were instructed to "play" for several hours. A highlight of the evolution—if you can call it a highlight—involved shinnying out over the swamp on a tightrope, then telling a joke for the entire class to hear. The real punch line came when the class would vigorously shake the rope and deposit the student into the shit and mud below.

Eventually, as morning gave way to afternoon, we made our way back to the compound on Coronado Beach. Of course, we didn't just walk back; instead, we conducted one last elephant run. We all knew that the end was near, but sleep deprivation has a way of screwing with your head; it seemed possible under these conditions that Hell Week could go on for several more hours, or even days. But as we assembled on the beach, soaking wet and caked with mud and shit, completely exhausted, and the instructors gathered as a group in front of us, it was apparent that something was different. The instructors planted a flag, and then one of them took a bullhorn in hand and shouted, "Class 246, Hell Week is secured!"

At first, there was stunned silence. A few guys looked like they might cry. There were weary hugs, and then shouts of "Hoo-yah!" rang across the beach. We stood up as the instructors walked through our group, shaking our hands and smiling, and offering heartfelt congratulations. These men, who had spent the previous five days treating us like dirt, now embraced us as brothers. I had never felt so proud in my life.

Afterward, I took a shower and put on some dry clothes. The instructors ordered pizza for everyone—and by pizza, I mean an entire large pizza for each surviving candidate. I sat outside on the grinder, shoveling pizza into my face, and called my father to give him the news.

"Hey, Dad," I said . . . and then for some reason, a mischievous thought crossed my mind. And I paused.

"What's up, Will? How's it going?"

"I'm sorry, Dad. I wanted to let you know that I didn't make it. I just quit."

There was a short pause before my father finally broke the silence.

"Bullshit," he said.

And that was it. I laughed into the phone.

"Yeah, you got me, Dad. You're right. I'm okay. Hell Week just ended. I made it."

There was another pause. I could almost see my father smiling.

"Good job, boy."

After pizza, we were escorted back to our rooms (not the tents on the beach, but our real rooms) by some students who were going through Indoctrination. Under medical advice, they helped us put drawers and cabinets under the base of our beds, so that our aching and swollen legs would be elevated when

we passed out. Early that evening, I fell into bed and lost consciousness almost immediately. For the next twelve hours, I
slept like the dead.

It was, and remains, the best night of sleep of my entire
life.

# Chapter 4

Hell Week was followed by Heaven Week.

Well, not really, but that's the way it felt. Technically, it was known as *Walk Week*. We survivors of Class 246 were given the next nine days, including weekends, to let our bodies heal and to regain the physical strength and mental sharpness to continue with BUD/S. It wasn't like we just sat on the beach and worked on our tans, but the stress was minimal and there were no tests or timed evolutions.

Then came the last two weeks of First Phase, which consisted primarily of more physical training and evenings spent in classrooms, studying hydro reconnaissance. In plain English, this meant that we were learning effective ways to approach or attack a target using underwater tools and tactics. Old-school frogman stuff.

All of this helped set the stage for Second Phase, eight weeks of diving instruction and practice, conducted in pools, training tanks, and San Diego Bay. There were few, if any, serious beatdowns during the last two weeks of First Phase. While still embracing the time-honored persona of hard-ass that the job demands, our instructors were noticeably less negative in their rhetoric. They did not address us as losers; they did not preface every interaction with some comment designed to reinforce the fact that we faced overwhelming odds in our desire to become SEALs.

That's because the odds were now in our favor. Including rollbacks, Class 246 ended First Phase with slightly more than fifty students. We'd lose a dozen more in Second Phase, but obviously this represented a dramatic slowing of attrition. In comparison to First Phase, it felt like the sound of the DOR bell was as rare as a smile from one of the instructors.

Not that it was easy. BUD/S is never easy. But once you get past First Phase, the focus of the program shifts rather dramatically from thinning the herd to teaching and encouraging those who remain. It is presumed that if you get through First Phase, you will become a SEAL, and the remaining four months of instruction are staged accordingly.

Safety is a big concern during Second Phase. While exhaustion can lead to injury and illness in First Phase, it is in Second Phase that training can be legitimately dangerous. For this reason, we spent the first week studying physics and physiology and the basics of diving. We got to hear in great deal about all the terrible things that could happen to the human body and brain if you screwed up underwater. For example, a panic-induced uncontrolled ascent can trigger an embolism. We read and studied and took written tests, which we were required to pass before actually getting in the water.

And then we moved on to Pool Week, where we got our first taste of actual scuba diving. But, this being BUD/S, it was far from the sort of gentle indoctrination you might receive during a vacation in the Bahamas. For one thing, we either rode to the pool in a bus, while wearing scuba gear and breathing through hoses, or we humped it on foot, a distance of roughly a mile, with air tanks on our backs. Sometimes we did push-ups in the sand, while wearing our gear—including our breathing apparatus. By this point, we'd all gotten pretty good at cranking out forty or fifty push-ups while barely breaking a sweat, but 125 pounds of scuba gear and a breathing hose adds a degree of difficulty to the equation that is hard to imagine until you do it.

Worse were the relentless training exercises designed to induce panic, usually by making you think you couldn't breathe. Similar in philosophy to drownproofing, this was the navy's way of teaching students how to become comfortable in and under the water, even when facing the possibility of losing consciousness.

While the majority of students who reach Second Phase eventually graduate from BUD/S, it's also true that some of the strongest and seemingly most competent candidates are brought to their knees by the diving portion of training. There is no way to know who will placidly accept the horror of oxygen deprivation and water rushing into his lungs, while calmly finding a way out of the situation . . . and who will unabashedly freak out. Make no mistake: the second option is by far the more natural response. I don't care how tough you are or how adept you are at swimming. When outside forces cut off your air supply or promote the leaking of water into your equipment, the first inclination is to seek relief. The second is to panic.

Second Phase was packed with evolutions and training designed to test a student's ability to deal with situations that seemed not just beyond his control but life-threatening. You might have to go back to childhood to dredge up the memory, but just about everyone has experienced the sensation of drowning. Maybe you stumbled into the deep end of a pool before you were ready; maybe you got rolled by a big wave while surfing; maybe you went a little too deep while snorkeling and nearly passed out while scrambling frantically to the surface. Whatever the scenario, you remember it. And it sucks.

Much of Second Phase was devoted to replicating that sensation and to instilling in students the discipline and experience necessary for coping calmly with what feels like a near-death experience. Although no one liked it, most of us did all right with even the worst aspects of the training. A few students, however, simply couldn't deal with it and ended up dropping out.

The scary stuff started with the very first time we were allowed to try out our scuba equipment in the pool. Although most of us were decent swimmers and comfortable in the water, I'm not sure anyone in our class had any formal scuba training whatsoever. So when we turned on our air valves and sat down in the shallow end of the pool, and let our heads dip below the surface, imagine the surprise we felt as water seeped into our mouthpieces. We choked and gasped. We spit and looked for relief. A couple of guys panicked and tried to get out of the pool. All of this was intentional and designed to induce fear and dread. I had never used a hose or regulator before, but I knew right away that something was wrong. I also figured it was part of the program, and so I did my best to go to my happy place again.

*Stay calm . . . stay calm.*

Zen-like focus, while helpful in First Phase, was critical to surviving dive training. In addition to continued beatdowns on the obstacle course, four-mile runs on the beach, and endless calisthenics on the grinder, we were tossed into various bodies of water and forced to flirt with the sensation of drowning. As with much of BUD/S, the idea was not merely to educate and train but to see how you would respond under intense pressure. Can you stay calm when your life is at stake? It was all hard and occasionally frightening, but after a while, you got used to it. And if you didn't, you were gone.

A lot of the drills and tests were designed to foster teamwork and trust. For example, we'd sit at the bottom of the pool in pairs, sharing one mouthpiece. This was known as *buddy breathing*, the idea being that in the midst of a mission, your swim buddy might experience a problem with his equipment, necessitating the sharing of oxygen. It encouraged both camaraderie and courage. Other tests were more physical in nature, like treading water without using your hands while wearing a weighted belt and all your scuba gear. Sometimes an instructor would swim by in the middle of an exercise and rip off your mask or regulator hose, just to see how you'd respond. The proper response was to calmly replace the gear as quickly and efficiently as possible. In the real world, during amphibious assaults, any number of outside forces—from rough surf to a capsized boat—can cause you to lose your equipment. It's crucial to remain calm under even the most difficult conditions. But some guys would just immediately streak to the surface. In another test, instructors would tie our hoses into knots, and we would have to try to untangle the knots while submerged—preferably before passing out. And indeed, some guys did pass out. You'd see them flailing away at the knots, working feverishly. Then they'd begin to slow down, and finally their arms would barely move. They were virtually unconscious, but still trying to complete the exercise! Instructors were always nearby during the evolutions and would immediately rush in and rescue the struggling candidate. Still, it was a scary situation whenever someone passed out.

Roughly halfway through Second Phase, we were subjected to a test known as *pool comp*, in which our fitness, knowledge of basic diving techniques, and our ability to remain unshaken under pressure were severely challenged. Pool comp came at the end of Pool Week, and it had a well-earned reputation for weeding out BUD/S candidates with almost as much efficiency as Hell Week. It was a lot shorter, but in some ways equally challenging. The pool comp test involved jumping into the water with full scuba gear, and then sitting on the bottom while awaiting "orders."

The orders involved two or three instructors diving in after you and conducting an all-out assault known as a *surf hit*. It was pretty simple, really. The instructors were on me in a heartbeat, tearing off my mask, pulling out my air hose, and generally doing their best to instill a sense of complete panic. That's all there was to it: a series of roughly a half dozen situations, each designed to cut off breathing. The natural inclination is to rocket to the surface and take a big gulp of air. But in pool comp, that response gets you a failing grade. We were expected to work through each of the challenges—untying knots in hoses, fixing problems with our tanks, and so on—without coming to the surface. As with most tests in BUD/S, we were given two chances to pass pool comp. I passed on the first attempt, which was a huge relief, since it was a widely held opinion that if you made it through pool comp, you'd make it through Second Phase.

Not that it was easy. After the completion of pool comp, we did a lot of night dives in San Diego Bay. Most of us had never experienced night diving, and coping with the blackness was as challenging as it was it was disorienting. There was also a lot of tedious but important work in pools and tanks. Eventually, near the end of Second Phase, we did get to make one really cool dive, a two-hundred-foot descent to a sunken ship that felt like the sort of scuba diving I'd always heard about, instead of the tortuous and tactical stuff we had been doing for the better part of two months. It was all part of the process—the navy didn't want us out in the ocean, a couple of hundred feet below the surface, until we had demonstrated proficiency in a controlled environment.

By the time Second Phase ended, there were roughly forty

members of Class 246 remaining. We were nine weeks away from becoming SEALs. Finally, it began to seem real. Not just because the distance to the BUD/S finish line was now shorter than the distance we had traveled from the starting line but because Third Phase, as we all knew, would be devoted to training that would most closely resemble life while on deployment as a SEAL. While the handbook description is a mouthful of words about basic weaponry, small-unit tactical training, and demolition, Third Phase is known most commonly as *land warfare*. Like everything else about BUD/S, it was a knee to the nuts.

It was also, at least part of the time, a lot of fun. If you were to ask a civilian to describe their idea of SEAL training, they would probably come up with something like Third Phase. With evolutions that focus on marksmanship and rappelling, as well as explosives and navigation, Third Phase does in fact provide trainees with an opportunity to apply their skills and training to tests that loosely approximate the kind of work they might expect to encounter on deployment.

Loosely. There's nothing quite like going out on a mission, but Third Phase does a pretty good job of introducing the concept. We still did daily training runs, with the expectation that our times would decrease. We still beat ourselves up on the obstacle course. But the pain and stress of physical training was generally incorporated into field exercises that, while challenging, were often interesting and even fun in a weird sort of way. I mean, I'd be lying if I didn't admit that it was cool to blow things up or to become proficient on a variety of weapons— from a 9 mm pistol to an M4 rifle to an M60 machine gun. You don't become a SEAL if you don't like guns and explosives. It's part of the job.

For the last five weeks of Third Phase, we moved offshore to the same training facility, where I'd helped out before starting

Indoctrination some six months earlier. It was strange to think of how far I had come in such a short period of time. Back then, I had been utilized in a variety of ways, including playing the role of an enemy combatant to be dispatched by trainees during an ambush or other simulated mission. Now I was one of the trainees, back on that same jagged, rocky island, with only a few weeks standing between me and graduation.

There were still no guarantees. For one thing, the training facility had its own obstacle course, which, while not as nasty as the course at Coronado, was still no picnic, especially since we covered it while carrying a rifle and other gear, and even learned to negotiate it through a cloud of tear gas. I only ran the entire O Course once on the island, but that was enough, especially since we constantly incorporated long and difficult hill runs into our physical training.

The offshore facility was also the site of one of the most notorious and hated evolutions of BUD/S: a 5.5-nautical-mile swim.

This one had worried me since the start of BUD/S. Even as I survived Hell Week and the lung-popping fear of dive training—experiences that should have, and did, make me more confident—I still kept in the back of my mind an image of the open-water swim that had caused a great many men to DOR or get rolled back just as the end of BUD/S was finally in sight.

It's hard to convey just how hard it is to swim five and a half nautical miles. Or just how much the entire experience sucks. Five and a half miles. In the ocean. In sixty-degree water that is often turbulent, with strong currents. And did I mention the sharks? Okay, I'll say it now. There are sharks all around this island. Big, nasty, man-eating sharks, including the granddaddy of all ocean carnivores: the great white shark.

Now, the truth is, in all the years that the navy has conducted BUD/S training, there has never been a single case of a shark attack on a trainee. But when you step into the water for the five-and-a-half-mile swim, knowing you're going to be out there for more than four hours, wearing a slick black wetsuit and fins that might confuse any hungry shark into thinking he's looking at a seal, rather than a SEAL, it does give you pause. As most people know, the seal is at the top of the great white's preferred menu, and the training facility is home to a large seal colony. Where there are seals, there are sharks, and there were lots of seals nearby.

The possibility that one of us might get eaten was a source of great humor among the instructors in Third Phase, who were, in some ways, even more sadistic than their counterparts back in Coronado. It might have been the distance and the remoteness of the location that brought out the best—or worst—in these guys. Regardless, they took great delight in letting us know that we'd probably have company during the ocean swim. Rumor was they even chummed the water before the evolution. I have no proof that this happened; nevertheless, it would not surprise me. We were told very explicitly that shark encounters were not just possible but likely, and that if we came in contact with one of the toothy monsters, we were to hold our ground and fight back.

Sure.

In all honesty, while the shark talk might have upped the fear factor prior to the ocean swim, once in the water and dealing with the reality of the situation, I never gave much thought to being attacked. Oh, sure, I might have joked about it a little with my swim buddy, Connor (we did the ocean swim in pairs), but it wasn't a practical concern; there were too many other things to worry about and too many other ways in which this evolution sucked. Like many days in BUD/S, there were moments during the ocean swim when I was so exhausted, and in such discomfort, that anything that could put an end to the suffering seemed almost acceptable.

Including being eaten by a great white shark.

That's the sort of thing that slips into your mind when you spend a few hours slogging through frigid ocean water, getting tossed about by the waves—some guys vomit from seasickness—and experiencing cramps in muscles you didn't even know you had. The current can be quite strong, so we were given swim fins (flippers) to wear during the exercise. Sounds generous, right? Well, the truth is that the fins, while helpful in battling the current, put an enormous strain on your calves and feet, which had the unfortunate effect of causing you to tire more easily and increasing the likelihood of cramps. And yet, it wasn't very practical to attempt the swim without them.

For the first couple of miles, Connor and I would stop occasionally to rest and talk. We screwed around a little to take our minds off the pain and exhaustion. I'd been worried about this evolution for months, but I tried to take the same approach that I did to everything during BUD/S: stay calm and keep moving forward. Go to the happy place rather than dwell on the pain. Kick and glide, kick and glide.

At one point, a seal began swimming alongside us, which was one of the coolest things I had ever experienced. And not just for a couple of strokes, either. He was with us for quite a while, maybe a half mile or more. You don't realize how big seals are until one is swimming next to you; nor do you realize how beautiful and graceful they are. They really do look a bit like dogs, and if you get close to one in the water, they have similar personalities. We even played around with him as if he were a puppy. Maybe he was just curious, but this particular guy seemed to be enjoying our company. It occurred to me only later that we might as well have been swimming with shark bait!

At the halfway point, some two and a half hours into the swim, one of the instructors' boats pulled up alongside us and offered canteens of water and protein bars. BUD/S is brutal in its intensity and capacity for inflicting discomfort, but pushing the envelope is not the same as being reckless. You can't complete a five- or six-hour ocean swim without hydrating and eating at some point along the way. It just isn't possible. So we refueled and went back to work.

I have nothing catastrophic to report about the ocean swim. It was long and boring and painful, but at some point, it became apparent that we were going to reach the finish line, and I was filled with a sense of pride and accomplishment. This, I believed, was the last serious obstacle standing between me and graduation from BUD/S, and now it was nearly over.

But as my swim buddy and I broke the surf line and slogged up the beach, we were hit with a surprise. Instead of congratulating us, one of the instructors told us that even though we had finished, we had failed to complete the swim before the mandatory cutoff time.

"Get some rest, gentlemen," he said. "You'll be doing this again tomorrow."

This was perhaps the worst thing I had ever heard in my life. Not since Hell Week had I felt so completely exhausted, and instead of being allowed to celebrate this accomplishment, we were told that we would have to repeat the torture, in less than twenty-four hours. I was angry and confused—I didn't even know there was a cutoff time for the ocean swim (guess I should have paid closer attention); we thought it was one of those evolutions in which mere completion was considered success. It sure as hell seemed like that was a high-enough bar to clear. But I was too tired to question the instructor's mandate, and I figured it wouldn't have mattered, anyway. This was BUD/S: as bad as something was, it could always get worse.

I ate a big meal that evening and passed out as soon as I hit the bed. It was the second-best night of sleep I had ever experienced, surpassed only by the night that Hell Week ended; however, this time I woke not to the sweet relief that comes with knowing the worst is over but to the stark realization that today would be even worse than yesterday. I was so sore I could barely walk. Despite a solid eight hours of sleep, I was foggy and exhausted. The idea that we were going to get back in the water and swim five and a half miles all over again seemed not just crazy but completely unrealistic. They might as well have asked us to swim to Hawaii. For one of the few times during my entire BUD/S experience, I felt a sense of creeping dread. And even a sliver of doubt.

*This can't be happening . . .*

But it was. While the rest of the class slept in, Connor and I, along with a half dozen other "shitbags" (that's what the instructors labeled us for failing to meet the cutoff time), dragged our sorry asses out of bed and began to dress. Included in this group were two guys who had somehow managed to get lost during their first attempt at the swim. I don't know how this was possible, since you basically were supposed to simply follow the shoreline. But apparently, at some point, they had veered out into the ocean and become disoriented, a screwup so incomprehensible that the class paid tribute to it by writing a song in honor of the two wayward students; I don't remember the words, but it was sung to the tune of Queen's "Bohemian Rhapsody." In the fresh light of the morning, we were instructed to prepare all our gear for the ocean swim. We went through the entire pre-swim inspection, just as we had the day before. We were yelled at and told we were useless and threatened with expulsion if we didn't perform better on this day. We had one more chance, they said, to meet the cutoff. Fail, and we'd be rolled back.

We went to the beach, limped into the water, and prepared for a second consecutive day of anguish. Only a few times during BUD/S did I feel defeated before an evolution even began. This was one of those times, and the feeling of impending doom was heightened by the fact that while I was standing in the water, a wave crashed over me, causing me to lose one of my swim fins. Without the fins, the five-and-a-half-mile swim would have been almost impossible. With only one fin . . . well, I can't even imagine the result.

I looked at Connor. He shook his head.

"We've got this," I said, trying to sound encouraging. I don't think it worked.

And then, just as were about to begin swimming, a miracle happened.

"Okay, everybody out!" an instructor yelled. "Today's your lucky day. We're going to give you credit for yesterday's swim."

*Wait . . . what?*

I looked at Connor. We both smiled. And then we laughed. As did the others in our little group of shitbags. Along with the instructors. Turns out, they were just messing with us. In six months of mind fucks, this was the biggest of them all. It was evil. And if I were not so tired, I might have been tempted to say something about it. But I was just happy it was over. In a matter of seconds, the worst day of BUD/S had become the best of days. I even caught a lucky break—one of the other guys found my missing swim fin and handed it to me as we walked out of the water, so I didn't get chewed out for losing my equipment.

A few minutes later, we joined the rest of our classmates for the ceremonial raising of the flag, which we did every morning, usually accompanied by a recitation of the Pledge of Allegiance. With the sun on my face, and the ocean swim behind me, I spoke the words aloud. They had rarely sounded quite so sweet.

Graduation was held on November 21, 2003, on a clear November morning in Coronado, right on the grinder, appropriately enough. This place where we all had worked and suffered for the previous six months was now the site of our greatest celebration. We all wore crisply pressed dress blue uniforms, with white caps and spit-shined shoes.

I'd always been a fairly easygoing guy, not really all that emotional—traits that helped me get through the roller-coaster ride of BUD/S—but I'd be lying if I said that graduation wasn't a powerful day. Although rollbacks from previous classes left Class 246 with roughly 40 graduates, only 22 of the original 168 remained. You could see the pride on everyone's faces, and the joy of being reunited with friends and family, with girlfriends and wives. My parents both made the trip out from Texas to attend graduation, which was nice. They didn't get out of Texas very often, so this was a treat for them. And it gave me a real sense of satisfaction and pride to walk up and receive my certificate, and to then turn around and see their smiling faces.

The hated DOR bell in this setting was transformed from a symbol of individual failure into one of teamwork and triumph. At the end of the graduation ceremony, three different students—the officer in charge, class honor man (the outstanding class member, as determined by a vote of his fellow students), and lead petty officer—all were asked to ring the bell exactly once. As the final bell sounded, we threw our hats into the air and shouted.

"Hoo-yah!"

In reality, BUD/S was just the first step in the long journey to becoming a SEAL. There would be many more months of training—more than a year of Airborne School, SEAL Qualification Training, and Cold Weather Training. Along the way, I'd receive the Special Warfare insignia, also known as *the Seal Trident*, that signifies official membership in the SEAL brotherhood. While we might all have felt like SEALs that day in Coronado, and rightly proud of having survived BUD/S, there was so much more to learn.

A Navy SEAL, after all, is years—not months—in the making.

# Chapter 5

What most people do not realize is that SEALs spend a lot more time training than they do on deployment. There are years of training before the first time a SEAL embarks on a mission, and months of training between deployments. It never ends. Sometimes the training is pretty much what you expect it to be: a lot of time hiking and camping in the wilderness, or jumping out of airplanes, or becoming proficient with a certain type of weaponry.

You know, exactly the kind of stuff you dreamed about doing when you were going through BUD/S. The crazy, fun stuff.

But other times, the training is not at all what you expect. Sometimes it's quieter, more cerebral. Sometimes there are opportunities that you never imagined would come your way, and if you keep your mind open, they can change your life.

By 2006, I was solidly entrenched as a member of SEAL Team 4, stationed in Virginia. I loved everything about the job; it was my entire life, and I threw myself into it with every ounce of energy I possessed. As laid-back as I might have been while growing up in Texas, I was driven and focused when it came to my career as a SEAL. I knew almost from the minute I completed BUD/S that one day I wanted to be part of the navy's most elite team.

Just being part of the SEALs was great, but everyone knew that SEAL Team ████████ was the best of the best: an elite counterinsurgency and fighting unit that drew the most challenging missions around the globe. Just as not everyone who joins the navy wants to be a SEAL, not every SEAL dreams of making it to Team ████████. But many do, and I was certainly one of them. I knew it would be a long journey through an ever-narrowing funnel, but I did everything I could to make myself a strong candidate by going to the right training schools, getting certified in multiple areas, and, most important of all, by doing the best job I could possibly do while I was on SEAL Team 4. The most critical factor in being selected to try out was a recommendation from your current team leaders, troop chief, and master chief, so I knew I had to have a stellar reputation. I wanted to hunt down the baddest of the bad guys in the world's hot spots, and it was no secret that you'd have the best chance to do that if you were on SEAL Team ████████.

I knew what my future would look like.

Or at least I thought I did.

In 2006, while on a training exercise in the mountains of Kentucky, I was exposed to a relatively new program within Naval Special Warfare, and while it didn't change my career plans, it did open my eyes to the possibility that there might be roles within the SEALS that I did not even realize existed. I'd been to South America by this point. I'd spent several months on deployment with Seal Team 4, primarily doing security work in Iraq. It was, for the most part, a quiet deployment, with only a handful of operations, and I was eager to see more action. For now, though, the days and months were filled with training exercises as we waited for the next deployment.

We were doing some urban-warfare training, and in between the excursions, we were invited to take part in a unique demonstration. Unbeknownst to me, the military had recently begun incorporating working dogs into special operations, and they wanted to give us—the guys who would be on the front lines—a sneak preview.

Now, I had a vague notion that dogs were used in law enforcement and some aspects of the military, but I knew almost nothing about military working dogs and even less about how they might be employed in Special Operations. I did, however, love dogs. My mom owned some little dogs, while my dad and I had some big dogs—rottweilers and pit bulls rescued from shelters or just picked up as strays in the street. I'd never done an ounce of training with any of our family dogs—most of them were boisterous, goofy, and prone to getting out of the house and wreaking havoc. But they were harmless enough. We raised them with lots of love, took good care of them, and generally got the same in return. I never expected more from any of my dogs than a good game of fetch and someone to curl up beside me when I was watching TV. That was enough.

What I saw on this day opened my eyes to other possibilities.

It was a short demonstration, just two men and a dog. But what a dog it was! The handler explained that the dog was a Belgian Malinois. I'd never even heard of the breed, but it looked like a German shepherd, only slightly smaller and leaner, and more muscular. The Malinois, the handler explained, was extremely smart and athletic and had been successfully utilized by law enforcement agencies and some aspects of the military for years; more recently, it had been integrated into Special Operations.

"Let me tell you a little bit about this guy and what he can do," the handler said.

There were probably sixty of us in attendance—roughly thirty members of SEAL Team 4, and thirty support people. We all stood around, sort of marveling at the dog's physical strength and beauty, but unsure what to expect, and certainly unconvinced of how he might be of much use to us on deployment. I'm not saying we were skeptical or negative in any way—*curious* might be a better word. In my time as a SEAL, I was open to the idea of using any tool that could make my job easier and safer; I think most guys felt that way. Arrogance and narrow-mindedness will not only make a mission more difficult, they're liable to get you killed. Why not entertain all possibilities?

The handler told us all about the Malinois's incredible sense of smell, how he could detect an explosive odor better than any man-made technology currently available. Obviously, there were any number of ways in which this skill could be utilized: sniffing out roadside bombs in Iraq before they had a chance to kill a Humvee full of American soldiers; detecting an improvised explosive device (IED) that might be hidden near the perimeter of a compound in the mountains of Afghanistan. The dog's ability to track scents could also be used to ferret out bad guys hidden within the compound's walls. Or, as we were about to discover, to run down "squirters" (insurgents fleeing from a building or other target) in a manner that was at once brutal and efficient.

There were actually two handlers. One of them put on a bite suit—basically a heavily padded outfit that covered his torso and extremities, but not his face—and began walking away from the dog and the other handler. He moved a little like the Michelin Man, wobbling awkwardly from side to side because of the bite suit. Meanwhile, the other handler kept a firm grip on the harness of the Malinois. The dog clearly knew what was happening. He did not strain or pull against the handler's grip, but his body was tight, his eyes fixed on the target moving slowly away from him. I noticed the Malinois shifting his weight subtly, bouncing lightly on his paws. Like a racehorse in the starting gate, he was eager to run and simply waiting for the command.

The man in the bite suit kept walking, walking, walking across an open field, until he was perhaps fifty meters away. He stopped and turned to face the other handler and the dog. Then he waved his hands and began running. Well, shuffling, really, but still, he had a head start roughly equivalent to half the length of a football field. How quickly could the Malinois make up the distance? And what would happen when he reached his target?

The answers to both questions came soon enough. The handler released the dog and shouted a word I did not recognize. Instantly, as if shot out of a gun, the Malinois burst into a dead sprint. An audible gasp went up from the crowd, the sound of appreciation and wonder. I had some fairly strong and athletic dogs when I was a kid, but I had never seen anything like this. The Malinois, seventy-five pounds of muscle, looked more like a greyhound, skimming across the ground so effortlessly that he seemed almost to be flying. I figured it would take him maybe a half minute to catch the fleeing Michelin Man, but it took less than a fraction of that. The dog devoured the distance between them in what felt like a heartbeat, finishing with an explosive pounce that brought the target to the ground like a wide receiver getting blindsided by a free safety.

As the man fell, the dog attached himself with his teeth, wrapping his muzzle around the man's arm and hanging on with an intensity and fierceness I had never seen. And remember—I had owned pit bulls and rottweilers! There were more gasps from the crowd, followed by laughter, and then some shouts of approval and respect. It was like watching one of those nature videos where a cheetah runs down a gazelle, or a shark launches itself into a sea lion. Although there was no blood, it was still impressively violent. The dog was less than half the size of the man, but completely and utterly in control of the situation. As the guy writhed on the ground, yelping and flailing his arms in a futile attempt to discourage his attacker, the other handler jogged across the field, a big smile on his face.

I found it interesting that the Malinois was so precise in his attack. He could have bitten the man's neck or face, but instead he simply held tight to the arm with a viselike grip. There was, in fact, no attempt to bite any other part of the target. It was like the dog understood his job: to track down the runner, bring him to the ground, and restrain him until the other handler arrived. And this he did with stunning effectiveness. As the other handler arrived at the scene of the attack and put a firm hand on the dog's harness, the dog at first maintained his bite. But when the handler shouted again—issuing another command I could not understand—the Malinois loosened his grip. The handler then easily pulled him off the target, giving the Michelin Man time and space to climb to his feet. As he did so, we all broke into spontaneous applause.

And that was about it. The handler in charge of the demonstration thanked us for our time and reiterated that this was not merely a project in development but an inevitability: military working dogs had been integrated into the highest levels of Special Operations, including the Navy SEALs, and soon enough we'd find ourselves on deployment with them. I suppose it's possible that a few guys were skeptical. After all, things do not happen quickly in the navy. And maybe there were some people who, despite what they had just witnessed, simply didn't see the value of bringing a dog out on a mission. I saw the Malinois for what it was: a weapon. And an impressive one, at that.

Still, I never imagined that the fledgling canine program would have much of an impact on me personally. At the time, I was focused on being a shooter. An operator. A SEAL. There wasn't room in my head to fantasize about all the ways a dog might one day work itself into my life. That would happen much later.

In late 2006, I deployed for a second time to Iraq with SEAL Team 4. A generally accepted prerequisite for screening for Team ▮▮▮▮▮▮ is to have two deployments under your belt. This makes sense; you get more responsibility with each deployment, which helps you build a résumé—and gives the navy a better opportunity to assess the capabilities of each applicant and to narrow the pool through evaluations and recommendations of superiors. Basically, what you are told is this: "Don't even think about asking to join SEAL Team ▮▮▮▮▮▮ until you've been around a couple of years."

I was not that patient.

In fact, I started asking about the screening process early in my second deployment. I knew it wouldn't happen at that point, but I wanted to make sure that my career goals were clear and that my interest was conveyed right up the chain of command. I figured everyone would appreciate my honesty and enthusiasm; this turned out not to be the case.

As with everything in the military, protocol must be followed. I had taken the first step in the application process by signing a simple form expressing my interest. It wasn't a big deal, since a lot of guys had expressed interest. Most of them knew enough to just sign the form and let it go—do their job and hope for the best. I signed the form and then made a habit of following up with verbal requests.

"When can I screen? I'm ready."

"Shut up and relax, Cheese [my nickname]. We'll let you know."

This continued throughout my second trip to Iraq, which was roughly twice as long as the first deployment (six months instead of three months), and significantly more intense. Baghdad was the scene of heavy urban fighting in those days, and had been since the Siege of Sadr City had begun some two years earlier. This particular deployment put us in the heart of the action at the beginning of a massive U.S. surge, ordered by President George W. Bush during Operation Iraqi Freedom, that sent an estimated twenty thousand additional troops into Iraq, ostensibly to help the Iraqi government stabilize a wildly unstable region and to protect locals against insurgents.

Baghdad at that time was one of the most dangerous places on the planet—a steaming cesspool of terrorists and heavily armed insurgents who were often indistinguishable from the people we were trying to protect. It was, for me, an eye-opening job. But it was precisely where I wanted to be. From the first time we barreled through Sadr City, evading roadside IEDs and often with guns blazing, I knew I was right where I belonged. I never questioned the logic or politics of our work; I had a job to do, and I did it to the best of my ability. I'm not the first person to say this, but I'll say it again: when you are a solider, on the ground, in the middle of a battle, you fight not just for your country, or even primarily for your country, but for the brothers on your right and on your left. There were times, in both Iraq and Afghanistan, when the ever-changing rules of engagement made our jobs more difficult, if not downright confounding, but we did the best we could.

In Baghdad, in late 2006 and early 2007, we had a lot of latitude when it came to general combat and removing high-value targets. And I felt like a sponge; every day, I was learning new tactics and doing a job that I felt was important. I was saving lives. Sometimes, in the process, I took lives. That's just the way it worked. I can't remember the first time I killed someone; I'm not even sure I realized it at the time. The fighting in Baghdad was often chaotic and frantic and a lot less personal than it would be in Afghanistan. We'd be driving through Sadr City, taking sniper fire, and we'd sometimes spray an entire building in response. These were not precise, strategic attacks; they were an appropriately heavy-handed response to deadly force, and I'm sure that opposition forces were obliterated as a result. I didn't lose a minute's sleep over it.

Nor did I anguish over the more intimate encounters that resulted in death. The fact is, that was the role of Special Operations: not just to support ground troops in battle—although we did that—but to locate and eliminate targets that were deemed by U.S. intelligence to be of significant importance, as well a threat to Iraqi civilians and American troops. *Targets* is a clean and benign term. Sounds like it could be an office building or a facility for manufacturing weapons. Sometimes that's exactly what it was. More often than not, though, in the context of Special Operations, the term *target* referred to a person or a group of people.

*Bad guys.*

We'd get our intelligence and go after the target. This usually meant going door to door, sometimes breeching a locked or fortified building, interviewing locals to determine whether they were friendly or helping the insurgents. Sometimes the night would end quietly, with no engagement. Sometimes it would result in close-quarters combat. Sometimes it went smoothly, with only a few shots being fired, all from our side. The end result, more often than not, was the elimination of a target.

Other times, new and unanticipated targets presented themselves suddenly in the heat of battle or during the course of a strategic operation. In other words, one target sometimes led to another. These were the most challenging circumstances, for they required not only technical skill and combat acumen but the ability to think on your feet . . . and the confidence to make decisions that might have large and lasting ramifications.

And deadly consequences.

There was, for example, a day early in my second deployment with Team 4, when I found myself on the roof of a building in Baghdad, surveying the scene on the roof of a second building across the street. This was typically the way we worked: one group of operators would enter a building, while one or two snipers, often accompanied by a translator or an Iraqi soldier (one of the "good guys") would hold down security from another vantage point. In Iraq, the fighting was such that any building might not only be occupied by insurgents but rigged with explosives or overseen by snipers. It was imperative that we had another set of eyes, or multiple sets of eyes, on activity outside the building to ensure the safety of our guys.

At first, everything was pretty quiet, until the Iraqi soldier called my name. I walked over to another part of the roof.

"There," he said, pointing to a man in street clothes on the other building, hustling around the roof.

"What do you think?" I asked.

The Iraqi shook his head. "No good."

I fell to my stomach, flipped open the tripod on my MK-12, a highly reliable semiautomatic sniper rifle loaded with a 5.56 mm cartridge, and peered through the scope. And then I watched. I followed his movements for the next minute or two as he scurried about the roof of the building. At one point, he took out a cell phone—usually, although not always, a bad sign—and began talking to someone. He put the phone away, moved around the roof some more. He went to the edge of the roof and stared at the street below for a few seconds and then backed away.

By any reasonable definition, his behavior was suspect. By

the standards of urban warfare in Baghdad, his behavior practically screamed, "Trouble!" I had buddies in that building. My
job was to protect them so that they could safely complete their
mission. Intelligence had told us the building was occupied by
insurgents, and now, on the roof of that building, was a young
man in street clothes, talking on a cell phone and nervously
surveying the landscape below. He seemed unusually skittish—
moving around anxiously, hopping over small rooftop walls,
peering over the side of the building and then retreating to a
sheltered spot, and talking on his phone.

Among the tactics utilized by insurgents in Baghdad at that
time was a relatively low-tech assault in which hand grenades
were lobbed from rooftops into passing Humvees occupied by
U.S. soldiers. It was simple . . . and brutally effective. I didn't
know if the guy had a stash of grenades at his disposal; from my
vantage point, even with a high-powered scope, it was difficult
to tell. For all I knew, he might have had a box of grenades hidden out of sight.

Anything was possible.

I continued to watch and wait, all the while keeping the
guy directly in my crosshairs. I thought about the various ways
in which the scenario could unfold. If I shot the guy, and he
turned out to be nothing more than a harmless civilian, there
would be serious repercussions. Morally speaking, of course, I
did not want to kill an innocent civilian. Legally, I'd face some
serious shit, and there would be blowback for the entire unit.
It's one thing when a civilian is killed because he or she is in the
wrong place at the wrong time—near the site of an explosion,
for example. That is tragic, but it is unfortunately sometimes a
consequence of war. And it is more readily explainable, if not
necessarily acceptable.

These things are not always black and white, and occasionally mistakes are made in the chaos of combat. But SEALs are

trained in such a way as to minimize such occurrences; more-over, the intelligence we received was usually rock solid, which helped tremendously. Still, there were many times when diffi-cult decisions were left up to the individual, who had to use his head and his experience, as well as his instinct, to make the right choice.

I was still young and raw; nevertheless, this was my call. There was no one to ask for advice. I had been trained to make precisely this type of decision and to live with the consequences.

I squeezed the trigger. There was a slight hesitation as the bullet whistled through a couple of hundred meters of air. The man on the building across the street dropped to the roof.

This was one of my first kills—or, at least, one of the first that I was sure of. There were no exultations, no celebration or anything like that. In the moment after he fell, I mainly felt relief that a threat to my teammates had been eliminated. But I'd be lying if I didn't admit that a tiny part of me worried that I'd made a mistake.

As it happened, I'd made the right call. The guy on the roof was precisely the target we had sought. He'd heard our unit approaching and, with no way to get out of the building, had rushed to the roof. Did I have to shoot him? Maybe, maybe not. But if the alternative to taking him out was the possibility that he might throw a grenade at one of my buddies, then I'm at peace with the decision.

As a bonus, at a morning briefing a couple of days later, one of the battalion commanders informed us that the guy I'd killed had been responsible for the deaths of several American soldiers; they'd been after him for a while.

"Thank you," he said. "From everyone. Nice job, son."

I felt pretty good about that outcome, and it helped instill the confidence to make tough calls throughout my time as a SEAL. On balance, as I look back on it, I feel worse and lose more sleep over the shots I didn't take than the ones I did take.

I actually loved being a Navy SEAL on deployment. I found it to be exciting and highly challenging work—exactly what I had spent the previous several years training to do. There was no moral ambiguity for me, nor for any of the SEALs with whom I worked as far as I could tell. We were the good guys, they were the bad guys. Simple as that. The guy I shot? Given half a chance, he'd have done the same to me.

Killing is part of the contract for a SEAL; a big part, in fact. I never had any problem with that. We were always careful to minimize the risk to civilians or other friendlies. The elimination of a murderer—and that is precisely the way I viewed our targets, as people who killed freely and indiscriminately (terrorists, in short)—caused me not a second of unrest; not while I was on deployment, and not when I came home.

It was the battles lost, large and small, that broke my heart. It was the friends who gave their lives. That's the stuff that affected me the most, and it stayed with me a long time.

SEALs are very good at what they do. They are generally better trained than the enemy, better equipped, and more committed to the outcome. They win more than they lose, even when outnumbered. But the truth of war—including Special Operations—is that sometimes you take casualties, and no amount of preparation or training can prevent it from happening. My introduction to this reality came during my second deployment, when we lost a good friend of mine, Special Warfare Operator Second Class Joseph C. Schwedler.

I'd known Clarkie (his middle name was *Clark*, and most everyone referred to him as *Clarkie*) since BUD/S. We were both part of Class 246. Clarkie had grown up in Crystal Falls, Michigan, and went on to attend Michigan State before enlisting in the navy. Like a lot of us, he knew from the moment he signed up that he wanted to be a SEAL. He was a former high school football and basketball player—tough and athletic with a great sense of humor and unwavering good spirits. He wasn't a thrill-seeker. He was a patriot who believed in service. He was just the kind of positive person you wanted to be around, especially when going through the misery of BUD/S.

Clarkie and I were both assigned to SEAL Team 4, in Virginia, and although we were assigned to different platoons, in different parts of the country, when we got to Iraq, we remained good friends. He was just a solid, loyal guy, extremely competent and committed. But shit happens, and it can happen to anyone.

Like the rest of us on SEAL Team 4, Clarkie was coming up on the end of his second deployment to Iraq in early April 2007, when a coalition helicopter was shot down by terrorists near Fallujah, where Clarkie's platoon was stationed. Shortly thereafter, intelligence led to a raid on a home occupied by insurgents suspected of being involved in the attack. There was nothing unique about the raid, and I guess that merely underscores the danger of the job. As often happened in Iraq, the team encountered resistance, including a shooter who had barricaded himself behind a locked door. The door was breached, entry was made, and during the encounter, the shooter managed to squeeze off a few rounds, at least one of which hit Clarkie. He died almost immediately.

Clarkie's death, which occurred, coincidentally, on the same day as my father's birthday, hit me hard, both because of our friendship and brotherhood as members of SEAL Team 4 and because it was a reminder of the fragility of life. We weren't invincible. Despite all our training and preparation—despite the technology and intelligence that supported us—we weren't infallible. The job was dangerous and potentially deadly. But

Clarkie's death did nothing to dissuade my ambition. If anything, his passing provoked within me an even greater commitment to the cause. I'm not saying I wanted to avenge his death or anything like that; we were all a little more pragmatic and professional than that. We knew the risks of the job and accepted them without complaint. So while I was deeply saddened by the passing of my friend, I was not discouraged. If anything, I wanted more than ever to be in the thick of the fight. I wanted access to the missions that had the highest chance of providing lasting change.

I wanted to be part of SEAL Team ███████.

Throughout my second deployment, I continued to be a pain in the ass on this particular subject. Eventually, I was told in no uncertain terms that what I considered to be persistence was viewed as annoyance.

"If you don't knock it off, Cheese, you're going to eliminate yourself from consideration."

That's the last thing I wanted, so I toned it down to an acceptable level, while still making it clear that I was interested. When our deployment ended in May, we returned to Virginia. I had started to get the impression that the odds were against me screening, not because of my performance but because I was one of the younger guys on a team that had a bunch of highly capable candidates. There simply wasn't room for everyone. After all, it wasn't wise to deplete the ranks of one team. Someone had to stay behind and help train the newer guys. There was a pecking order, and while it was based partly on ability and performance, it was also based on age and experience. Despite having two deployments under my belt, I remained one of the younger guys on SEAL Team 4. I understood, and I wasn't going to make a big deal out of it. If I had to wait, I would wait. I figured eventually my time would come.

Fortunately, it came almost immediately.

# Chapter 6

No one quits the Training Team.

Well, that's not quite true—I'm sure it happens occasionally. But for the most part, a SEAL who is offered a chance to screen for Team ███████—in a demanding six-month process during which he will be part of an elite training unit—will not withdraw of his own volition. BUD/S is comprised of many months of ceaseless physical and mental pressure; the vast majority of trainees simply aren't up to the challenge, and they know it. They either don't want it badly enough, or they can't fight through the pain. Either way, the outcome is the same: they quit.

The Training Team is different. The training is physically intense and demanding, but focused as much on performance as misery. It's all geared toward practical application of skills that will be used on deployment. The goal is not to force candidates to quit but rather to determine which ones are best suited to the job. And since everyone who joins the Training Team is already, by definition, pretty damn good at his job, with a minimum of two combat deployments as a SEAL on his résumé and a proven ability to endure the six-month suckfest that is BUD/S, the navy has to come up with other methods to thin the herd.

They do this through endless physical testing and performance evaluations during various forms of combat and survival training, as well as through psychological testing, all of which led to a Training Team attrition rate of roughly 50–60 percent. But at this level, guys don't quit. They are simply asked to leave.

I joined the Training Team in the fall of 2007. Most of the training took place in Virginia, although some of our marksmanship training was held in Mississippi. For me, the hardest thing about the Training Team was knowing that I couldn't simply will myself to the finish line. As in BUD/S, my generally low-key personality helped make it easier to withstand the constant shitstorm of abuse from instructors. The stress came from trying to achieve required scores and times in a variety of evolutions—and from not knowing whether I was considered an appropriate psychological fit. All I could do was work my ass off every day, try to maintain a good attitude, and hope I wouldn't be asked to leave.

I never was.

At the end of six months, I graduated from the Training Team and became one of the youngest members of SEAL Team ██████. Training Team graduates are assigned to one of four squadrons, each denoted by color. Regardless of a squadron's particular reputation or area of expertise, it's fair to say that every member of the team is, first and foremost, a fighter.

An operator.

Squadrons choose their new members in a mysterious process that resembles the NFL or NBA draft. Training Team graduates are assigned to a particular squadron based on that team's openings and needs. Personality and fit can factor into the process, as well, with prior relationships sometimes playing a role. I would have been content with any assignment, but as it turned out, I was assigned to a squadron where I happened to have a couple of friends.

The best thing about going to Team ███████—and this was obvious from day one—was the increase in resources. Simply put, there was more money. By that, I don't mean that we were paid better (there was a modest bump in salary, but I barely noticed it and didn't care, anyway). I am referring to the fact that it was obviously a step up: I knew we'd be getting the plum assignments on deployment and going after the most important targets, but even at home in the States, while training, it was apparent that the team got almost anything it needed in terms of equipment and other resources. It was all first rate.

If there was a downside, it was simply that I went back to being low man on the totem pole, so to speak. The new guys from the Training Team got all the shit jobs and worked the longest hours. First to arrive, last to leave—which, by the way, is exactly as it should be. I got used to taking out the trash or cleaning up, carrying stuff nobody else wanted to carry during training exercises, and generally just doing whatever scut work I was assigned. I kept my mouth shut and my eyes open.

Training provided endless opportunities for the new guys to find their niche, and then they would naturally gravitate toward concentrating on that specialty. Some guys liked skydiving, for example. Other guys liked sniper training or climbing.

I liked dogs.

I mean, I liked a lot of the other stuff, too, but I found myself drawn to the dogs, probably more out of curiosity than anything else.

The history of working dogs within the Navy SEALs can

be traced back as far as the Vietnam War, although their use was not widely implemented until after the events of 9/11. Because of the nature of the conflicts in Iraq and Afghanistan, which frequently involved hidden explosive devices and targets embedded within civilian communities, it became apparent that specially trained MWDs, with their extraordinary sense of smell and ferocious prey drive, could be not just useful but invaluable. As a result, demand for the dogs worldwide soon outstripped availability, leading to an expansion of programs designed to train both dogs and handlers across a broad spectrum of military Special Operations.

Rather than simply acquire dogs from other sources, the SEALs began training their own dogs, much as the army had been doing for years. A small, fledgling program in Virginia, specifically designed to provide combat assault dogs for the elite SEAL team, had been in place for a couple of years by the time I arrived.

Although I had never seen MWDs utilized on deployment, my one interaction during that training exercise in Kentucky had left a strong impression; more so, I would guess, than it had on some of my teammates. There certainly wasn't any animosity toward the canine program—indeed, the more people were exposed to it, the greater their appreciation. Still, a lot of guys weren't particularly interested in a deeper involvement. But to be integrated into the ranks, the dogs had to become comfortable with their human counterparts, and we, as SEALs, had to be comfortable around them. As one of the new guys, I was a bigger part of this desensitization process than perhaps some of the more experienced members of the team.

It was all pretty basic stuff. We'd watch the handlers work with the dogs, then take a turn at moving them around—very gently, just guiding them through spaces. The dog would be passed from soldier to soldier. Sometimes, while we were doing shooting drills, the dogs would walk around us or weave through our legs. The idea was to simulate for them, as well as for us, the conditions of battle, so they would be comfortable around gunfire and explosions and respond positively to anyone in the unit. You didn't want a dog freaking out and biting one of his own soldiers when the bullets started flying.

Everyone took a turn at this. Some guys merely tolerated it, while others, like me, found it fascinating. I wouldn't say I had any intention of making a career out of being a dog handler—I was more interested in being a traditional operator—but I liked the look and temperament of the dogs, and I was curious about how they would perform in the field of battle.

The answer came during my next deployment in the spring and early summer of 2008. We were based in Kandahar, but ended up spending as much time out on operations as we did on the base. In just about every way imaginable, it was a very different experience from my two previous deployments with SEAL Team 4.

For one thing, the fighting was quite different. In Iraq, especially in Baghdad, we usually hopped in an armored vehicle and rode through the crowded city streets. In Afghanistan, our missions took us out into rural and mountainous regions, or to small villages, on an almost nightly basis.

Despite the mountainous terrain and the comparative lack of population density, it was a very busy deployment. This was, in part, because our team, by design, was kept very active with a seemingly never-ending stream of quality missions and high-value targets presenting themselves. We'd sleep until late morning or early afternoon. Then we'd eat a big breakfast or lunch, hit the gym to work out, and wait for a late-afternoon briefing, during which details of the next operation were revealed.

The rhythm and tempo of a deployment are usually established early, and this one was active from the beginning. We went out on missions four or five nights a week, usually with a couple of teams, each consisting of six or seven assaulters and roughly an equal number of support personnel. Sometimes we'd hit long stretches during which we would go out virtually every night.

Rarely were these excursions quiet and uneventful. We had solid intelligence behind us and the capability to neutralize targets with efficiency. In most cases, this meant fighting stealthily, in close quarters, to minimize the risk to both our own troops and Afghan civilians. It was dangerous, intense work, but this was what we had been trained to do, and I found it exhilarating and rewarding.

But here's the strange thing: most of the time, I didn't even get nervous before we went out on missions. It was a job, and I felt like I was completely prepared to do the job to the best of my ability. Sometimes we'd have to fly an hour and a half or more to reach our drop-off point for the evening mission. On the flight, some guys would listen to music, some guys would just think. Some guys would read by ChemLight. Talking was difficult because of the noise in the chopper. A surprising number of guys would fall asleep almost as soon as they climbed aboard. I was often one of them. I don't share that as an illustration of toughness but merely as an example of the professionalism and temperament of the guys on the team. We approached it as though it were work, not a video game or an adventure.

If there was ever a temptation to become overconfident or complacent, something would happen to remind you of the stakes involved. Our squadron did not lose anyone on that deployment, but we were involved in one firefight, alongside a Ranger unit, in which one of the Rangers was killed by a squirter who had bedded down in an open field. Those were some of the most dangerous scenarios—when a target got out of a secured area and lay in wait, hidden by grass or trees. Usually, when that happened, the squirter became less a fighter than a suicide bomber. He knew he was going to die; he just wanted to take as many people with him as he could. All the training in the world won't save you if you happen upon someone with a bomb or a grenade. Wrong place, wrong time.

In this regard, a military working dog was an exceptional asset.

We had two dogs embedded with us on that deployment. Their names were Falco and Balto. Night after night, I watched them do amazing work, catching or neutralizing one bad guy after another. There were virtually no restrictions on where we could take them. If we had to jump out of a helicopter while hovering fifty or a hundred feet above ground, the handler would hook the dog into his line and fast-rope with him. If we had to parachute in—which wasn't common, but did happen—the dog would be placed in a harness and a large pouch attached to his handler, and the two of them would jump together. It was awesome to witness this, especially since the dogs always seemed so calm. Dogs instinctively do not like high, open spaces. For example, some dogs wash out of SEAL training because they freak out when climbing stairs. But just as SEAL candidates either overcome these sorts of phobias and deficiencies or find themselves dropping out of BUD/S, so, too, does the stock get thinned during canine training. The dogs who were deployed with SEALs in Afghanistan were the best of the best. They were genetically gifted and temperamentally suited to the assignment; whatever weaknesses they might have had were mostly trained out of them.

So, when it came time to jump, they jumped, or at least they were cradled without much fuss.

You had to see the dogs on a nightly basis to truly appreciate their contributions. It wasn't just that Balto and Falco could sniff out explosive devices or run down a squirter before he had time to take out one of our team. They could also be sent into a building, where their movement could be tracked with cameras. This naturally made it possible for us to have a better idea of what we would see once inside, and it would minimize the likelihood of surprises. Not only would the dogs provide us with a clear picture of a structure, but they would also frequently find bad guys and either hold them at bay until we arrived, or literally start ripping them apart. Since the insurgents were generally reluctant to reveal their position, they would avoid shooting at the dogs unless absolutely necessary. Often, by the time they tried to fire, they already had a dog's powerful muzzle wrapped around their arm or leg.

It always seemed to me that the bad guys feared our dogs more than they feared us. And maybe with good reason.

At first, I barely noticed the dogs. They were just sort of there, behaving appropriately, sometimes being used extensively and getting involved in the action and sometimes not. Then I started to pay closer attention, and I started to see the little things they did and how fiercely loyal and reliable they were. It was common to come back from a mission and sit around afterward and debrief casually over a few beers about what had gone down. We'd tell stories about shit that had happened, targets we'd eliminated, close calls, and the like. Invariably, someone would bring up one of the dogs.

"You see what Balto did out there, man?"

"No, I was on the other side of the compound. What happened?"

"Practically took a squirter's arm off. Guy never had a chance."

Sometimes the stories were more dramatic than mere run-downs. There was one time, for example, when a group of our guys were walking through a field, in a line. The dog was on the left end of the line, off lead, and actively following a scent. He was excited, which is usually a sign that a dog is onto something. This type of situation is ripe for the possibility of an ambush, so the dog's handler gave a command to let him go. The dog sprinted down the line of men at full speed, from the far left to the far right, near a tree line. He stopped suddenly and tore into the ground in front of him. A human cry went out, loud and piercing. There was a flutter of grass and leaves and other debris as an insurgent popped up, with the dog still attached to his feet, and AK-47 in his hands.

They weren't more than a few meters from our unit.

I was a good distance away from the engagement, so I didn't see the way it ended, but there was no shortage of guys who wanted to talk about it afterward. As the dog ripped into his leg, the guy hesitated just long enough to present a close and easy target for our unit. He was shot and killed at close range, and the mission went on without incident and without any casualties on our side. But if not for the dog's intervention, that encounter would have ended very differently. I don't know how many of our people the insurgent might have taken out before he was killed, but the answer is definitely not *zero*. He had an automatic weapon, and he was close enough to have squeezed off a few quick and deadly rounds before we would have had time to react.

Sometimes, we'd say a dog saved our lives, and it was just a generally descriptive term for something he did that made our job easier. Other times, it was a literal description of what had transpired.

*"That dog just saved my life!"*

This particular incident fell into the second category.

More common were incidents in which one of the dogs would simply make our jobs easier by revealing a squirter's position or running him down. When that happened, the handler would let the dog get in a few good bites, then recall the dog through his transmitter or by yelling to him. Once the dog safely returned, we could eliminate the squirter by tossing a grenade onto his position from a safe distance.

As the deployment went on, I came to realize that a dog saving someone's life, in any number of ways, wasn't that rare an occurrence. When you're going out on operations practically every night, for four or five months, and coming in contact with the enemy on most of those missions, the close calls begin to add up.

I began to think of Balto and Falco as not just tools or weapons but as full-fledged members of the squadron. I began to think of them as members of our family.

I don't mean to imply that the dogs did all the dirty work for us; they were additional tools in the box, albeit tools that were highly effective. They were so reliable, in fact, that sometimes we had to remind ourselves not to break protocol solely because of something the dog had done. For example, let's say we were using the dogs to help clear a house. We might send one of the dogs in first to check things out. If the dog found nothing, that didn't mean the house was empty or that a particular room was empty. They were not infallible, and sometimes they could be distracted by outside factors: strange noises or funky smells. Livestock, in particular, was an ongoing problem, since so many Afghan compounds were overrun with animals like dogs, goats, chickens, and so on.

If the dog returned from a house search having detected nothing, we followed suit, and while training and experience dictated that we proceed as if a dog had not even checked the place out—in other words, that every room might in fact be occupied by someone with a gun or explosives—I can't deny that a clean search by Balto or Falco left me with just the slightest warm and fuzzy feeling. It didn't change the way I did my job, but it was reassuring. Like I said, the dogs weren't perfect, but they didn't make a lot of mistakes.

A bigger risk was the possibility of getting so caught up in the dog's performance that you might temporarily forget about your own job. Here's the truth: it's an absolutely amazing thing to see a dog attacking a bad guy, just effortlessly crushing someone who has a one-hundred-pound advantage. I'd been warned about this ahead of time; we all had.

"Don't watch the dogs," we were told. "I know it's fun. I know it's tempting. But it's dangerous as hell. Do your job."

More than once on that deployment, I caught a quick glimpse of a bad guy going down, shrieking at the top of his lungs as Balto or Falco ripped at his flesh. I never stopped working, but I might have taken a few seconds to admire the awesome display of power and violence. I mean, how could you not?

These dogs were fighting and tracking machines. They also could be cute as hell. Balto's handler actually taught him how to open doors! Which was one hell of a trick but also freaked people out a bit. Some dogs were more affectionate than others—like humans, each had its own personality and temperament—but in general, they could be trusted to hang out with us when we got back from a mission. They were tools, yes. They were weapons. But they also were . . . *dogs*. If you were a dog guy like I am, you were predisposed to feeling affectionate toward them. And the fact that they were such loyal and reliable soldiers, as well, only served to strengthen the relationship.

Occasionally, if things unfolded just right, we might get more than a brief glimpse. There was a night early in the deployment, for instance, when we were working our way through a compound. We had gotten word that our target—a male—was hiding somewhere in the compound, so we slowly worked our way around the perimeter and through each building. Every mission was different, and while our intel was usually solid, we never knew what we might find once we were on the ground. We might be looking for a lone male in his thirties and discover a houseful of his friends, all armed to the teeth and willing to die for the cause. Or we might find absolutely nothing. Dry holes were common, but you had to treat every mission as if it could be deadly. You just never knew.

We all learned how to interview the locals, since the bad guys often were embedded within their homes. It wasn't unusual for the locals to hate the insurgents—their existence complicated the locals' lives and put them at risk—but fear played into the equation, as well. The locals were often so frightened of repercussions that they would not easily give up the position of a bad guy who might in fact be hiding right in their home. We learned to ask the right questions and discern fact from fiction, but it was a constant struggle. Some of the Afghans welcomed our presence. Some of them hated us almost as much, if not more, than they hated the insurgents.

We never knew who to trust, so in the end, we mainly trusted our instincts. Dogs were immensely helpful in that regard, since they couldn't be bothered with extensive interviewing or logistical hand-wringing. Turn them loose and let them poke around. Sometimes the results were amazing. This particular night was one such instance. We slowly and methodically began clearing the compound, calling to the residents to come out of their rooms, most of which were doorless or otherwise open. At first, they all seemed to comply. One after another, the locals walked out into the center of the compound, hands up, offering no trouble or resistance, as we moved through the open courtyard. Near the end, a single doorway remained covered by a curtain.

We asked if anyone occupied the room. Several of the locals nodded affirmatively.

"Come out!" we yelled. (Although we almost always were accompanied by an interpreter, most of us had mastered a few important phrases or commands in Pashto: "Stop!" "Come out!" "Don't be a fucking idiot!")

No response.

Typically, we did not ask more than once. Refusal to comply usually indicated that the person inside the room was either the target we sought or a different bad guy. Either way, he was now officially considered dangerous. The next step would be an escalation of force: flash bombs, for example. Or . . .

"Come out now, or we send in the dog."

Still no response. The team leader nodded at Frank, Falco's handler. Frank unclipped the dog from his hip lead (a leash attached to the handler's belt), and Falco bolted away. It took him only a few seconds to reach the doorway. Instantly, there was contact—the sound of a man screaming. Ordinarily, the handler would have let this go on for a few moments before operators followed the dog into the room to make sure the target wasn't killed (ideally, he would be held for interrogation); more importantly, to make sure the dog wasn't harmed. Some dogs, especially newer dogs, were more aggressive than others. They would bite whenever the opportunity presented itself. Others preferred to "bark and hold," meaning they would corner a bad guy and immobilize him with fear. The danger was that an armed insurgent might shoot a dog that had opted to bark and hold rather than bite. Falco, in the beginning, was prone to barking and holding rather than biting. But this tendency was effectively trained out of him to the point that he became an absolute monster—in the best possible sense of the term.

Before anyone could react, Falco pulled the target out of the room and into the hallway. The man was seated on the floor, turned sideways, with Falco locked onto his arm. But instead of just holding the man in place, Falco began slowly backing up, dragging the man with short intense bursts of strength.

Rather than interfere, we all stood there watching in astonishment as this bizarre game of fetch played itself out. The man screamed and swatted at Falco, but every attempt to free himself only deepened Falco's resolve and, presumably, his bite. Blood poured down the guy's arm as he tried to dig in with his feet and prevent Falco from delivering the goods. An added benefit of Falco's determination was that it provided us with an opportunity to get a full view of the insurgent, and to see whether he was wearing a suicide vest—an enemy tactic that was, unfortunately, not uncommon during missions in Afghanistan. But he had no chance. Falco kept backing up, his muscular body positioned inches off the floor to gain the greatest leverage. Eventually, they came to rest at the foot of our line of soldiers. Falco let go and returned to Frank as the insurgent slumped to the floor, blood pouring down his arm, whimpering from pain and exhaustion.

*Good boy!*

We were probably halfway through that deployment when I decided that I wanted to be a dog handler. This was not a decision to be made lightly. While dogs were extremely important to our work—and by extension, so were their handlers—the job was quite different from what I had done in the past and from what I had always assumed would be my role as a SEAL.

Not everyone wanted to be a dog handler. First of all, you had to really like dogs. Second, you had to accept the fact that the job was, by design, a supportive position. One of critical importance, to be sure, but unlike other team members, a dog handler was expected to manage and care for his dog at all times while also serving as a shooter. It was an extraordinarily demanding and complicated job. It's true that once Frank released Falco, he became another soldier, armed and ready to fight. But he had to balance those two priorities: fighting and taking care of Falco. The dog handler was rarely the first guy in a room. Much of the time, he was outside, on the perimeter with his dog. This job was no less important than any other job on a mission.

But it was, indisputably, *different.*

Not only that, but the responsibility of being a dog handler never seemed to end. Operators (or *assaulters,* as we often were called) would return from a mission, take care of their gear and collateral duties, and then hang out and relax. The dog handler . . . well, he had to take care of the dog 24-7. Some guys, like Frank, loved it. Frank was a master-at-arms in the navy; he wasn't a SEAL. But he knew his shit when it came to dogs, and he could handle himself in a firefight. I was intrigued by the challenge of balancing these twin responsibilities. Others? Not so much. Most guys would look at Frank (or a SEAL dog handler) and think, *You're out of your fucking mind.* We were all grateful to have Falco and Balto on the squadron, and we respected the hell out of Frank for taking on the responsibility of making sure Falco was fit and well trained and ready for work—and for leading him into combat situations.

But make no mistake: almost no one wanted to switch places with Frank.

Almost.

As the deployment wore on, I spent increasing blocks of time with both dogs, but especially with Falco. I just liked his personality. I also knew that Frank was planning on giving up his role as Falco's primary handler after this deployment, which meant Falco would need a new partner. I spent a lot of time hanging out with Frank and Falco, seeing how they worked and trained together, and before long, I had talked myself into becoming a dog handler. I was not only fascinated by the job and totally enamored of the dogs themselves—I also figured it would be good experience if I ever became a team leader. Combat assault dogs were now fully integrated into the SEALS, and that wasn't going to change. A good team leader would have to fully understand and appreciate the roles performed by both dog and handler.

Frank liked the idea of my assuming responsibility for Falco because he wanted to know that his dog would be in good hands. The rest of the guys were only too happy to let me apply for the job because . . . well, somebody had to do it, and this way it wouldn't be one of them.

One night, late in the deployment, we went out on a mission. As often happened, we divided into two assault teams, each of us chasing a different target. I was not on Frank's team that night, so I didn't see exactly what went down, but I heard the story afterward. Apparently, Falco caught someone hiding in a ditch, lying in wait and preparing for an ambush. As he was trained to do, Falco jumped on the guy and immediately bit into his arm, immobilizing him as he shrieked in pain. Unfortunately, the bad guy wasn't alone. This was always the most dangerous situation for a dog: coming upon more than one target. In this case, as Falco held on to the first guy, doing his job with complete commitment just as he was trained to do, the second guy shot Falco several times.

The rest of the team quickly responded and killed both insurgents, but not before Falco was critically wounded. By the time I arrived and saw him being loaded onto a helicopter, he was already dead. The loss hit me hard, but not nearly as hard as it hit Frank. He was completely crushed, almost as if he had lost a family member or a fellow soldier. Which, in a way, he had.

Just as we would have with a fallen soldier, we held a memorial service for Falco back on the base. (Later, a memorial plaque in his honor was put on permanent display in Virginia.) Frank got up and said a few words, as did the master chief. There were tears and salutes. Afterward, we did what we would have done for any of our brothers: we talked about what a great soldier and friend Falco had been to all of us. We told stories. We shared a cake in his honor. We celebrated his life and service. We laughed more than we cried.

We said goodbye.

Falco was cremated; his ashes were placed in an ammo can and presented to Frank. They went home together.

# Chapter 7

The first and most important step in maintaining a self-sufficient canine program was the procurement of the actual canines. That may sound obvious, but it was nonetheless challenging, as the candidates most suited for the job of military working dog, and especially for the more demanding and technically advanced job of SEAL combat assault dog, were not readily available at the local kennel. The SEALS were looking for the best of the best, an elite animal that was the canine equivalent to its human counterpart. Sure, there were good dogs to be found at specialized kennels and training facilities in the United States. Since working dogs had become such a fixture in law enforcement and the military, an entire industry had sprung up in which devoted vendors and trainers supplied smart and capable dogs to an expanding clientele. Some of these dogs were bred domestically; the majority were not.

If you wanted a dog with the purest of bloodlines dating back scores of generations—a lineage likely to produce working dogs of uncommon ability and temperament—then you had to travel to Europe to places like Belgium and the Netherlands, where the breeding and training of working dogs has long been embraced as both a business enterprise and a sport or hobby.

Most dogs brought back to the United States for work in law enforcement and the military today are products of sport programs like Schutzhund in Germany or KNPV in the Netherlands. They have received certificates acknowledging their ability to track, bite, detect scents, and follow commands without hesitation.

It would be inaccurate to suggest that these dogs are ready for deployment the moment they are procured, but certainly they possess the basic attributes and foundational training likely to make them successful. These are not raw pups who need to be trained from the ground up; they are, in most cases, two to three years old by the time they are purchased by American clients. In many ways, they are at exactly the same point along the developmental timeline as their human counterparts in Special Operations: late adolescence or early adulthood. They are strong, fit, and ready to be molded into a unique asset.

The dogs aren't cheap, but in the beginning, at least, neither are they prohibitively expensive. A Malinois puppy with solid bloodlines might cost as much as two thousand euros, but often significantly less. If the puppy grows into an accomplished adult with a stack of certificates and trophies to his name, well, his value can easily quadruple by the time he is sold to a buyer in the United States.

The majority of combat assault dogs are acquired during whirlwind European excursions usually lasting no more than two to three weeks. These trips are not vacations in any sense of the word. They are, instead, frenetic and exhausting adventures across hundreds of miles and multiple countries, with stops at dozens of private clubs and kennels, at the end of which a buyer might have acquired as many as fifty dogs suitable for clients in the military, law enforcement, and sometimes private or government security.

Several months before I was introduced to Cairo, he was acquired during a European buying trip organized by the father-son team of Dave Reaver and Mike Reaver of Adlerhorst International, a Southern California–based business serving police K-9 units and the military, as well as private clients. Dave Reaver founded the business in the mid-1970s; Mike came aboard in 2004, after serving in the U.S. Army. Sometimes, the guys from Adlerhorst make this sort of trip alone; they like to travel light and fast, and allowing clients to tag along can complicate matters and slow everyone down. An exception is made for military clients, "because it's the right thing to do," according to Mike Reaver. The Reavers know exactly what they are looking for in a dog, so they don't waste a lot of time agonizing over the decision to buy or not buy. Practically speaking, their approach works—not only for them but for everyone involved in the process.

It's a seller's market, after all, and if you go to a place and they have eight dogs, and you spend a couple of hours with each individual dog, that might be the last time you're ever welcome at that particular club or kennel. In general, the Reavers spend about ten to fifteen minutes with each dog, relying not only on the reputation of the vendor and a mountain of paperwork and certificates but also on their own ability to test the dog as thoroughly as possible.

If that sounds like a contradiction—testing a dog as thoroughly as possible, in a window of only ten to fifteen minutes— well, it's more than adequate if the buyer knows what he's doing.

The purest and most reliable test is one that measures not just instinct or tracking and scent-detection ability but something deeper: the dog's heart. Mike or Dave Reaver climbs into a bite suit and then goes off to a secluded spot, hiding in a corner of a building or in a thickly wooded area. The dog is then unleashed and given the command to track down the target. It usually doesn't take the dog long to find his target, or at least to get in the vicinity, but once confronted, he meets an adversary that is less compliant than those he has likely faced in his previous training.

"When the dog gets within a few feet, before he tries to bite, I'll give him a little poke on the nose, just to see how he reacts," Mike Reaver said. "It's not hard, doesn't hurt him. But it does put him back on his feet a little bit. That's what we want. We want to see how he responds to that aggression. If he dives right in and bites, that's awesome. If he stands six inches away from my legs, barking, waiting for me to open up or give him a window of opportunity, that's okay, too. But if he backs up twenty feet, that's a problem. That means he's not comfortable with this level of aggression."

The poke test may not be a perfect gauge of a dog's spirit, but it can be an effective way to measure a dog's fighting instinct. If he's blessed with that instinct and is a product of the best European programs, then the rest can likely be taught. Of course, there are no guarantees. Sometimes a dog looks great in the club. He has impeccable breeding and a great résumé, and he pushes right past the poke test like a natural fighter. Then, for whatever reason, he gets to California or Virginia or wherever else he might wind up, and he starts going through more advanced testing and washes out.

"It happens," Reaver said. "We do occasionally buy dogs that don't work out. But hopefully the percentages aren't too high in that regard."

Don Christie had the same hope in May 2008, when he was one of two military clients (the other was a representative of Canadian special forces) accompanying Adlerhorst on a European buying trip. Christie, a former longtime sergeant with the Cook County Sheriff's Department in Illinois, worked for a company that had contracted with the navy to run the elite SEAL canine program in Virginia. Christie had been authorized by his employer to buy as many dogs as he wanted from Adlerhorst's stock; he was there to get a good look at the dogs and to view firsthand the selection process utilized by Adlerhorst.

On their first day in the Netherlands, the group traveled from their hotel in Oirschot to a KNPV dog club in the village of Best, located fewer than ten kilometers away. The Reavers immediately went to work assessing and testing the dogs, while Christie and his Canadian counterpart looked on and took notes.

Most of the dogs were either German shepherds or Belgian Malinois, with a handful of Dutch shepherds sprinkled in. They were uniformly fit and athletic. They were all well trained. When the selection process began, Christie and his Canadian counterpart joined the Adlerhorst contingent in another part of the club, along with a handful of private clients and a couple of members of club management. They watched as the canine candidates were put through their paces in scent detection and tracking, skills they seemed to possess in roughly equal measure—which is to say, they were all at least competent; several were exceptional.

Then it came time to test the intangibles. Dave Reaver climbed into a bite suit and went about the thankless task of transforming himself into human bait. Most of the dogs performed well on this test, although some were more impressive than others. Of the dozen or so dogs that the Adlerhorst contingent assessed at the club, an attractive young Malinois named Cairo, between two and three years of age, was among the more determined biters and thus one of the most promising candidates.

Cairo's résumé indicated a higher-than-usual score on his certification test, but still, those were just numbers. He was sturdily built, roughly seventy pounds of adolescent muscle, with good teeth, pronounced ears that did not flop over, and a thick, healthy coat. His coloring was darker than a typical Malinois: mahogany with flecks of black throughout the legs and torso, giving way to a darker hue along the head and snout. His big brown eyes were bright and alert, signaling an eagerness to work.

"He looked great," Don Christie recalled. "But at this level, they're all good-looking dogs. You try not to get caught up in the aesthetics."

In fact, Cairo was a "cross-Malinois," not a purebred, a quirk of lineage that might have disqualified him from certain competitions. He looked almost like a cross between a Malinois and a shepherd, with coloring similar to a Dutch shepherd. None of that meant a damn thing. Cairo wasn't a show dog; he was a working dog, and his workability was superb. By all accounts, though, his appearance was somewhat unique; so, too, was his performance in that day's assessment.

"Cairo was very strong," Christie said. "I remember him biting calmly on the suit and just hanging on. Dave Reaver was trying to knock him off, but Cairo wouldn't let go. In a bite test, you yell and scream at the dog; you poke him—not to hurt him, of course, but just to dissuade him. And Cairo was not easily dissuaded."

The group selected a couple of dogs from that particular club. Cairo was one of them. He was placed in a traveling kennel and joined the buyers in their utility van. Then it was on to the next club, and the next town . . . and the next town and the next club after that . . . for the better part of two weeks. By the end of the trip, Adlerhorst had acquired approximately thirty to thirty-five dogs. Don Christie was given his pick of the litter.

He selected eight dogs, including the Belgian Malinois named Cairo. Those dogs, each of which cost approximately $10,000, were shipped to Virginia to begin training as combat assault dogs.

Most of the dogs in this class were Belgian Malinois; a few were Dutch shepherds; there were no German shepherds. All three of these breeds are smart and energetic, but the Malinois is the most compact and athletic, which at least partially explains its popularity with law enforcement agencies and the military. Like the German shepherd, the Malinois is physically impressive. His mere appearance can be intimidating to those considering breaking the law and reassuring to those who aren't. This makes either breed extremely useful in common law enforcement scenarios like foot patrol and crowd control. Both the German shepherd and Malinois have an extraordinary ability to detect certain scents. All dogs have olfactory ability that far outstrips anything humans can imagine; their sense of smell is tens of thousands of times greater than ours. But even among dogs, both the German shepherd and Belgian Malinois rank near the top in this capacity. According to the American Kennel Club, the Malinois is ranked sixth among all breeds in scent ability; the German shepherd is fourth, surpassed only by a trio of hunting and tracking dogs: the beagle, basset hound, and bloodhound.

It probably goes without saying that you wouldn't want to take a beagle into combat, let alone a slow-footed basset hound. A very particular set of skills is required, and while they include scent detection, they also include raw physicality. For a long time, the German shepherd was the standard bearer for work in law enforcement and the military, but for many reasons, including practicality, the breed has been surpassed by the Malinois. Among the factors in favor of the Malinois are size and resiliency. While the Malinois has nothing on the German shepherd when it comes to brainpower or strength, it does have the advantage of being a smaller and more agile breed. The Belgian Malinois is built for military work, and especially for the sort of job commonly undertaken in Special Operations. While either breed can reliably detect the presence of explosives or a human target in hiding, the Malinois is quicker and stabler, simply by virtue of its smaller and more compact musculature. It is better suited to traversing uneven terrain, and, when necessary, more easily transported.

Simply put, it's easier to pick up a seventy-pound Malinois than a ninety-pound German shepherd. To say nothing of jumping out of a plane or fast-roping out of a helicopter with one of them.

Additionally, the Belgian Malinois has proven to be an impressively healthy breed, largely free of the structural and anatomical issues that have long been associated with the German shepherd, and that can certainly be exacerbated by the stress of military work. They're both great dogs, but the Malinois is simply better suited to the rigors of the job and thus a safer investment. For some of these same reasons, the Dutch shepherd, which is similar in stature to the Malinois, has also become favored for military work.

Once they arrived in Virginia, all eight dogs were immediately put through a series of selection tests by Christie and his training partner, Jim Hagerty, a former dog handler with the Los Angeles Police Department, to further determine not only their skill and fitness but the likelihood of their serving as combat assault dogs in a SEAL squadron. The trainers ran the dogs through various exercises and obstacle courses in a variety of environments. They exposed the dogs to gunfire and other explosions—the vast majority of "regular" dogs hate loud noises and become instantly skittish if not terrified by anything that sounds like an explosion; ask anyone whose house pet cowers in a corner for days after a thunderstorm or a neigh-borhood Fourth of July celebration. Through both breeding and desensitization, military working dogs are less prone to freak-ing out when exposed to loud noises or the sudden bursts of fire and light that sometimes accompany them. But a single clap of thunder or lightning strike is not the same as a firefight. These dogs would have to be unwavering under conditions that should, by all reason, incite panic.

Even a dog that is great at scent detection, tracking, and biting is virtually useless if he melts into a neurotic puddle at the first crack of gunfire, so you might as well figure out the dog's mental state right at the outset. All eight of the dogs in this particular class passed the initial screening process (all but one would end up serving with Team ▮▮▮▮▮▮▮. And as the testing and training progressed over the course of the next six to eight weeks, it became apparent that while all of the dogs were exceptional, a few stood out.

One of those dogs was Cairo.

"He was probably top three of the eight," Don Christie re-membered.

In addition to being strong in all the basic skills like odor detection and bite work, Cairo impressed the trainers by be-ing a dog of uncommon demeanor. He remained calm around gunfire and explosions. He scampered up multiple flights of stairs without hesitation. This might sound like a small thing, but in fact it can be a troublesome mental block for even the sturdiest of working dogs. They are instinctively distrusting of staircases, particularly open staircases, which seem mysteri-ous and dangerous. Often, the dogs have little experience on stairs when they begin training as MWDs, and certainly not the kind of stairs they would face when on deployment in Afghani-stan or Iraq, or even when working in an urban setting for a law enforcement agency. Some dogs balk at climbing stairs. Some freeze when they are halfway to the top. Some make it to the top and refuse to come back down.

None of those reactions is advisable in the middle of a SEAL mission.

Cairo, for whatever reason, had no compunction whatsoever about ascending or descending stairs. Even if they were open in the back and revealed a precipitous and spooky drop to the ground, he was unfazed.

And while being likable isn't a prerequisite for the job (some talented dogs, like some talented people, are prickly, to say the least), Cairo also had a personality—affable but not boisterous—that endeared him to his trainers.

"Cairo was a sweetheart," Christie recalled. "A very special dog—a fine example of what these dogs are bred to be. He was strong and enthusiastic. He was just . . . happy."

# Chapter 8

Cairo was not my first choice. Might as well be honest about that.

We met in the summer of 2008. I'd gotten back from my deployment, taken some time off for vacation, trained a little with my squadron, and now I was preparing to move onto my new role as a dog handler. I wasn't given a lot of time to become acclimated to the position or to become acquainted with my new canine partner. That's not to say that shortcuts were taken; it's just that, as is often the case with Special Operations, there was no coddling or hand-holding. Whatever the job, it was expected that we would embrace it completely and quickly. I had volunteered to be a dog handler, so that's what I was.

Of course, being a dog handler was not my sole responsibility; it was just another responsibility. This, I realized, might have been one of the reasons some guys had no interest in the job: it was intensely time-consuming, and yet it did not relieve me of my other training commitments within the squadron. Which was fine. If longer days were the price to pay for being a dog handler, I was more than willing to make the investment.

Hell, it wasn't like I had an especially busy social life. I was a young, single guy. No kids. Not even a serious relationship. I mean, I had girlfriends, one after another, pretty much, but none of them lasted.

I knew guys who had steady girlfriends while they were SEALs, and even some guys who were married, but frankly, I'm not sure how they did it. The job is so dangerous and demanding, with long blocks of time away from home. This is a challenge for all military marriages and families, obviously, but I think it's particularly daunting within Special Operations. It's not just the danger involved or the prolonged separation but the secrecy, as well. There are some things—details of missions, people you've killed, friends you've lost—that you simply don't share with anyone. Not even a girlfriend or a spouse.

Some guys managed it. They were mostly older, and I presume they all had partners who were incredibly patient and understanding. Me? I wasn't ready for anything like that. I knew what was important in my life at that time, and I wasn't willing to compromise it for anyone else.

Ten-hour or twelve-hour days didn't bother me in the least. I loved everything about being a SEAL—the training, the traveling, the deployments, the fighting. I was keenly aware of the fact that I had beaten long odds. Here I was, a kid with no military lineage, no great academic or athletic accomplishments, and I was part of one of the most elite Special Operations units in the world. I'd gotten there by working my ass off and by refusing to quit and by doing to the best of my ability whatever job was assigned to me. Don't get me wrong. I was proud to be there; I think I deserved to be there. But sometimes I'd look around at my teammates, and I'd think about the stuff they had done, the missions they'd been a part of, stretched out all over the world and over a decade or more, and I'd think, *Man, I haven't done shit. I'm just lucky to be a part of this.*

Being a dog handler was a chance to do something different. To me, it seemed like a role that cut to the core of what it
meant to be a SEAL. It might not have been the highest-profile
job or even the most exciting, but after what I had seen in
Afghanistan, where Falco and Balto had repeatedly saved our
asses, I knew how important a job it was. I also thought it was
a really cool assignment. I liked dogs, I was fascinated by their
expanding role within Special Operations, and I wanted to be
part of that expansion. Before I even showed up to the first
training session in Virginia that summer, I was excited about
the opportunity to be a handler. And once I met the dogs, I was
all in.

The introduction came during a half-day training exercise
at a site not far from our base. The trainers had been working
with this particular crop of eight dogs for the better part of two
months, preparing them to be part of a SEAL team, assigned
either to an operator or a master-at-arms. Roughly speaking,
there was one potential handler for each dog. I knew ahead of
time that, as a SEAL, I'd get my choice of dogs, or at least one
of my top choices. In all honesty, though, they all looked great.
I mean, I didn't know shit about working dogs at that time, but
every one of these guys looked like a thoroughbred.

Having already served with Falco and Balto, I felt quite
comfortable around the dogs, but before they were removed from
their kennels, we all were given a brief overview of the program,
including the training they had received and a reminder that,
while they were enormously attractive animals, these were, in
fact, attack dogs. They were also rather young and, unlike Balto
and Falco, still somewhat unaccustomed to the military life.

"I wouldn't try to pat them on the head or anything," one of
the trainers said. "Think of them as weapons, not pets. Treat
them with respect."

I thought that was kind of funny, but it was certainly a

warning that had merit. The Belgian Malinois and Dutch shep-herds introduced to us that day were gorgeous, but each one had to be treated less like a dog and more like a loaded weapon. As someone who had grown up around dogs—and mostly the kind of big, tough, muscular canines that a lot of people under-standably find scary—my first inclination was to befriend the dogs. I was accustomed to animals that looked nasty but whose bark was worse than their bite. In this case, exactly the oppo-site was true; by any objective standard, these were beautiful dogs, and most of them looked less imposing than the average pit bull. Beneath the beauty, though, beat the heart of a warrior. Each and every one of these dogs, we were told, was a ferocious fighter with an extraordinary prey drive. While it's true that they responded best to positive reinforcement during training, it was also true that they required a firm hand.

In short, you had to show them who was boss, and you didn't do this by crouching to snout level, scratching them behind the ears, and cooing at them like a baby. Not in the beginning, any-way. Not if you wanted to, quite literally, save your face.

For much of the afternoon, we were strictly spectators, watching as the new crew of dogs ran impressively through a series of training exercises. The training site included a series of dimly lit underground bunkers. Each of the dogs was given a human scent to track and dispatched into the maze of bunkers. Eventually, if successful, the dog would come upon a man in a bite suit. The dog's reward would be several minutes of ag-gressive biting until called off the attack by his handler. I had already witnessed Balto and Falco performing these feats on deployment, under harrowing conditions, multiple times, so it no longer surprised me that dogs could track so swiftly and at-tack so aggressively. Still, it was impressive to see them work-ing in the early stages, learning their craft when they were just youngsters.

I can recall only one of the dogs being somewhat reluctant or difficult to handle—and, in fact, he eventually washed out of the SEAL program and ended up finding a home in law enforcement. They were all well behaved and eager to work. That said, there were two dogs that stood out from the pack, so to speak. One was named Bronco; the other was named Cairo. It wasn't like they were obviously better than the other dogs. The differences were subtler than that: a slightly more aggressive bite and a reluctance to let go, and absolutely no hesitation when entering a dark room. I might not even have noticed some of this stuff if I hadn't already seen working dogs in Afghanistan, but once you walk into a compound with a dog, you understand what he can do for you. I just had a feeling in my gut that both Bronco and Cairo would do the job well. From the moment they were taken out of the kennel, they looked like awesome dogs.

Before that first session was over, we had a chance to meet the dogs, albeit briefly. Like I said, there wasn't a lot of petting or messing around, but we did get an opportunity to let the dogs walk among us, and sniff us, and see how they would react to us. I gravitated toward Cairo, mainly just because of the way he looked and how well he performed in the training exercises, but also toward Bronco. Bronco was the outwardly friendlier of the two; he nudged up against me and almost seemed like he wanted to play. Cairo was a little more laid-back—not unfriendly, but more serious about working. After a short introduction, the dogs were put back in their kennels, all of which were housed in large portable unit that was hooked up to the back of a truck and returned to the larger training kennel on the base.

For the next two weeks, prospective dog handlers spent large chunks of each day getting to know the new team of dogs. For the most part, we were spectators, watching as the dogs were put through exercises and scenarios, while the experienced trainers and handlers offered a running commentary. It was almost like a live-action classroom. With each successive day, we spent more time interacting with the dogs. A lot of it was very simple leash work: teaching the dog to walk at a certain pace and to obey basic commands. It should be noted here that this was not for the dog's benefit: it was for our benefit. These animals had already spent the better part of three years being trained at an extremely high level.

Their new handlers, on the other hand, had virtually no experience with dog training. Sure, I was a Navy SEAL, but when it came to being a dog handler, I knew almost nothing. So, naturally, we started with baby steps, walking around the kennel with a dog on a leash, directing him to heel or sit or whatever. Then we'd take him off leash and allow him to do what he was bred and trained to do: run, hunt, detect, chase, bite.

Being a dog handler on deployment involves becoming proficient with a wide array of equipment, but in the beginning, in Virginia, it meant first learning how to use a leash and a choke collar. I'm sure some people don't like the very idea of a choke collar, but it's vital in the beginning to communicating to such a strong and aggressive animal who is in charge. Then, more positive means of reinforcement are easily incorporated into the process. We also utilized an electronic collar (sometimes referred to as an *e-collar* or *shock collar*). This was another tool of the trade that, in civilian life, might seem unnecessary or even cruel but can save the life of a military working dog on deployment.

These are smart, complex animals instilled through generations of breeding with a fierce desire to track and hunt prey. Intensive training hones that genetic instinct to a razor's edge, so that you end up with a dog that will not only enter a dark

house with gunfire going off and track a bad guy into the creepi-
est of holes without hesitation but also bite and hold the target
until he is literally pulled off. Sometimes, the only way to get
the dog to let go, or to return to a safer spot, is to give him a
little zap with the e-collar. If that sounds unkind, well, it sure
beats the alternative: a dead dog. I found the e-collar to be a
highly effective training tool, one that gets an unfair rap. The
amount of electricity generated is minimal and can be adjusted
to varying levels of intensity. In general, it's no more than the
amount produced by the transcutaneous electrical nerve stimulation (TENS) units commonly used for physical therapy in
humans. It's harmless and causes no pain or damage to the dog;
it just gets his attention. And once he understands the meaning
conveyed by the e-collar, only the slightest amount of current is
needed.

Ideally, you wouldn't have to use the e-collar. You'd just yell,
"Los!" which means *let go* or *release*. Most of these commands
the dogs had heard since they were puppies undergoing early
KNPV or Schutzhund training. In terms of communication, we
had a good foundation on which to build. If I was playing fetch
with a dog, the dog would race to pick up a toy or a ball, bring
it back to me, and then, typically, refuse to let go. Instead, he
would want to play tug-of-war with the toy or ball. To get him to
drop, I would say, "Los!" If he let go, he would be rewarded with
a ball or strong, enthusiastic words of encouragement or both.
If he didn't . . . he'd get nothing. And then we'd do it again. This,
really, was the foundation of all training: convincing the dog to
work in such a manner that he would receive positive reinforcement. Working dogs need to work, and they want nothing more
than to please their handlers . . . their masters . . . their *dads*, as
we became known. And there was no more important or more
commonly used command than *Los!*

It was a tricky thing; you wanted the dog to bite, and to

bite aggressively, and to hold on. But you also wanted him to let go when instructed to do so. This is more easily achieved in training than in real-world application, in part because, well, let's be candid: in the real world, a bite leads to bloodletting, and when a trained attack dog gets a mouthful of blood, it can be intoxicating. To the point where he ends up being so committed to the bite that he gets himself killed. So it's absolutely crucial that he understands and responds appropriately to the word *Los!* Sometimes an accompanying zap from the e-collar is needed to drive the point home and keep him from getting hurt.

We all quickly became proficient in the vernacular of combat assault dog training. Obviously, we didn't learn all these commands during the indoctrination phase of the program, but we were introduced to the basic language of being a dog handler. I found it fascinating. The more time I spent with the dogs, the more I came to appreciate how intelligent and strongwilled they were. It was this, as much as their athleticism, that I admired.

Each prospective handler worked with multiple dogs each day. This makes sense on multiple levels. First, it's good for a handler to have a variety of experiences. While the dogs might all look similar and possess similar skills, the truth is that every dog is unique. There are subtle differences in personality and technique; understanding those differences can be vital on a mission. Cairo, I would come to realize, was a tremendous worker. I never had to worry about him. He was just so good at doing his job without acting up in any way. A lot of dogs—probably most dogs—aren't built that way. They take a lot of consistent work and effort to get them to behave a certain way.

I could tell Cairo was exceptional in the first few days as I cycled through the whole group, and it wasn't long before I began to have doubts about my choice. I still liked Bronco—he was such a fun dog to be around—but I could tell Cairo was going to an easier dog to work with. In a lot of ways, I felt like he could teach me as much as I could teach him. Nevertheless, it was important to have the experience of working with different dogs, since you never knew what might happen on deployment. You could lose a dog—your dog—and suddenly have to adjust to a replacement. Similarly, it was beneficial for the dogs to become accustomed to a variety of human personalities and styles.

All of it made sense. All of it was very methodical and well planned and extremely labor intensive.

It was also fun. Can't lie about that. I had volunteered to be a dog handler because I thought it seemed like an important and interesting job; nothing I saw in those first two weeks did anything to dissuade me.

As the end of our two-week indoctrination period drew near, I started to wonder which dog would be assigned to me. All the new handlers would soon be leaving with their dogs for a much longer and more intensive training school in California, and I hoped that Cairo would be my new partner. One morning, I was approached by Jim Hagerty, one of the program's trainers. He and Don Christie were running the canine program, and it was up to them, along with command staff, to determine which dogs should be paired with which handlers. As I understood it, this was based on vacancies within a particular squadron, as well as the temperament and personality of the handlers. I had expressed an interest in both Bronco and Cairo, and I knew I'd get preference. But I never said explicitly, "I want Bronco," or "I want Cairo." And no one asked. These guys knew a lot more about dogs than I did, so I trusted their judgment. They watched all of us work with the dogs for two weeks, tried to assess our personalities as well as our strengths and weaknesses, and in the end made the assignments they felt were most appropriate.

"You're getting Cairo," Jim Hagerty said to me. "He's the right dog for you."

I shrugged. "Okay, cool."

At the time, I'm not sure I agreed with Jim's assessment, but I was satisfied with the assignment. I liked Cairo a lot, knew he was an exceptional working dog and probably would be an easier dog to train than Bronco. I just liked the fact that Bronco seemed a bit more playful when I first met him. To some extent, though, I had misjudged Cairo. He would prove to be not just friendly and affectionate but as loyal and loving a dog as you could ever hope to find. It took a little time to peel away the layers, but he was well worth the effort.

# Chapter 9

*I remember meeting Will and Cairo for the first time and thinking,* This is the perfect dog. *Well, maybe not perfect, but if you're looking for a police dog, or a military dog, he had the perfect personality. He was social, happy-go-lucky, not one of those dogs where you can't just be easygoing around him. Cairo seemed like he was happy to be there; I don't think he made life too hard on Will, as far as training. I could be wrong, but it didn't seem that way. He was a very friendly dog. And when it came to working, he was never on my radar as far as needing extra help. Sometimes you have to sit down with a handler and say, "Hey, this one might not work out," but I can't remember anything like that ever happening with Cairo. He never seemed to have any kind of problems. And Will was the same way. He never seemed to get stressed out or frazzled. It just seemed like he was having fun. He was happy to be working with the dogs. We had some students, guys who maybe would do a little bit of complaining, or they would critique their dog too much and look at every exercise and say, "Jeez, my dog didn't do that well compared to this other dog." And sometimes you see a guy who wants to be a dog handler and he's okay with it, but he really doesn't like dogs all that much. That's a huge issue. But Will? His personality—he's like a Malinois. He's like rock 'n' roll. He likes to have fun, but at the same time, when it's time to work, he's all business. Just like Cairo.*

**—Mike Reaver**

Just a few short days after Cairo and I were assigned to each other, we flew to Southern California for seven weeks of intensive training at a program run by Adlerhorst International. Most of the new dogs and their handlers made this trip. It was an opportunity to bond and work almost exclusively on the skills we would use as dog handlers on deployment. Instead of splitting time between the normal duties associated with being both an operator and a dog handler, we would be able to concentrate almost exclusively on the tactics and training that go into making an elite military working dog.

And an elite dog handler.

Let's be clear about that: when we arrived in Southern California, I needed just as much training as Cairo. Maybe more.

In what I guess you'd call a type of immersion therapy, Cairo became my roommate, training partner, and best friend. And it happened almost instantaneously. The navy handed me the reins, literally and figuratively, one morning in Virginia, and suddenly Cairo was my full-time responsibility. We would live together, work together, sleep together, and sometimes even eat together. I was no stranger to the symbiotic relationship between man and dog. Like I said, I'd had dogs before and even had a pet Doberman at home at the time I became a dog handler.

I was totally comfortable around dogs and liked spending time with them. But this was different. Cairo wasn't just a dog. He was a finely tuned instrument, a model of exceptional breeding and training who was now being groomed for some of the most vital Special Operations work in the U.S. military.

For me, and for Cairo, it was an awesome responsibility.

Not that he necessarily noticed.

Very early in our time together, I took him to one of the training sessions at Adlerhorst. We drove together in a rental car, a small SUV, from our hotel to the training site. The parking lot was filled with trucks and SUVs, all with their windows down or liftgates raised, and kennels in the back. I lifted the hatch so that Cairo would have plenty of air, told him I'd be back in a little while, and then went inside for the classroom portion of the session. The days were often broken down in this manner: an hour or two of instruction, like any other class, followed by practical application involving the handler and his dog. Well, when I went back outside to the car, I noticed the door to the kennel was . . . missing. It had been completely blown off and was lying on the ground some six feet away from the truck. Cairo was gone.

*Holy shit!*

A thousand horrible scenarios ran through my head, not least of which was the possibility that a seventy-pound attack dog—a purebred fighting and killing machine—was loose in the area and might run into another dog, or, worse, some unsuspecting, dog-loving civilian. Forget what this meant for my future as a dog handler; I was worried about a potentially fatal attack.

A few minutes passed as I searched the area and called out for Cairo. There was no response. Eventually, I made my way back to the car, sweating, fretting, angry at Cairo for breaking out, but even angrier at myself for not exercising greater caution.

When I got to the car, I was stunned at what I found. There was Cairo, sitting quietly in the back of his kennel, just chilling. As I drew near, I had to stifle the urge to yell at him. After all, it wasn't really his fault. And anyway, as noted earlier, scolding a dog long after the infraction does nothing but confuse the poor guy. If I had yelled at Cairo in that moment as he sat in his kennel, lightly wagging his tail, he would have assumed that merely sitting there was some sort of correctable offense. Which, of course, it was not. So instead, I swallowed my anger and embarrassment, gave him a pat on the head, and pulled him out of the kennel.

"Let's get to work, buddy."

So . . . what happened? I can only speculate. Knowing Cairo the way I do now, I imagine he felt the call of nature and decided to bust out of his kennel; he was strong enough and smart enough to do that. Once he'd done his business, he was also smart enough—and reliable enough—to jump right back into the car and into his kennel while he waited for his handler to return. When I reached in and patted his head, he simply panted and gave me a look that seemed to say, *Where've you been, Dad? I had to take a shit.*

We stayed at a Residence Inn near Ontario International Airport, and while I trusted Cairo implicitly, I tried at all times to remember that his generally pleasant demeanor could sometimes mask the inarguable fact of his lineage and training. He was an attack dog, and as such, it warranted caution around the civilian population. Some people are "dog people" to a fault. They will wander over to even the biggest and strongest of dogs and insist on introducing themselves. This is especially true of children, to whom even an unknown dog is often little more than a potential furry companion, no more or less harmful than the stuffed animals in their bedroom. A child, and even some unwise adults, are all too quick to put their hands on a dog they've never met, or to kneel at face level, thus giving the dog—if he is badly trained or grumpy or otherwise predisposed to this sort of thing—an easy target.

With this in mind, I took no chances with Cairo, especially in the beginning. When I brought him back to the hotel after a day of training, I'd try to go straight to my room. If, for some reason, we had to walk through the lobby or another part of the hotel, I'd make sure he was harnessed and leashed and usually tightly muzzled. Eventually, as Cairo grew older, this would no longer be necessary, but for now, I treated him with an appropriate level of respect and caution.

Once in our room, I'd take Cairo out of his kennel, or remove the muzzle and leash, and let him have the run of the place. On the first night in California, he slept in his kennel; by the second night, we were sharing a bed, although I do recall pushing him off in the middle of the night for being such an aggressive snuggler and blanket hog. This was a pattern throughout our time together, and it was established early on. With some dogs, boundaries are critical; they must know their place. If you let them in your bed, or on the couch, they won't respect your authority or understand their place in the pack. If you try to push them away, they will growl unhappily; it's a sign of dominance, and you have to be very careful about letting this behavior go unchecked.

Fortunately, this was not the case with Cairo. As far as I could tell, he just liked sleeping on a bed rather than in his kennel or on the floor. And he liked curling up next to his dad. This concession to comfort and security had absolutely no bearing on his perception of our relationship. If anything, it strengthened our bond.

While Cairo was a reliable and tireless worker during the day, he was laid-back and content to chill out in the evening. I'd give him a couple of scoops of food after a long day of training, take him outside to poop, and then we'd sit together on the bed or the couch and watch TV. It was almost like hanging out with one of my buddies. And as with many close friendships, I almost felt like I could read Cairo's mind.

Once in a while, though, he would do something that would remind me of the differences in our DNA. Like the night he suddenly sat up in bed and started growling, his gaze fixed on a spot high in the far corner of the hotel room. I was halfheartedly watching something on TV at the time and at first ignored his response. But then it continued, a low, guttural growl.

*Grrrrrrrrrr* . . .

I hopped off the bed and walked around the room. Checked the doors and windows.

Cairo was a highly sensitive attack dog, so maybe he had heard an intruder. But there was nothing.

"What is it, boy? What's wrong?"

*Grrrrrrrrrrr* . . .

He sat up on the bed, head motionless but tilted slightly upward, toward the ceiling above the television set. I walked to a point just below where his gaze was aimed.

"Here?"

*Grrrrrrrrrrr* . . .

I ran my hands along the wall. "Nothing here, bud. All good."

*Grrrrrrrrrrrr* . . .

Eventually, I went back to the bed and gave Cairo a pat on the head. Ordinarily, he would have given me a lick and pushed up against me. But this time, he did not move. Instead, he sat perfectly still on the foot of the bed, eyes unblinking, teeth bared ever so slightly.

Finally, since this was beginning to piss me off just a bit, I decided to turn him loose and let him have some fun.

"Go!" I yelled. "Get him!"

Cairo did not budge. Did not move a muscle. He just sat

there on the bed, motionless, and continued to express . . . what? Fear? Mistrust? Suspicion? I have no idea.

*Grrrrrrrrrrrrrr . . .*

It went on like that for fifteen to twenty minutes, until finally, for no particular reason that I could pinpoint, Cairo's body relaxed, and the growling ceased; he curled up into a tight ball against me and fell asleep. Whatever it was that he sensed—a threat . . . a *presence*—it apparently had dissipated. I patted him on the head.

"Okay," I said. "All clear."

I'd like to say that Cairo's vigilance and hypersensitivity was in some way reassuring, but the truth is, at this point in time, when I barely knew him and had no idea what the hell he was doing, it kind of freaked me out. Only later would I come to realize that dogs, especially those as gifted as Cairo, are uniquely aware of their surroundings; they have a way of sensing things—not just danger but almost anything out of the ordinary. And while it might have been a bit unnerving sitting in a hotel room in Southern California, this heightened sense of awareness would sure come in handy down the road a bit in the mountains of Afghanistan.

The days in California were long and filled with variations on some of the things I had been exposed to during my introduction to dog training in Virginia—scent detection, bite work, command response, desensitization to sound, physical training—although in much greater depth. The bite work, to me, was the most fascinating part of the process, and it took up a great deal of time in the first few weeks. You see, while Cairo had already been taught the basics of biting and tracking, his tactics and technique were unrefined. We spent a lot of time teaching the dogs how to bite safely and appropriately to maximize the effect of a takedown, while minimizing the risk to the dog itself.

For example, I had to learn how to properly "catch" a dog while bogged down in a lumpy bite suit. A dog's natural inclination when he attacks is to simply leap at a target and grab the first thing he hits. This might be the target's face or chest. Now, on the surface, this might not sound like such a terrible thing—after all, if a seventy-pound Malinois jumps on a bad guy and latches onto his neck, the bad guy surely is going to be subdued. And perhaps killed. But there are problems with this strategy, especially in training. First, when a dog leaps at a target's chest or head, there is a greater chance of injury to the dog, either through blunt-force trauma or through the victim responding to the leaping dog like a baseball player swinging at a pitch. If it happens once in a while on a mission, that's fine—you don't want to dissuade the dog from attacking hard and fast. But to lessen the chance of injury, we were careful to protect the dog during training exercises. It's a similar philosophy to football; hard contact is limited to game days.

Ideally, the dog would go for an arm or a leg. This was the safest landing spot, and once attached, he would not let go. It simultaneously gave the dog the satisfaction of a bloody bite and immobilized the target. There was a possibility that the bad guy would be armed and respond to the attacking dog with gunfire. Usually, though, he was in too much pain and too overwhelmed by panic to offer much in the way of resistance.

Bite work, therefore, was vital and meticulous. To help steer the dog toward the desired part of the body (arm, leg), the person in the bite suit would offer up a thickly padded arm or leg. Then he would guide the dog in by pulling back slightly as the dog's teeth found their mark. To borrow another sports analogy, think of it like a football player learning to catch a pass. You don't stand perfectly still and let the ball rocket into your hands—that provides a trampoline effect. Instead, just as the ball reaches your hands, you pull back slightly, in time with the pass, cradling the ball as it lands.

It was all about protecting, as well as teaching, the dog.

I didn't understand this strategy until I put on the bite suit and felt the power of these dogs firsthand (in the beginning, we wore thin rubber suits and were subjected to short bites so that we could really feel the bite pressure of the dogs; it was, to say the least, impressive). At seventy pounds, they were less than half my size, but getting hit by one of these animals when it was running at full speed was like being thrown into a wall. And that was while wearing several inches of protective foam rubber. For the dog, the risk was much greater. If he hit his mark in a solid place, such as the chest or back, or if the target swatted him in the face as he leaped, it was possible for the dog to severely damage his jaw or perhaps even break his neck. The idea, then, was to train the dog to aggressively attack and neutralize the target without injuring the dog him in the process. The dog was doing what came naturally to him; it was up to the handler to help him remain safe during instruction.

All of this was much harder than it probably sounds. I remember the first time I played the role of the squirter and how I thought very clearly, *Oh, shit, this isn't going to work.* I could barely move in the bite suit, so the dog quickly and easily made up the distance between us. As he ran toward me, I had the sudden and sinking sensation that the dog was going to go right for my throat. Which was possible. Fortunately, that didn't happen. Instead, I held out an arm and waved it frantically. As if on cue, the dog jumped at me from maybe six or seven feet away and hit my arm perfectly. He hung there for a second in midair before the force of the blow took us both to the ground.

And you know what? It hurt! I mean, the bite suit did its job—the dog's teeth did not penetrate the padding—but still . . . just the sheer force of the impact, combined with the strength of his jaws, left me with bruises on my left forearm. This, I soon discovered, was common, and in fact most of the handlers went through the entire course with arms and legs that appeared almost to be covered with ink.

It was all part of the job, and I certainly didn't mind. The bruises were daily reminders of the awesome power of Cairo and his fellow working dogs. I suppose it's possible that Adlerhorst could have spared us this daily punishment by permitting only the program's instructors to wear bite suits—after all, it wasn't like any of us were going to be dog targets once we went on deployment. But there was, of course, a method to the madness. For one thing, the bite work brought us closer to the dogs, instilling within us greater understanding of their role and the skill they brought to the job. And this, in turn, helped us be better dog handlers. Second, the bite work was a crucial part of the training of a military working dog, and the more firsthand experience we had in training the dogs, the more likely it was that we would be able to share this knowledge and experience with others who might have to step into our roles on deployment. Simply put, a dog handler had to be extremely well versed in every aspect of the job.

It should be noted that I never wore the bite suit while working with Cairo; only while working with other dogs. An inviolable rule of training attack dogs, I learned, is this: never teach your own dog to bite you. That one is self-explanatory, I guess.

Sometimes we'd do bite work without actually letting the dogs bite. Instead, we'd install a muzzle and put the dog through exercises in which he was expected to find and engage a target, even though the target was not wearing a bite suit. Now, obviously, it would be exceedingly dangerous to allow one of these dogs to attack an unprotected target, so we simply muzzled the dogs to prevent anyone from getting hurt.

And yet . . .

It's a testament to the strength of the elite military working dog that in fact some of these encounters resulted in a handler sustaining more bruises than if he were in a bite suit. The muzzle, comprised of thick nylon mesh and steel, was a serious contraption, creating a sort of canine Hannibal Lecter. While it was quite effective at restricting the animal's ability to bite, it did turn him into a veritable battering ram. With a good head of steam, a dog wearing a muzzle could do some significant damage simply by launching himself headfirst at a handler. This was risky for both the dog and the handler, which is why exercises involving muzzles typically were designed not for confrontational purposes but simply to encourage the dog to bite even when the target was wearing street clothes—in this case, the loose-fitting garb (which we called a "man dress") favored by Afghan males.

To this point, the dogs had been taught to bite primarily when presented with a human in a bite suit. There would be no bite suits in the field, so it was critical that the dog's biting instinct be linked more to smell and command, rather than a particular image—one he would never encounter in real life. The dog would be muzzled and presented with a target, often either fleeing or shouting, and instructed to attack. Once engaged, the handler would roll on the ground and scream, offering up various parts of his anatomy for the dog to vigorously poke and prod with his muzzled snout. In this way, while the dog was not rewarded with an actual bite, he at least enjoyed the thrill of a good "fight."

But sometimes even the muzzle was barely sufficient protection. One of the venues we used for training was an old abandoned movie theater. It was a perfect spot—dark, musty, with plenty of places to hide and inspect. On this particular day, we took turns running the dogs through a bite scenario in which they would seek out a target hiding in the dark in street clothes. The dogs had nothing but their sense of smell in this exercise, and they used it impressively. Like most of the dogs, Cairo adapted easily and did well; he found his mark almost immediately, mauled the guy for a few minutes, and then ceased the attack upon command. But there was one dog, a Dutch shepherd named Nero, who was not so easily dissuaded. Nero was a big dog, well behaved and good looking, but something about this exercise brought out the best—or worst—in him. He went after the target so aggressively that he somehow almost ripped the muzzle apart. Now, it's hard to convey just how difficult a feat that would be, but Nero nearly did it. Afterward, as we all stood around outside, Nero's handler showed us the muzzle. The metal portion had been bent and twisted, and the mesh was ripped and frayed.

"Another minute," he said with a smile, "and he would have gotten out."

I had two reactions to this—one, I got a little chill thinking of what Nero might have done to the poor handler playing his target; two, I was seriously impressed. I'd seen working dogs in action on deployment, and I'd been working closely with Cairo for a while now, so I was intimately aware of the dogs' capabilities, but the sight of that supposedly inescapable muzzle, now twisted and useless, left me speechless.

"That," I said, "is sick."

When Cairo was learning to attack and bite, my role was one of supervision and oversight. As Cairo wrestled with his flailing target, I'd approach with gun in hand. Then I'd hook my hip lead to his harness and give him a pat on the ribs or on the top of his head—being careful not to interfere with his mouth, obviously.

"Good boy!" was the appropriate first response, as it indicated to Cairo not only that he had done exactly as instructed but that we were in fact in this thing together. We were a team. His job was to find and bite; mine was to reward him afterward and let him know that he could safely release the target. Most dogs are usually reluctant to give up a bite, and Cairo was no different, especially in the early phases of training. The cessation of a good bite, therefore, had to be executed with a combination of caution and reward. I'd praise Cairo for a job well done, and after giving him an affectionate pat, I'd gently pull up on his collar, making sure that any pressure was applied to an area around the jawline, rather than the neck. The last thing I wanted to do was choke my own dog, not only because it would hurt him but also because he would interpret the response as a punishment. This would confuse him:

*Wait, you just told me good job for biting this guy, but now you're choking me because I won't let go? What's up with that, dude? Make up your mind!*

But if I lifted the collar at the right angle, I could apply just enough pressure to loosen his jaws. This would cause him to drop the target (although sometimes his teeth would be deeply embedded in the foam of the bite suit, necessitating a bit of extra effort), without causing him any discomfort. Then I'd give him another pat or even a quick hug.

"Good job, buddy."

Regardless of how quickly or slowly the situation resolved, I would do everything possible to make sure that Cairo found the experience to be a positive one so that the next time he was instructed to bite, his drive would be even stronger. And no matter how well I knew him, and how much I thought he respected me, I would never put my hands near his mouth when he was on a bite. Release was always achieved through firm, easily understood commands and effective collar pressure, coupled with common sense and patience. Then, as the training progressed, and the bite drive was firmly established, we incorporated other methods of release—incorporating the e-collar or yelling, "Los!" from a distance. By the time we left California, I could usually convince Cairo to return from an attack without even approaching him physically. Most of the dogs were great in this regard; Cairo was exceptional.

The entire California trip was a great experience, as it not only made me a much better handler and Cairo a better assault dog, it really brought us closer together. At the end of the seven-week program, there was a competition involving all the dogs and their handlers. We were put through various exercises and given scores, mostly based on time, for each event. In one of the events, we had to paddle across a pond in a light canoe, with our dog as a passenger. What we didn't know is that when we were halfway across the water, a bad guy in a bite suit would jump out from behind some rocks and begin waving and shouting. Several of the dogs, predictably, went nuts and capsized their boats. Not Cairo. For one thing, Cairo wasn't a big fan of water, so maybe he just knew that it was in his best interests to sit tight until we reached the other side. More likely, it was just in his nature to wait until he was told what to do.

We ended up finishing second in the competition, getting caught right at the end by a SEAL from a different squadron. But it wasn't Cairo's fault. It was all on me. I was just a little slow. Cairo did his job.

*What I liked about Will is that he wasn't pretentious at all. A lot of those guys—Rangers, SEALs—they're like that. You think of them being like superheroes or whatever, but they're really just regular guys in a lot of ways. Although they do some pretty extraordinary stuff. Will was just humble. I remember one exercise, one night, we were out with the dogs, hiking up a mountain. It wasn't huge, not ten thousand feet or anything like that, but it was steep and rocky. At one point, I said, "Look, you guys all know how to suffer. You know how to walk with a bag of rocks on your back." And I'm not saying this was suffering like they're accustomed to, but a walk is a walk, and when you've got a dog with you, and you're on a ridgeline, in the dark, it can get frustrating. I wanted them to get just a little taste of that before they went to their unit. It would be a lot worse in Afghanistan, obviously. So we were at maybe two thousand or three thousand feet, and we got to the top and then walked down a ridgeline. And I knew that on the other side of that ridgeline was a cave. And in that cave was a guy in a bite suit. That was the reward for the dogs at the end of the exercise. We did it multiple times with every patrol. It's a long and tiring exercise. Anyway, we got down to the last couple of dogs going through the bite work, and some of the students, Canadian special forces, started complaining. "Hey, this is stupid, we don't walk up mountains; we take helicopters." Now, in my limited knowledge, I think they're wrong, and I tell them so. "Actually, I think you guys do a lot of walking, and you're going to be doing it with dogs." A couple of the other guys jumped in and told the Canadians to stop their complaining. One of those guys was Will. So that's kind of my lasting memory of Will. We're walking down a ridgeline at night, everyone is really tired, and some guys are whining and complaining and feeling sorry for themselves, and Will is quoting movie lines and laughing and trying to keep everyone else upbeat. Truthfully, though, I didn't have to pay much attention to Will or Cairo. When it came to an exercise, I knew they were probably going to knock it out of the park. It was like, "Here come Will and Cairo; this should be easy."*

**—Mike Reaver**

# Chapter 10

Cairo might have been better at skydiving than I was. I mean, he never jumped on deployment, simply because he didn't have to—more often than not, we would land by a chopper and hike in to the target, or fast-rope from twenty to fifty or even one hundred feet overhead. But he jumped in training. A lot. And he was as cool as could be.

When we finished the program in California, we returned to Virginia for more training and to prepare for our next deployment. We took trips to various sites to work on different aspects of training—we'd go to Arizona, for example, to work on skydiving for a couple of weeks at a time. Of all the things I learned to do as a SEAL, skydiving was probably the one I found most challenging. Not because of the fear factor, necessarily; like I said, even though my knees would weaken and my stomach would rumble when climbing a utility pole on a summer job in high school, I didn't really mind jumping out the back of a plane. That might sound illogical, but it actually makes perfect sense. Or, at least, it does to me and to a lot of guys with whom I served.

When you're only a few stories above the ground, everything

looks real—and yet, just distant enough to envision the damage that will be done when you splat against the pavement. From ten thousand feet, however, the earth seems distant and almost unreal. I rarely felt even the slightest flutter of butterflies when skydiving. Over the course of my navy career, I made at least three hundred jumps, nearly all of them during training exercises. I became competent enough that I never caused any problems or suffered any injuries, but it was not a strong suit. I knew some guys who were extraordinary skydivers, with thousands of jumps to their credit. They loved it! Didn't matter if it was day or night, windy or calm. These guys just wanted to jump. They were the ones you wanted leading a string of guys out the back of a plane because that is a huge responsibility. You read the wind wrong, by even the slightest margin, and you can get fifty men hurt or killed in a hurry.

One of the reasons I regret not becoming more proficient at skydiving is because I never got the opportunity to jump with Cairo. The dogs, as you can probably imagine, did not jump alone. They were muzzled, harnessed, and tucked safely in a big pouch, almost like a baby carrier, worn by a human skydiver. Together, they would float to Earth under a huge tandem canopy. Typically, the dog carrier was one of the strongest jumpers in the unit. Practically speaking, for this particular exercise, skydiving skill was more important than dog-handling experience. Some dogs naturally found the experience terrifying.

Interestingly, though, most of the dogs seemed to almost enjoy the skydiving experience. Cairo fell into that category. I'd load him into the pouch of a more seasoned jumper and give him a big pat on the head before each jump. When it was time to exit the plane, I'd usually be somewhere in the middle of the line—the best jumpers would go first, leading the excursion, while the tandem jumpers (those carrying dogs, or paired with support personnel who had no jump training) would go last. I'd turn to Cairo and his handler, give them a thumbs-up, and leap out the open bay. A few second later, Cairo would be on his way. Sometimes, I'd look up and get a glimpse of him floating gently above me. I could almost see him smiling. He never freaked out. Not once.

I'll admit that in those moments, I sometimes wished that Cairo had been attached to me. It would have been a cool experience. But it would have required significantly more advanced jump training, and I wasn't sufficiently motivated. I have tremendous respect for the guys who dedicate themselves to it; it's a vital part of the job, and it's dangerous as hell. I've seen a lot of skydiving accidents in training. I just didn't want to push my luck. Besides, I had my hands full with Cairo, even if he wasn't jumping out of planes with me.

For the next six months, from December 2008 to June 2009, Cairo and I were virtually inseparable as we trained for our first deployment together. Technically speaking, military working dogs resided in kennels on the base, but Cairo often came home with me at the end of the day and slept in my house. This was frowned upon but usually ignored, as everyone understood the importance of a handler forging a tight bond with his dog. What better way to do that than by taking Cairo home and splitting a steak with him?

The training was ceaseless and at times challenging. I discovered quickly that Cairo, like all combat assault dogs, preferred bite work to almost any other aspect of training. This was both understandable and problematic. From our perspective, odor detection was the most important skill a dog could possess. The ability to sniff out weapons or explosives could save dozens of lives on a mission. To Cairo, though, the reward for even exemplary scent detection (a hug or a pat on the head, or even a treat of some sort) was far less satisfying than the rewards associated with the successful tracking of a target.

A bite.

Once a dog got his first taste of human flesh and blood, he naturally became even more committed to bite training. For Cairo, this happened during an exercise at a training center, while we were preparing for our first deployment. My friend Angelo, a master-at-arms, was playing the role of target as Cairo did some scent-detection work inside a very basic concrete building meant to simulate some of the places we would encounter in Iraq and Afghanistan. Angelo had positioned himself on top of a closet-like structure, some nine feet off the ground, while Cairo went about his business. Angelo was not wearing a bite suit because he was presumably safe from such a high vantage point. But when Cairo found Angelo—his target—he went absolutely nuts, jumping and barking like crazy. We all just sort of stood there watching as Cairo leaped higher and higher, until, somehow, Cairo soared high enough to sink his teeth briefly into the back of Angelo's ankle. It wasn't a serious wound, but it did hurt like hell.

It was one of the most impressive athletic feats I had ever seen from Cairo, and for the effort, he was rewarded with his first official bite.

The taste of blood.

Good luck competing with that. Cairo was a great dog, friendly and playful and trustworthy around strangers, but he was still a dog. Centuries of breeding, combined with the best training money could buy, had made him a highly adept hunter. Nothing made him happier than to sink his teeth into his prey. That's just a simple, irrefutable fact. As a result, Cairo, like all combat assault dogs, required endless refresher training on the less enjoyable and (to them) more mundane aspects of their work, primarily scent detection. Once exposed to biting, especially real biting with bloody results, a dog wanted nothing more than to bite again.

Consequently, I began spending more time with Cairo working on scent detection than bite work. This had already been trained into him, but reinforcement was especially important given his natural inclination to be more interested in bite work.

Cairo was pretty good about maintaining a businesslike attitude, but there were days I could almost tell he was disappointed and bored:

*Wait a minute. All I get is this tennis ball? I don't give a shit about that anymore. I want to go find that dude we're after and bite him. Okay?*

This was especially true as the dogs became more seasoned. Therefore, it was important to work regularly on scent detection and find new ways to make the training interesting and fun. I frequently took Cairo to the beach and worked on odor detection with him. In Arizona, we'd do a full day of skydiving, and then, even if we were both exhausted, I'd make sure we got in some scent work. Once in a while, as a reward for good odor-detection work, I'd let him go after someone in a bite suit. For both of us, the bite work was more fun, but the scent work was more important, and it was a skill that deteriorated swiftly, so I tried to stay on top of it.

On a more fundamental level, dog handlers were constantly reminded of the fact that we were dealing with working dogs. I don't mean we were reminded by navy brass or anything like that. No, I'm talking about the irrepressible DNA of a Belgian Malinois that has been bred for generations to be among the best working dogs in the world. I constantly worked Cairo not only because that was my job but because I knew how unhappy he would be if he didn't get enough high-quality exercise.

Any working dog will make your life miserable if you are too selfish or lazy to recognize and respect his genetic makeup. When I was a little kid, we had a Siberian husky for a little while. His name was Smokey—appropriate enough, I suppose, because most of the time this guy ran around like his fur was on fire. I was too young to be his primary caretaker, and although I played around with Smokey a fair amount, I always ran out of gas before he did.

I remember one day he literally pulled a tree out of the ground. It wasn't a huge tree, but neither was it a little wisp of sumac or some other shallow-rooted wannabe. Nope. It was at real tree, maybe ten feet tall, young, with a narrow trunk and low-hanging branches. New growth, no doubt, but settled enough to have sturdy roots. Well, one morning, Smokey started digging around the base of the tree, pawing and scraping and shoveling like a maniac. I sat out on the porch and watched with amazement as he dug frantically for what seemed like hours. Every so often, he would stop digging, rest for a minute or so, and then begin tugging on the tree. He'd wrap his jaws around the trunk and pull. Then he'd jump up and grab one of the branches and pull on that. Pretty soon, the tree was bent over at a forty-five-degree angle. Then a ninety-degree angle. At one point, I went outside and tried to coax Smokey away from the tree, figuring he'd have a heart attack if he kept it up much longer. But he wouldn't quit.

It went on for most of the day—Smokey alternately digging and pulling, digging and pulling. At first, just his muzzle and paws were covered with dirt, but after a while, he almost seemed to change color. The entire front half of his body was caked with dirt. Periodically, he would stop and work his jaws and run his tongue over his teeth and the outside of his mouth. He would cough and do something that looked like spitting. Clearing the sand from his airway, no doubt.

But he would not quit, because, well, he was a husky, bred to run and race and fight. Every time I hear about someone buying a husky as a family pet, usually in response to some movie they've seen—or worse, because their kid had been following the Iditarod in school and thought the dogs were cute—I can only roll my eyes. You want to know what it's like to own a husky? It's like this: sitting in the backyard, watching Smokey pull a tree out of the ground with his teeth.

That's the way the battle ended, with Smokey backing up and backing up, his paws dug into the dirt for leverage, his jaw clamped around the trunk, blood dripping from his teeth after hours of effort. There was no way he was going to give up. Either that tree would come out of the ground, or Smokey would die of a heart attack. And you had to respect him for that. Eventually, Smokey's ceaseless effort was rewarded. The tree wiggled like a loose tooth and began to give up its roots. I remember being amazed at how much of the tree had been hidden beneath the surface: a couple of feet of tendrils, caked with dirt and debris.

When it was over, I applauded and ran over to give Smokey a hug, but he wasn't all that enthusiastic. He sniffed at the roots, circled the tree for a minute or two, and then walked away and took a well-deserved nap.

That, in a nutshell, is what it's like to own any type of working dog. Most people, I believe, are aware of what they are getting into, but not everyone. A few years ago, there was a movie called *Max* about the relationship between a military working dog and his handler, which predictably caused a spike in interest in Belgian Malinois. I can only imagine how unprepared most of these owners were for handling such a magnificent but demanding animal. This concept holds true for any dog bred to work. If you buy a hunting dog just because you like the way it looks and expect it to be happy lounging around your living room all day and night . . . well, be prepared to buy new furniture. I mean, you bought a hunting dog, right? Take him hunting!

Cairo was a military working dog, bred and trained to be part of the most elite fighting unit on the planet. He needed to work, and so I worked him. At least twice a day, I'd let him run until he'd had enough. As winter gave way to spring and our first deployment together loomed on the horizon, we spent less time at the beach and more time training on less forgiving surfaces: concrete, pavement, rocky hillsides, and mountains. Military working dogs don't often wear boots, after all (I mean, booties are available, but the dogs hate them!), so they had to be acclimated ahead of time to the rough and uneven terrain they would face in the mountains of Afghanistan.

If Cairo had trained only on grass or sand, his feet would have been devastated by the shock of suddenly running all night over rocks and concrete. Even a properly prepared dog could find the transition challenging and end up with sores and blisters on his paws so severe that they limited his ability to work. To minimize the likelihood of foot problems, I worked Cairo daily over surfaces that ordinarily he might have found unpleasant. But he was such a happy and energetic dog that he quickly adjusted. We'd run together on sidewalks and uneven, rutted trails. We'd play fetch in parking lots. Slowly but surely, Cairo began to develop calluses on his pads—thick, crusty shields that would protect him against the brutal terrain he was soon to face.

By April he was ready—physically, temperamentally, tactically—for his first deployment.

And I couldn't wait to see him in action.

# Chapter 11

Nothing triggers memory quite like a powerful odor.

Even now, all these years later, when I smell shit, I think of Afghanistan. Might be dog shit, horse shit, cow shit, or even human shit. Doesn't really matter. If I smell shit, under just the right circumstances—a hot and dusty day, or a moonlit night, in a field somewhere—the scent pulls me back in time to a place I both loved and hated. Does that sound like a contradiction? Well, it really isn't. It comes with the territory when you are fighting and killing and trying to stay alive—when you are doing a job you love and that you know is important but that sometimes seems like the craziest job imaginable.

I could never quite figure out the smell of Afghanistan, especially when we were out on target. It was only later, when I came home and left the service, that I realized how much I associated my service there with the pungent smell of waste. Animals were ubiquitous: goats and horses in the mountains, cows and chickens and other livestock in the villages and compounds, dogs everywhere, and of every shape and size and degree of domestication. With the animals came mountains of manure. Great, steaming piles of shit that could be smelled for miles in every direction. Coupled with the primitive sewage systems common in the Afghanistan hinterlands, where human waste was often dumped raw into the ground or in nearby streams and rivers, and clean water was scarce at best, the effect was like that of a fecal storm system that never seemed to dissipate.

It was nauseating, but after a while it also became normal. If I'm on a farm today, or even cleaning up after my dogs, I'm still sometimes transported back to Afghanistan. The smell of shit can do that to me. So can the smell of jet fuel. I don't fly much these days, mostly because I have a few dogs and one or more of them usually travels with me—it's easier to throw them in the truck and just drive. Sometimes, though, I find myself at an airport, walking through a jetway, and just as I get to the door, I'll get a big whiff of exhaust, and I'll reflexively start to smile. See, when I smell jet exhaust, I think of being a SEAL and being in that environment. I think of flying halfway around the world in the belly of a cargo plane, with Cairo at my feet, sleeping in his kennel. I think of being in a briefing room in Afghanistan, going over the night's mission, and then grabbing my kit—my helmet and pack and night-vision goggles and rifle—and boarding a chopper with some of the greatest guys I've ever known.

Was it dangerous? Without question. But it was also beautiful in its simplicity. At home, we were busy with a multitude of tasks. On deployment, we had one job.

Go after the bad guys.

Night after night after night.

Cairo and I arrived at Forward Operating Base Sharana, in the highlands of Paktika Province, Afghanistan, in June 2009. Originally constructed in 2004, under the name Camp Kearney, Sharana was one of the largest U.S. military bases in Afghanistan (it was closed in 2013 and returned to the Afghan government). We had a group of roughly thirty to forty members of the squadron stationed at Sharana, along with an approximately equal number of support personnel. Although Sharana was a large base, we were mostly segregated in a handful of huts set up to meet our particular needs and work schedules. We shared a chow hall with the regular troops but had our own living quarters and a nice private gym tricked out with more equipment than we needed and a giant flat-screen television.

There were perhaps fifteen SEALs sharing a hut, and Cairo slept right alongside us. It was a big, well-appointed camp, but there were no designated kennels built for the dogs. This wasn't a big deal because we only had two dogs at this location. I stayed in one hut with Cairo, while the other dog and his handler stayed in a different hut. This lessened the chance that the dogs might get into a disagreement—a turf war, so to speak—and also reduced the impact of their presence on the other members of the assault team. The huts were divided into small, individual sleeping sections for each assaulter, along with a big area at the end of the hut for relaxing and hanging out when we weren't working. The living area was furnished with couches, a refrigerator, an ice machine, and a television.

I kept a small kennel in the living area for Cairo to sleep in, but he was just as likely to share my sleeping quarters. Since the sleeping rooms were tiny, they accommodated only a twin bed, which was raised off the floor to create additional space; Cairo would usually sleep on a rug beneath my bed, although sometimes he'd try to jump up on the bed. At home, where I had a queen-sized bed, I didn't mind. But sharing a twin mattress with a full-grown Malinois?

Sorry, Cairo. Gotta draw the line somewhere.

My first deployment with Cairo was a four-month assignment with a pretty steady operation tempo. We went out five or six times a week. Sometimes seven. A typical night consisted of locating and determining the legitimacy of a target. This was done through the accumulation of a wealth of intel from various

sources. Once it was confirmed that a target was indeed a legitimate fighter, and overwhelmingly likely to be at the location we
planned to hit (and that the odds were in our favor), a briefing
would be conducted. Outlined during the briefing was the identity of the target or targets, the reason we were going after him,
and the basic movement and responsibility of each of the two
assault teams in the squadron. I would get together with the
other dog handler and team leaders, and together we would de-
cide who would support each of the teams. Most of the time, we
stayed with our assigned team unless circumstances required a
change. Then we would each brief our team about the dog and
its capabilities and responsibilities and the gear we would be
carrying. By the end of a deployment, most of this information
was old news to the rest of the team, but we shared it, anyway,
every night, as a matter of protocol.

If a chaplain were available, the briefing ended with a prayer.
Then we would swing quickly into action. Each operator would go
to the ready room to prepare his personal gear and make sure he
had everything he needed. (The ready room was a separate building where we kept all our gear in cubbies, packed and ready to go,
so that we could embark on a moment's notice at any time of the
day or night). My first responsibility was to check my weapons
and be certain that they were functioning properly. Then I'd go
through a mental checklist of supplies and preparation that included fresh batteries in my optics; enough water for myself and
Cairo; and a fully functioning radio. Then I'd check all of Cairo's
gear. I always carried a small, collapsible bowl to give Cairo water
on patrol, and a medical kit designed to treat canine injuries.

In every way, Cairo was one of the guys. Except he was
a dog, which by nature made him somewhat unpredictable, regardless of his training or genetic gifts. We were only a few days
into the deployment when we went out on our first op—looking
for bad guys, as usual.

We had trained for this mission, discussed every possible scenario we might encounter. Or so we thought. Usually, we brought two dogs on each mission: one positioned at the front of the patrol, the other in the middle. On this night, Cairo and I were at the front. I remember feeling a surge of adrenaline as we hiked in, loaded down with the usual complement of gear, just as on every other mission, only this time with a full-grown Malinois at my side. This was my fourth deployment as a Navy SEAL and my second to Afghanistan; it wasn't like I was unfamiliar with the terrain—figuratively or literally. Although each mission was unique, I knew basically what to expect.

And yet . . . the excitement of being on deployment again, coupled with the fact that I had a new role and expanded responsibility, added a layer of unpredictability and excitement. In some ways, I felt as if I were starting all over. I knew there was a good chance the night would end with gunfire and the elimination of a target. Maybe we'd encounter resistance; maybe not. Regardless, my job would be different from how it had been in the past.

I was a dog handler, and my first responsibility was to take care of Cairo, to make sure he did the job for which he had been so exhaustively trained. This was his first mission. I wondered how he would do—and how I would do as a handler. If Cairo messed up, after all, that was not merely a reflection on me but a potential danger to everyone in the squadron.

With Cairo on my hip lead—I rarely held the leash, as I had to keep my hands free to hold a weapon—we walked across a moonlit field toward a small compound. He seemed comfortable in his surroundings, neither hesitant nor overly eager, but rather content to wait until he was given some type of direction. I wondered if he had any idea that this was not merely an exercise but rather the real deal.

And since it was the real deal, and since this was Afghanistan, you never knew quite what to expect.

We entered the compound and crossed a little courtyard and then walked through a doorway, where, to my surprise, we encountered a herd of a few dozen sheep. This could have been a bloody disaster, of course. In all our months of training, through countless scenarios designed to teach Cairo and his fellow working dogs how to respond while on a mission, the one thing we had not simulated was a courtyard filled with farm animals. Cairo had chased down hundreds of bad guys in bite suits; he had ferreted out explosives in fields and darkened movie theaters. He had jumped out of planes and calmly crossed a lake in a canoe.

He had been damn-near perfect.

But he had never been presented with a scenario in which dozens of helpless, crying little animals stood between him and the successful completion of his task. There was no way of knowing how he would respond, but I didn't like the odds.

I heard a voice whisper from behind me, "You got him, Cheese?"

I nodded, even though I wasn't sure I had anything.

As the little animals began to bleat, I reached down and grabbed Cairo by the harness. Immediately, he stopped in his tracks.

*What's wrong, Dad?*

Without speaking—because I really didn't have a command for what was about to happen—I scooped up Cairo, while still holding my weapon, and tossed him over my shoulder like a sack of laundry.

The last thing we needed at that moment was for Cairo, who was in full hunt mode, to be distracted by a giant, all-you-can-eat lamb buffet. I had no idea how he might react to being suddenly withdrawn from his usual position. In training, I had never encountered a situation like this. For all I knew, Cairo might have responded by barking and yelping and struggling to get out of my arms. It was also possible that if I had left him on the ground, he would have walked right past the little critters, so focused on doing his job that he would ignore a free meal.

I couldn't take any chances. In that moment, a decision had to be made, one based on instinct and probability. Cairo was a dog. A highly trained and even-tempered dog, yes. But he was still a dog. And I figured that given half a chance, he might just run a bloody path through the entire menagerie.

Cairo, however, was as cool as could be. He didn't try to wrestle away from me; instead, as we stepped quietly through the herd, his body pressed against my back, he just sort of looked at the sheep quizzically until they were out of sight. Then I put him down, gave him a firm but approving pat on the head, and let him go back to work.

As it turned out, that was the highlight of the evening. We methodically worked our way through the compound, cleared all the rooms, interviewed a few locals, and let Cairo get his first taste of real work (our other dog had been stationed outside on the perimeter with his handler, which is the way we usually operated: one dog outside, one dog inside). There were no bites, no bad guys, no explosives . . . nothing. As often happened in Afghanistan, this particular hole was dry. Or, at least, it was dry by the time we arrived.

Nevertheless, I considered the mission to be a success and one that demonstrated in no uncertain terms that, despite all our training, it was impossible to plan for every contingency. Cairo had done everything that was asked of him that night. He had adapted to new surroundings without so much as a hint of anxiety or trepidation. Best of all, when confronted with a distraction of potentially catastrophic proportions, he had merely shrugged.

What more could you ask of the guy?

As far as I was concerned, this mission had been the perfect little shakeout—an opportunity for Cairo to test his training and temperament in the field with, as it turned out, minimal risk. And for me, it was a chance to see how my new partner would respond to both stress and stimulation. You can train forever, but until you're on a mission facing the potential of real danger with serious consequences, you never how someone will respond. That is true of dogs as well as humans.

Cairo had passed the first test. And everyone was happy to have him on the team.

That was Cairo. He understood his job to a degree that never ceased to amaze me. On many missions, our objective could be distilled to this: capture or eliminate one or more known targets. This was intense, dangerous work, often complicated by the presence of not just unexpected wildlife and heavily armed insurgents but civilians—women and children—who were sometimes deliberately placed in harm's way. Human shields, for lack of a better term. More than once, I held my breath as Cairo raced into a building in search of a target—a bad guy who had refused to come out when summoned—unsure of what the outcome might be.

When Cairo got his very first bite, I was startled by the damage it did—the guy's arm had been nearly severed, and arterial spray covered a nearby wall, so clearly, he was fortunate to have survived—but also by the sight of a tiny, bundled baby not far from where the man had been hiding.

To get to his target, Cairo must have run right past the infant. Given his extraordinary sense of smell, he surely would have stopped to investigate. I don't quite know how to explain the fact that he didn't harm the child—any more than I can explain the infant's presence, untended, while an insurgent hid from view nearby—except to say that Cairo was indeed a special dog. He knew right from wrong, good from bad.

When Cairo worked, he did so with a singular purpose. His job was to protect us, to alert us to the possibility of danger in the form of explosives or insurgents hiding within closets or behind walls or outside in tall grass or tree lines. He looked out for us, and we, in turn, looked out for him. Not that Cairo couldn't take care of himself; it's just that's sometimes he was so focused on his mission that he failed to notice outside threats. And those threats could come in many forms, including another dog.

It was a sad fact of life in Afghanistan that dogs were everywhere, and most were not particularly well cared for. Many were either feral or semi-feral. They roamed the countryside and city streets alike, foraging for food wherever they could find it. Some were harmless; many were not. We grew accustomed to seeing stray dogs everywhere, but we had to be vigilant when it came to their unpredictability. You didn't just stop to scratch an Afghan dog behind the ears, for you never knew if he had been raised in someone's home or birthed in the wild. As someone who had grown up with dogs, loved dogs, and now considered a working dog to be among his closest allies, this was something of a conundrum for me. But I got over it quickly. Dogs in Afghanistan, especially in the mostly rural provinces, were mainly a nuisance. They were neither cared for nor loved. Even those that managed to find a home among villagers appeared to hold no higher a place in the societal pecking order than the goats and sheep and chickens being readied for slaughter.

For the most part, the dogs were untethered and untrained but nonconfrontational. Sometimes we had to chase them away while on a mission, simply because they were getting in the way or otherwise hampering our objective. A few wound up on American bases and were treated loosely as pets. Occasionally, however, their presence was more than just a nuisance.

We were only a few weeks into the deployment when a mission was compromised by an Afghan dog. We were searching a compound during a rare daytime patrol, trying to calmly deal with the distractions and other variables that come with working without the cover of night. Everyone, of course, was wide awake and going about their business. The first step was to secure the compound, which we did by placing the children in a safe and secure spot, sequestered in the center of the courtyard, along with most of the adult women. The men were separated and questioned.

Meanwhile, I began working Cairo around the perimeter of the courtyard, methodically moving from one building to another, looking for explosives.

As usual, Cairo did exactly as he was told. He sniffed around the outside of each building, then went inside and searched bedrooms and closets and other hidden spaces. It was a painstaking process and involved a lot of downtime as I directed Cairo from one spot to another, off leash. Suddenly, as we worked our way to the back of the courtyard, a large, mangy dog emerged from one of the buildings and began sauntering toward me. I'd been through this before, so at first, I didn't even worry.

Trying to remain quiet, I lifted my fist, figuring he would just flee, which is the way most Afghan dogs responded, especially those that were semidomesticated and living among villagers. The dog didn't budge. Instead, he held his ground, maybe ten to fifteen feet away. He was bigger than the usual mutts you'd see in Afghanistan—bigger than Cairo, for sure—and a whole lot uglier. I held the dog's gaze, since I didn't trust him enough to turn my back, and waved a first at him again.

Again, he did not move. Instead, he crouched low and inched a couple of steps closer. Now I had a problem. I didn't know whether the dog was rabid or just ornery. He wasn't growling or baring his teeth or otherwise acting in an aggressive manner. He was just . . . there. And refusing to leave. That was disturbing enough. But it really didn't matter. We had a job to do. Intel had told us there was reason to believe insurgents were utilizing the compound, and where there were bad guys, often there were explosives. Cairo's job, of course, was to sniff out the bombs or weapons or any bad guys in hiding. The Afghan dog was putting that job at risk.

Not that Cairo seemed to care. Even as the dog inched closer, Cairo went about his business. Once locked into odor-detection mode, there was little that would distract him—except perhaps the scent of a human he was supposed to bite. But another dog? He could not possibly have cared less.

I kept waiting for the dog to get tired of the standoff and retreat. That's the way these things usually resolved. But this guy was stubborn, and that made him unpredictable. He would take a couple of steps toward me and tilt his head to the side. I kept working, watching Cairo, and periodically looking over at the dog—multitasking to the best of my abilities. Then I'd stick out my chest and raise my hand, which caused him to back off for a moment. Unfortunately, this also had the effect of turning his attention toward Cairo.

The dog stopped, turned to face me, and went back into a crouching position. Although I wasn't all that experienced with wild dogs, I knew enough about canine behavior to recognize an aggressive position. This guy was ready to move—either at me or Cairo. The only question was, which one of us would he target?

I glanced at the center of the courtyard, where a small group of women and children were gathered, watching with diminishing interest as our search progressed. I imagined how they might react if the dog suddenly attacked and I was forced to shoot him.

I took a deep breath and glanced at a nearby room, where Cairo was hard at work. Then I looked back at the dog. He remained low and tight. Suddenly, he turned his head toward Cairo. I knew what was coming. The dog leaped to his feet and within a heartbeat was at full throttle, sprinting toward Cairo, who was oblivious to the coming assault. I didn't hesitate. As soon as the dog took off, I raised my rifle, took aim, and squeezed off a single shot. The bullet caught him square in the head. He fell to the ground in midstride, dead on impact, no more than ten feet from Cairo.

*Shit . . .*

Instantly, I felt a mix of conflicting emotions: sadness and disappointment at having to shoot a dog; relief that the threat had been neutralized and that Cairo could go on with his business; and guilt over exposing a group of locals to the death of a dog. Maybe a dog they cared for. At the very least, a dog they knew.

I turned to face them. They seemed oblivious to what had just transpired. There were no tears, no shrieks of horror. This poor dog lay sprawled on the ground, bleeding out from a gaping head wound, and no one seemed to be affected by it or to care in the least. Apparently, I was the only one who felt bad for the big mutt. I was a dog handler. And now I was a dog killer. In this world, so far from home, those two things somehow went together.

# Chapter 12

On June 30, 2009, FOB Sharana—and, subsequently, the entire U.S. military—was rocked by the news that an American
soldier named Bowe Bergdahl had been reported missing. At
the time, I didn't know anything about Bergdahl; no one did.
But over the ensuing days, months, and years, he'd become
famous—or infamous—in military circles.

Private Bergdahl was a young guy, twenty-three years old,
who had enlisted in the army in 2008. But that was not his first
experience with the military—previously, he'd enlisted in the
Coast Guard but did not even make it through basic training.
Why or how he ended up in the army is anyone's guess. Regardless, Bergdahl eventually was assigned to the 501st Infantry
Regiment and sent to Afghanistan on his deployment. Had he
not decided to stroll away from his post one night, I doubt our
paths ever would have crossed. I mean, not that I ever met the
guy, but his actions had a profound impact on me and a lot of
other people, sometimes with grave consequences.

The circumstances surrounding Bergdahl's disappearance were a source of debate almost from the beginning. Did
he walk away from his post? Was he captured while on patrol?

Around the base, it was generally accepted that Bergdahl had simply deserted. Regardless, it wasn't long—fewer than twenty-four hours—before word came down that he had landed in the hands of the Taliban. With that news came an abrupt shift in the war in Afghanistan. Suddenly, we weren't just looking for insurgents and other Taliban forces and generally trying to root out the baddest of bad guys throughout the country. Instead, it seemed, the entire might of the U.S. military was temporarily redirected to a singular cause:

Find Private Bergdahl and bring him home.

Understandably, there was an urgency to the mission—and to call it a *mission* was to undersell the task; it was actually an objective that included dozens of missions. Generally speaking, the longer a captive remained missing, the less likely he was ever to be found alive.

For the remainder of that deployment, much of our work revolved around trying to rescue Bergdahl. This led to many dry holes and a lot of nights without contact, as well as some nights with unanticipated and violent contact. I'll be candid here: it was tough on morale. Bergdahl's actions put a lot of people at risk. I understood the importance of finding him. Politically speaking, Bergdahl's capture was a nightmare for the U.S. military. And from a human standpoint, it was the right thing to do. Bergdahl was an American. Thousands of miles away, back in the States, he had a mom and dad who hoped to see him again. It was our job to bring him home.

On the night of July 9, 2009, just ten days after Bergdahl was taken captive, an assault force was dispatched on a hostage rescue mission. Now, the truth is, for the last two months of that deployment, basically everything we did revolved around the search for Bergdahl, so it would not be inaccurate to say that every operation was, in fact, a hostage rescue operation. These missions were unsuccessful in terms of recovering the hostage, although some did provide collateral reward in the form of capturing or eliminating other targets.

I was not part of the unit involved in the July 9 rescue mission—I was out with another unit, helping to clear the area in support of the mission—but I had friends who were there. The operation, which resulted in American casualties, is a matter of public record, so I'm not giving away any secrets by discussing it here. Suffice it to say, we had strong intel that led us to believe that Bergdahl was being held in a specific place, and we acted on that intel. But apparently the Taliban knew we were coming, for according to official accounts of the mission, the two helicopters carrying U.S. forces came under heavy enemy fire from machine guns and rocket-propelled grenades before they even touched down.

Outnumbered and under withering attack, the unit nevertheless advanced steadily toward its target position: a large, strongly fortified building on the edge of a field, where intel suggested Bergdahl was being held captive.

Among those on the mission were Senior Chief Petty Officer James Hatch and Senior Chief Petty Officer Michael Toussaint. I knew both of these guys well. Jimmy was an older member of the squadron whom I liked personally and respected professionally. He was a funny, sweet-tempered guy, as well as a courageous and reliable fighter, having completed hundreds of missions as both an operator and a dog handler. Obviously, we had some things in common. Three years earlier, in Iraq, Jimmy had lost a dog named Spike. I know that Jimmy was shattered by the dog's death. He often said that Spike had saved his life many times over, which isn't hard to believe.

By the time of our deployment, Jimmy was no longer a dog handler, but as he moved toward the target that night, he did so in proximity to a combat assault dog named Remco. A big, beautiful Belgian Malinois who was part of the same training

class as Cairo, Remco was accompanied by Mike Toussaint, a
master-at-arms (MA). As previously noted, it wasn't unusual
for MAs to be involved in combat missions, and some of them
fought not just well but every bit as effectively as their SEAL
counterparts. Mike was one of those guys. I'd gotten to know
him when I first began working with Cairo and considered him
a friend. He had my respect as both a fighter and a dog handler.

As the platoon advanced toward its target, a small group
that included Jimmy, Mike, and Remco broke off in pursuit of
two men they spotted running off into the field. The group pursued the two men until they disappeared. Then Remco was dispatched with the hope of revealing their hiding place.

Moments later, as Remco dashed forward, one of the insurgents, hiding in a nearby culvert, stood up and fired his AK-47
directly at Remco, hitting the dog in the head from a distance of
only a few meters. He died instantly, but that act of sacrifice revealed the insurgents' position, which led to an immediate and
deadly confrontation. Seconds after Remco was killed, Jimmy
Hatch was shot in the leg. As another member of the team ran
to Jimmy's aid, Mike Toussaint charged at the culvert, through
heavy fire, and killed both insurgents. Mike also retrieved Remco's body and dragged him back to the same position where
corpsmen were treating Jimmy Hatch.

Private Bergdahl, as it turned out, was not in the vicinity.

Some two years later, Mike Toussaint was awarded the Sil-
ver Star and a commendation for extraordinary heroism from
the chief of naval operations. Befitting his status as a member
of an American fighting unit who gave his life in the line of duty,
Remco was also awarded a Silver Star. His heroic actions, according to the citation, drew enemy fire that gave the members
of his unit "the split seconds needed to change the balance of
the fight."

Jimmy Hatch received the Purple Heart, but his military

career was effectively ended by the injuries he sustained that night. He spent several months in hospitals, enduring multiple surgeries and endless physical and emotional pain, which are so often a consequence of a soldier's time in battle. Like I said, it's not so much the things you do that follow you home; it's the stuff you didn't do, or the things you think you could have done to alter the outcome. Jimmy is a great guy and a heroic SEAL. Like all of us, he lost friends during his service. And two of those friends were dogs that saved his life.

Trust me, that shit will weigh on you.

# Chapter 13

Cairo was one of the boys.

He lived with us, ate with us, slept with us, played with us, trained with us, fought with us. Sometimes he even pranked with us.

On July 29, 2009, I woke early in the afternoon. This wasn't unusual, as we'd been out the night before and would be going out again on this night. You learn to sleep almost anywhere in the military, and to nod off on a moment's notice—thus the somewhat jarring sight of guys snoring their way through a loud and bumpy chopper ride into a drop zone. I've seen men go from a dead sleep to a firefight in a matter of seconds. It's amazing what the mind can do under the right circumstances.

That said, constantly changing schedules, sleep deprivation, and frequent travel can go a long way toward messing up your circadian rhythm, and it wasn't unusual for guys to lean on pharmaceutical assistance (e.g., Ambien) to ensure sufficient rest. This could be tricky. Ambien was perfectly fine as a way to help pass the time on a fourteen-hour trip from Virginia to Afghanistan, but you had to be careful when using it in the field. The last thing anyone wanted was to feel hungover or foggy when heading out on a mission. Nevertheless, we all used it to varying degrees, mostly without incident.

I was a pretty good sleeper, so I didn't use it much, but on this particular day, I took a small dose to catch some much-needed rest between missions. When I woke, Cairo was wandering anxiously around the hut, breathing heavily. I had raised my bunk off the ground to create more space on the floor of the hut, and Cairo was pacing below me, giving me a look that was instantly recognizable as guilt.

"What's up, buddy?"

Cairo whimpered a little and kept walking. I went into a corner of the hut to retrieve my boots and found them practically swimming in a puddle of liquid. The smell—pungent and fresh—left no doubt as to the source. Cairo had peed in my boots.

"What the hell, dude?"

I hooked him up to a leash and led him outside, where Cairo quickly lifted a leg. But he managed only a dribble. No surprise—after the flood he'd left indoors, there couldn't have been much left in the system. I stood there for a moment looking at Cairo. He was an enormously reliable and well-trained dog. Honestly, I couldn't recall him ever having an accident like this. Bad enough that he pissed all over our living quarters, but to do it in my boots?

I wondered for a moment. Was it really an accident? I mean, obviously the poor guy had to relieve himself. Ordinarily, if he had to go during the night (or whenever I was sleeping), he would just whimper a bit and I'd wake up and let him out. This time I must have slept through the alarm. And maybe, because he was unhappy and wanted to send a message, he opted to decorate my boots, rather than just peeing harmlessly on the floor.

Like I said, a prankster.

Or maybe he was just looking for a familiar and friendly smell. Who knows?

Regardless, when we got back in the hut, I decided to have some fun with Cairo. Like I said, he was one of the boys.

"You're gonna mess with my feet, I'll mess with yours," I said. "Let's do a little booty work."

This sounds worse than it was. *Booty work* meant the application of small boots over a dog's paws. As noted, I didn't often use these with Cairo, but sometimes—when crossing particularly jagged terrain, or in urban settings where broken glass was a consideration—they were a well-advised, temporary precaution. Some dogs adapted to the booties better than others. Cairo greatly preferred to go natural and absolutely hated the booties, so I didn't force him to wear them often; in fact, I only occasionally even trained him in booties, especially on deployment.

But I was a little grumpy now and figured some booty training would be a fitting but harmless punishment for peeing in my boots. As usual, he fought their application; and once on, he walked about the hut gingerly as if tiptoeing across a hot beach. Watching him, I started to laugh. He was so damn cute. He would take a step forward, then two quicks steps back. Then two steps forward, and one step back, like a little cat dance. I grabbed a pair of doggles and strapped them loosely to Cairo's head. And then a pair of earmuffs—the kind we'd wear to protect ourselves from the eardrum-shattering roar of explosives. As the cat dance grew increasingly sloppy, I snapped a few pictures while laughing so hard I could barely breathe. He actually looked like a little superhero, all dressed up like that.

At that moment, a couple of guys from the team walked into the hut.

"Cheese, what the fuck are you doing?"

"Just having some fun with Cairo," I said, laughing. "He pissed in my boots."

"Aw, come on, man."

They were both trying hard to stifle laughs as Cairo lurched about like a guy who had drunk too much at a Halloween party. But they were right: even though Cairo was one of the boys, I knew better—and he deserved better—than to use him for our amusement. So I stripped off the glasses and booties and ear-muffs and gave him a big hug.

"All right, pal. Sorry about that. I know you didn't mean to piss in my boots. My fault, anyway."

This was 100 percent true. If I had woken and let Cairo out, he would not have peed in my boots. It was totally my fault.

I led Cairo outside with some of the other guys, and we took turns working him in a long and tiring game of fetch. I still have pictures of Cairo from that day, doing his superhero cat dance in the hut. They always make me smile.

A few hours later, I boarded a helicopter with Cairo for the next mission. We were still looking for Private Bergdahl, although by this point, the trail had begun to cool. At the same time, we had received intelligence about a possible IED-manufacturing operation. We flew roughly a half hour to our destination, in two choppers. The plan, as usual, was to set the choppers down and hike quietly to the target, but as sometimes happened, the insurgents found out that we were on our way. I'm not sure if someone tipped them off or they simply heard the choppers; regardless, as we approached, word came down that four men were seen, via drone, hurriedly leaving the target—a large, seemingly unoccupied building in the middle of nowhere. We had no choice but to pursue from the air.

As we drew near, I could see the scene unfolding below: the four men had split into two groups. Each duo had hopped on a motorcycle—more of a moped, really—and was racing away from the building. Each moped was weighed down with an abundance of gear, some of which appeared to be RPGs and other explosive devices and guns.

Now, you might wonder how this even presented much of a dilemma. We had two helicopters carrying a couple of dozen Navy SEALs, armed with highly sophisticated and accurate weaponry. Why not just blow the fleeing bad guys into the next universe?

Simple question, complicated answer. While these guys certainly passed the eye test and the common-sense test—they were bad guys engaging in obviously bad behavior (i.e., running from a known explosives manufacturing site while carrying explosives)—the rules of engagement demanded 100 percent certainty before raining fire from the sky. We had to be 100 percent certain that these were grown men and not boys who had been conscripted into the terrorist ranks while barely in their teens; we had to be 100 percent certain they were really carrying RPGs and IEDs; we had to be 100 percent certain there were no civilians in the vicinity.

We needed 100 percent certainty. On all counts.

This did not always happen; in fact, it rarely happened, which is why we usually put the chopper down and engaged on foot. And that's what we did now, despite the fact we no longer had the advantage of surprise. As we closed in, the two mopeds veered off in opposite directions, so we did the same. Divide and conquer, so to speak.

For the most part, the pursuit happened in a vast open area, but eventually, the moped made it to a cluster of trees near the top of a hill. The two passengers jumped off, grabbed some bags of gear from the moped, and ran away. We set the helicopter down as close as we could to the tree line and pursued on foot. This was risky, as we knew the insurgents were armed with automatic weapons, RPGs, and who knows what else. They also had the high ground, which was a tactical advantage we rarely surrendered. But we had no other option. We weren't going to just let them get away. These guys were the target for the night, and our job was to swiftly and safely neutralize the target.

The wind was blowing left to right, so I worked Cairo from the far right, into the wind, figuring he'd pick up the scent of the bad guys and work his way upwind to their hiding spot. But we couldn't just walk blindly into the trees because we knew they were armed to the teeth and prepared to fight; they weren't going to just walk out with their hands up. Ordinarily, we would have carefully established control of the scene through air support or sniper teams on adjacent buildings. Circumstances, though, left us naked and vulnerable.

In this highly volatile scenario, the next step is to rely on your dog. You let him pick up the scent and then send him in to pinpoint the enemy's position or to flush them out. If this sounds like exceedingly dangerous work for the dog, well, it is.

As I led Cairo into the wind on a hip lead, he lifted his snout in excitement. I made my way to our team leader, Daniel.

"He's got it," I said. "We can send him in anytime."

Daniel nodded. "Okay. Whenever you're ready."

I unhooked Cairo's lead and gave him a pat on the behind.

He raced toward the tree line and quickly picked up on an odor. I'd seen Cairo do this dozens of times, but it never failed to impress. Oddly, there was a low concrete or stone wall, perhaps three to four feet in height, running parallel to the tree line. Cairo easily hopped the barrier and continued working. With his head bobbing up and down, he aggressively worked the tree line, moving steadily from east to west. Whenever I sent Cairo off to find a target, there was a possibility that he could be injured or killed; it was part of the job description. But this was the riskiest sort of scenario: sending him into a hidden area occupied by insurgents who were heavily armed and almost certainly desperate.

I don't want to make it sound like we were at a complete disadvantage here, or that we weren't accustomed to fighting in this manner. We had every advantage in terms of training and technology. State-of-the-art night-vision goggles allowed us to scan the field and trees as if it were daytime. We had them outnumbered and outgunned by a substantial margin.

And we had Cairo to help neutralize the one advantage the enemy held—the advantage of the unknown.

Cairo continued to follow the scent; he was clearly responding to something. For a while, I could see him weaving in and out of the trees, but as Cairo continued to work the tree line, he faded from view. He was on the far left of the tree line while I was on the right, closest to the team leader.

Suddenly, a few seconds later, I heard gunfire. While we had been holding our position on this side of the hillside, a few other members of the team had positioned themselves farther to the left. From my vantage point, I could not tell what was happening. But as shots rang out across the field, it was obvious that contact had been made.

"Cairo!" I yelled. "Los!"

Even if I couldn't see what was happening, gunfire was a signal to retrieve the dog. The best-case scenario was that our team had found the bad guys and were in the thick of a firefight; one we'd likely win. But there was no benefit to having Cairo in the way once bullets started flying. His presence was a distraction to the team, and, obviously, he was in danger.

I said his name again, gave him a quick hit with the e-collar, and began moving toward the left end of the tree line. A dog handler's job in that scenario quickly becomes complicated, for he is at once a member of the assault team but also someone who is responsible for the safety of the team's dog. I hit the e-collar again, yelled, "Cairo! Los!" and continued to move. As I looked to my left, I could see the muzzle flash of AK fire coming from above the ground, apparently in the trees. And I could see our guys returning fire.

I continued to call for Cairo, all the while holding my rifle at the ready, but not yet close enough to engage. I'm not sure how much time passed, but as the minutes went by, it became clear that something had happened to Cairo. He was a smart and obedient dog; even when locked into a bite, he always responded well to the e-collar. Given the intensity of the fight at this moment, and the amount of gunfire, it seemed unlikely that Cairo had taken down one of the bad guys. In fact, it seemed increasingly likely that something very bad had happened.

"Cairo!" I repeated, still moving upwind along the trees. "Come on, buddy! Los!"

Finally, in the distance, I saw something move. It was Cairo! He emerged from the trees maybe thirty or forty meters away. I called his name again, this time loud enough to be heard through the night air, above the crack of gunfire even. Everything was happening very quickly, and yet time seemed to stand still. This was not an uncommon occurrence on missions, the sense that events unfolded in slow motion. I watched as Cairo walked toward me. I was struck immediately by the fact that he was not running but rather lurching awkwardly. Still, he followed my voice, my scent.

I ran to him as quickly as I could, but he fell to the ground just a few feet before I reached him. And he didn't just stop and lie down; he basically tipped over in midstride.

*Shit . . . he's dead.*

It was as simple as that. I didn't mourn. I didn't panic. We still had a mission to accomplish, and Cairo was no longer a part of that mission. He was gone.

Or so it seemed.

I knelt beside him as the gunfire ebbed. Under a moonlit sky, I could see that Cairo's fur was wet and matted with something dark. His eyes were slits, his breathing labored. Instinct and experience told me that the battle was over, or at least under control. We had more than a dozen men; they had two. It was highly unlikely that another thirty insurgents were hiding in the trees. It was now mop-up time, and my responsibility was to Cairo. I ran a hand along his vest, felt a hole soaked with something sticky. I patted him on the head.

"Hang in there, boy."

It seemed a miracle that Cairo was still alive; honestly, when a dog was wounded, it usually happened at point-blank range, and the dog rarely survived. But Cairo was tough. Or lucky. Or both, I guess.

As I stayed with Cairo, another member of the team peeled off and made his way back to us. Word had already come over the radio that we had suffered a FWIA—*friendly wounded in action*. This is the worst thing you want to hear during or after a fight, and the fact that the *friendly* was Cairo barely registered as consolation. He was part of the team. He was one of us.

The guy who had come back to help was a former combat medic. He immediately went into action, treating Cairo with just as much urgency and professionalism as if he were a human. I removed Cairo's vest and handed the medic my canine medical kit, which I always carried with me. Then I gently slipped Cairo's muzzle over his snout. Although Cairo was usually friendly and knew both of us, there was no telling how he would respond to the pain and trauma of being wounded. I kept waiting for him to lapse into unconsciousness, but he remained awake, if not exactly alert.

"We'll fix you up, Cairo," the medic said. "Don't worry."

Cairo barely reacted as the medic ripped open packages of gauze and stuffed them into his chest wound. One after another, deeper and deeper, his fingers disappearing into the hole. There was so much blood, so much damage. At one point, as the medic rooted around, trying to stem the flow of blood, Cairo yelped and turned his head. The muzzle smacked against the medic's hand.

"Sorry," he said.

I rubbed a hand along Cairo's back, trying to calm him down. After what seemed like only a few moments, the medic declared Cairo's chest wound to be stable—at least by field standards—and began gently moving his hands around Cairo's entire body. By now, he was covered in blood, and we didn't have much light, so it was hard to tell whether there were any other wounds. As it turned out, there was—another bullet had hit Cairo in the right foreleg. Must have hurt like a son of a bitch, but compared to the chest wound, it was a minor concern. In humans or canines, battlefield chest wounds are very bad, and often fatal.

Within a few minutes, a medevac helicopter was called in. I boarded with Cairo, along with the medic, and we flew back to Sharana, where a team of doctors worked on him for the better part of two hours. And when I say doctors, I mean *physicians*. The kind who treat human soldiers. See, there were no veterinarians at Sharana, so Cairo was treated just like any other soldier. I was there the whole time, and these folks—doctors, nurses—were just incredible. I couldn't believe how quickly and efficiently they worked, and how they didn't treat Cairo like a dog but simply as a wounded member of the U.S. armed forces. They performed an emergency tracheotomy to clear his airway so that he wouldn't drown in his own blood. They inserted chest tubes. They put a brace on his leg to stabilize that wound and to keep his femur from falling apart.

Simply put, they saved his life.

And the night wasn't over yet. As soon as Cairo was out of immediate danger, he was put on a plane bound for Bagram Airfield, the closest military base with a veterinary staff. Bagram was the granddaddy of all U.S. bases in Afghanistan, and as such, it was equipped to deal with a wide variety of medical issues, including those pertaining to working dogs. Technically speaking, I didn't have to make the trip with him. He was an attack dog, and as such in need of experienced oversight, but there would be dog handlers at Bagram.

I went because Cairo was my dog. I wanted to be with him. While I didn't feel responsible for his injuries—they came with the territory and were a known risk—I did feel responsible for him. He had been wounded doing a job I had assigned to him. And as I would later discover, when debriefed on the mission, he had done that job exceptionally well.

It wasn't unusual for the details of a particular mission to trickle out slowly. Hours or even days could pass before a clear and concise picture was presented. In this case, I was in the air with Cairo as the mission was being deconstructed. But I later found out that he had performed heroically and in so doing had probably saved lives and certainly impacted the outcome of the mission.

Here's the way it went down:

As Cairo followed the scent between the wall and the tree line, he came upon the two bad guys. One of them was on the ground, using a flashlight as an attempt to misdirect us and draw us in; the second guy was in a tree, hiding in some lower branches. As Cairo engaged the guy on the ground—I can only hope he got in a good bite—the other guy began shooting at

Cairo from above. Two of the bullets struck Cairo, one in the chest, one in the leg. This effectively ended the battle for Cairo; it also immediately revealed the insurgents' position, which allowed our guys to move in and kill them both.

As soon as the gunfire started, I had called out to Cairo and punched his e-collar to get him to come home. Remarkably, he did exactly as he was told, despite being gravely wounded. Unable to jump back over the wall because of his injuries, Cairo had to go all the way around it to make his way back to me. I had no idea what was happening to him at the time, no clue as to the struggle he faced. I just kept calling him and buzzing him with the e-collar, trying to get him to withdraw from the fight. And he made it. With a nearly shattered leg and a gaping chest wound, Cairo staggered home to Dad.

So, yeah, I accompanied him to Sharana, and then to Bagram. It was the least I could do.

# Chapter 14

I spent the night on the floor of Cairo's room in the veterinary hospital at Bagram, one arm resting on his back, trying to comfort him. He looked to be in a world of hurt, although, thankfully, I don't think he was aware of much in those first few hours. He had bandages on his chest and a cast on his right foreleg (later signed by the veterinarians and staff who had inserted a metal plate to hold it together). His face and body were bloated from steroids and intravenous liquids.

The poor guy looked exactly like what he was: a wounded warrior.

I didn't sleep much that night. I was too worried about Cairo and whether he would succumb to his injuries. If something happened, I wanted to be awake and alert so that I could call his treatment team right away. And if he were to pass, I wanted my face to be the last thing he saw. I wanted to hold him close and tell him how much I loved him, and how much everyone on the team respected him and appreciated his sacrifice. He deserved at least that much.

Would this have meant anything to him? I have no idea.

Probably not. But it was important to me, and it would have been important to everyone in the squadron. As the night went on, I inched closer to his puffy torso and gently rubbed the back of his head. I told him again what a great job he had done, and how proud of him I was. Over the course of the previous year, I'd spent a lot of nights nudging Cairo off the bed or pulling blankets away from him so that I could get a decent night's sleep, but right now, on the cold tile of a hospital recovery room, I just wanted to keep him close. I stayed right by his side, just as he would have stayed by my side if the situation had been reversed.

Still sedated by anesthesia and painkillers, he seemed unaware of his surroundings. His breathing was shallow and labored. The medical staff had done a fantastic job patching him up, but I still couldn't help but wonder whether he'd pull through. Honestly, it was a miracle that he'd even made it this far. It was a sad fact of life on deployment that when a dog was engaged by an armed bad guy, the end result was usually fatal for both of them. Bad guy shoots dog. Good guys shoot bad guy. End of story.

But not this time.

By morning, Cairo had started to come around. His face remained almost comically bloated, and he was clearly in a great deal of discomfort, but as he opened his eyes and gave me a little lick, it was apparent that he was becoming more lucid.

"Hey, buddy," I said, giving hm a gentle rub on the neck. "Welcome back."

Cairo burrowed into me and let out a little moan. Pretty soon, the docs were in the room, checking him out, declaring his wounds to be clean and healing well, and expressing an appropriate amount of respect and appreciation for Cairo's toughness and durability.

"Hey, boy," one of the nurses said. "Let's try to get you on your feet."

Obviously, Cairo had no idea what she had said, but his expression indicated something along the lines of, "Are you nuts?"

Together, very slowly and carefully, we helped him stand up. A day earlier, he had been as healthy as could be—a fit and eager working dog going off on a mission. All military working dogs are enthusiastic and full of energy, but even within that narrow subset, Cairo was unique. He never seemed to tire, never wore down. He could outwork all of us.

But now here he was, bloated and bleary-eyed, unable to take even a step without a couple of humans guiding him along the way. He gave me a sad look as he lurched slowly forward, just a few inches at a time.

"You're doing great," I said. "Proud of you."

I thought he might not cover more than a few feet of ground in the recovery room, but I had underestimated him. As Cairo stumbled along drunkenly, he seemed to gain confidence. His gait straightened. His pace quickened ever so slightly. Don't get me wrong—compared to his usual speed, which was roughly one hundred miles per hour, day and night, Cairo was in slow motion. But the very fact that he was walking on his own, albeit with glassy eyes, a fat face, and a definite hitch in his step, was cause for celebration. Although the doctors tried to temper their enthusiasm and advised only cautious optimism, I couldn't help but feel as though Cairo had weathered the storm.

"Yeah, you're going to be all right, aren't you, boy?"

His response was to continue walking—out of the room, down a hallway, and out the back door, where a large, open stretch of dirt and rocks awaited. When it comes to recovering from surgery or life-threatening injuries, the protocol for dogs is similar to humans in a few significant ways. In both cases, ambulation is important. Getting a patient up and out of bed promotes healing and a positive attitude. Cairo was moving. Good sign. Second, you want to know that the plumbing is working properly. Humans are often catheterized during surgery or after lengthy sedation; a wounded soldier who can urinate on his own is a patient on the way to recovery.

For Cairo, catheterization was unnecessary. He dropped his nose instinctively as he walked outside into the desert sun. I put a pair of sunglasses on his head to protect his swollen eyes from the glare, which he didn't seem to mind in the least. Then he went about the business of sniffing for an appropriate place to pee. It didn't take him long. Given all the IV fluids that had been had pumped into his body, the poor guy's bladder was probably ready to burst. Ordinarily, Cairo, being a young, unneutered male, would have lifted a leg and sprayed his territory. On this day, however, he was so tired that he simply squatted and peed gently into the ground below him. As he peed, I laughed and gave him another pat on the back.

"No shame, big guy. Whatever gets the job done."

That first little walk took a lot out of Cairo—he came right back inside and took a nap—but it was also the first solid reassurance that he was going to be okay. By the next morning, the IV line had been removed, and he walked with more of a bounce in his step. He also ate a small amount of solid food without getting sick. When anyone said his name, his tail wagged reflexively, which was another indication that his spirits had improved.

For three days, I barely left Cairo's side. My commanding officer and my teammates were completely understanding about my desire to stay with Cairo until he was stable. I hung out with him, took him for long, slow walks, fed him by hand until he was able to eat on his own, and generally just tried to let him know how much I cared. His recuperative powers were impressive. By day two, the doctors were confident that Cairo was out of danger; he would make a full recovery.

Now, the words *full recovery* are always open to interpretation. The medical staff used this term to refer to a patient regaining health and resuming a full life relatively unimpeded by the effects of his or her injury or illness. My definition was slightly different. Cairo, after all, was a combat assault dog. That's what he was bred and trained to do.

"Will he work again?" I asked one of the docs.

He shrugged, smiled. "Hard to say. Maybe."

After three days of rehab, it was time to get back to work. For me, that meant flying to Sharana and rejoining my squadron. For Cairo, it meant a trip home.

Well, not exactly home. His destination was Lackland Air Force Base in Texas, where the 341st Training Squadron oversees the Department of Defense Military Working Dog Program, which procures and assigns dogs for military installations all over the world. With more than sixty training areas and seven hundred kennels spread out over some three thousand acres, Lackland is easily the largest and most well-equipped MWD training center in the world. As such, it also home to the best canine medical care and rehabilitation facilities, which was exactly what Cairo needed.

The very fact that he was going to Lackland was a positive sign that Cairo was not ready to be placed on long-term disability. Not just yet. He would be given every opportunity to recover from his injuries and to resume his life as a critical member of the team. Selfishly, I hoped he would recover and return to our squadron not just because he was a great working dog but because he was my partner. He was my dog, and I was his dad.

If he were retired, I would miss him. Although the military had a long-standing practice of trying to reunite handlers with their service dogs after the dogs' careers ended due to injury or age, there was no guarantee. Especially since I was still an active dog handler. And even if Cairo's injuries proved severe enough to preclude a return to active duty as a Special Operations canine, there might be other jobs for which he was still suited—working for law enforcement, for example, as an odor-detection specialist. He didn't have to be a superhero or even particularly athletic to sniff out explosives or narcotics.

Cairo was only four years old. The military had invested tens of thousands of dollars in his care and training, and he'd proved himself to be worth every penny of that investment. Bum leg or not, there was unquestionably still a place for him as a working dog—whether in the military or in law enforcement. He was far too young to be sent out to pasture. The only question was, how badly was he damaged? At Lackland, an assessment would be made and a training and rehabilitation regimen implemented.

The U.S. military is one of the biggest bureaucracies on the planet. As a result, sometimes things within the navy can move very slowly, but there are other times when the military is incredibly quick and efficient. Just three days after he was nearly killed on the battlefield, Cairo was airlifted out of Bagram on the first leg of a long journey to Texas. He was accompanied by a master-at-arms named Mike, who was another buddy of mine. This was actually the second half of Mike's assignment that week; the first part was to accompany another combat assault dog from Virginia to Afghanistan. That dog was Bronco, the very same Malinois who had nearly become my dog during the initial assignment phase of training.

Mike and I hung around for a day, swapping stories and playing with both dogs. Bronco and I had to become reacquainted since I would be his handler for the remainder of the deployment, roughly two more months. And Mike, who loved dogs as much as I did, wanted to spend a little time with Cairo before taking him back to the States.

Late in the afternoon, I packed up Cairo's gear and helped load everything onto the huge cargo plane that would carry him halfway around the world. Before putting him in his kennel for the trip, we posed for some photos. I asked Mike to take good care of Cairo and promised to do the same for Bronco. I gave Cairo a hug and closed the door on his kennel.

"See you around, boy."

More than two months passed before Cairo and I were reunited. Work is work. As a SEAL, you learn to push down the emotional stuff and get on with the job. Wives and girlfriends and children are left behind for months on end. Friends and fellow soldiers are maimed and killed. You grieve like anyone else when it happens; you suffer from homesickness and sadness. But you try not to let it show. The job is bigger than you or any of your problems, and you knew that when you signed up for it. Five minutes after I said goodbye to Cairo, I took Bronco's leash from Mike and began making arrangements to return to Sharana. A few hours later, I was back in my hut, introducing our new working dog to the rest of the squadron.

Some of them had met Bronco before; he was, as I'd said, a friendly, fun-loving dog, more personable than Cairo upon initial introduction, and so he easily assimilated into the team. We went out on our first mission together the next night. It was smooth and uneventful. Indeed, the same could be said about much of the remainder of the deployment. The search for Bowe Bergdahl remained a persistent and frustrating thorn in our sides, with false sightings and sketchy intel periodically leading to missions that resulted in . . . well, nothing (it would be five years before he was finally released from captivity). There were other missions, though, that were more fruitful in terms of finding bad guys and weapons—the kind of stuff we did best and that provided a high degree of immediate feedback and positive reinforcement.

Bronco was a perfectly fine working dog—better than that, actually. Like Cairo, he was extremely smart and reliable, with a good nose for odor detection and a strong prey drive. There was absolutely nothing wrong with him. In the beginning, I would have been happy to flip a coin to determine which of the two dogs was a better match for me; they were that close. Now, though, after spending so much time with Cairo—and after, quite literally, going to war together—my opinion had naturally shifted somewhat.

I thought Cairo was the best dog I'd ever known—in or out of the military. And my affection for him—my respect and appreciation for the sacrifices he had made—may have clouded my opinion of Bronco. There was nothing wrong with Bronco; I just didn't know how to handle him properly. Any shortcomings in our working relationship were my fault, not his. Bronco was a great dog.

He just wasn't Cairo.

A lot of the guys really liked Bronco. As I remembered from our initial meeting back in Virginia, he was a playful and personable dog, very easy to have around the hut. Ironically, this characteristic is what had drawn me to Bronco in the first place, but by now, I had come to appreciate Cairo's more restrained and businesslike manner. It's not that Cairo wasn't friendly, but you had to work a little to gain his affection and respect. I'd spent nearly a year doing exactly that, and in the process, I had become quite attached to Cairo. We worked together seamlessly. I could rely on him as surely as I could rely on any other member of the team when we were out on a mission. He had my back, and I had his.

Had I been Bronco's handler from the beginning, it might have been different, but now, after Cairo and I had been together for so long, and in the aftermath of a mission on which Cairo had nearly been killed, and in the process ensured the safety of his teammates . . . well, let's just say I struggled a bit with the transition. There were no glaring mistakes, no fights between man and dog or anything like that. I just felt like Bronco and I did not really connect. He was a bit of a handful, somewhat rambunctious in an adolescent kind of way—at least compared to Cairo—and thus did not inspire in me quite the same degree of trust and confidence. In time, I suppose, that might have changed, but we had only a couple of months together, and while I knew it was possible that Bronco would be my dog for quite some time, I treated our alliance as a temporary thing.

Until someone told me otherwise, Cairo was still my dog.

Throughout the rest of the deployment, I got periodic reports on Cairo: his wounds had healed and he was doing well with rehab. I'd heard great things about the dog program at Lackland—I had friends there and knew that Cairo would have access to the finest medical care and the most state-of-the-art technology and equipment. He was in good hands. What I didn't know, of course—and no one could really predict this—is whether he would ever be fit enough to return to his role as an active duty military working dog.

Would he lose a step because of his shattered femur? Would he have trouble breathing because of his chest wound? Even if he did somehow manage to make a full physical recovery, what of his mental state? Cairo might not have been a human being, but neither was he a machine. Dogs can be notoriously skittish, and even the most gifted and well-trained CAD is susceptible to post-traumatic stress. Cairo had been shot at point-blank range. We all knew men who had gone through exactly that same amount of trauma, and it wasn't unusual for them to disappear from active duty, or at least from duty that included combat. Same thing with dogs. You get shot, you get blown up or otherwise severely wounded, and sometimes you're never quite the same. It's an illusion that SEALs are different. I mean, yeah, we're different. We have better training and presumably a greater willingness to fight and not quit.

But the truth is . . . getting shot sucks. Even if you are lucky enough to survive, it will mess you up mentally as well as physically, and it will change your life and the way you look at things. That is simply a fact. We aren't superheroes; neither was Cairo.

I got back from Afghanistan in October. At the time, Cairo was still in Texas, receiving world-class training and rehabilitation. I continued to receive good reports. Physically, the docs and trainers indicated, Cairo had made a nearly full recovery; there was no reason why he couldn't return to active duty. But what of his spirit? I wondered. What about his heart? Would he be the same dog I'd come to know and love? Would he be nervous or frightened? Would he have the same drive to work?

And what would happen if we deployed again? How would he respond to bumpy helicopter flights in the middle of the night? Or to tracers and gunfire and explosions? Would he rush into a darkened room with the same fearless zeal he had exhibited in the past, or would he sit down and refuse to perform?

*Hey, Dad . . . I really don't want to do this right now. I'm scared.*

And how would I respond? With compassion? Anger? The bottom line is this: if you can't do the job, then you shouldn't be on the mission. Lives are at stake. It's as simple as that. Over the years, I saw a lot of guys disappear suddenly from Special Operations; guys who had once seemed invincible suddenly lost a step or began to question themselves in one way or another. When that happened—poof! Gone. Everyone felt bad for these guys, but we also understood the need for a zero-tolerance policy when it came to battlefield fitness. If you weren't 100 percent certain that you were up to the job, then maybe it was time to step aside.

There was no margin for error.

Cairo didn't exactly get a vote in any of this. He would be observed and tested, and if he appeared fit for duty, then he'd be back in the game. Time would tell.

A few weeks later, I got a phone call saying Cairo had returned to Virginia from Lackland. I drove straight from my home to the kennel to see him. It was the strangest thing—to feel such a strong sense of excitement and anticipation over greeting a dog. Then again, Cairo was much more than that to me, especially now. I wondered how he would react. Would he remember me? Would he be anxious? Would my presence trigger some sort of flashback to the worst night of his life?

I parked my truck and walked straight to the kennel— didn't even stop at command to talk with any of the guys. Cairo saw me approaching from several yards away and immediately began jumping around. The sound of his playful whimpering brought a smile to my face. I opened the gate, and he leaped right through my arms and into my chest; Cairo liked to greet me that way—standing on his hind legs and letting me hold his forelegs in my hands or against my chest. This time, though, the force of his enthusiasm nearly knocked me on my ass.

I laughed. "Hey, buddy! How have you been?"

Cairo danced around me, jumping like a rodeo bronc, and butting me with his muzzle. I put a hand through his collar and pulled him close, let him breathe right in my face. His breath was terrible, as usual. I didn't care in the least.

"It's okay, Cairo. Dad's back. Everything's going to be all right."

For much of my first year with Cairo, the dog program was

run in much the same way as the SEAL program—which is to say, with a high degree of professionalism and accountability and access to the best equipment and training that money could buy. But, also, with a certain looseness. SEALs, in general, were given more leeway than traditional sailors or soldiers in such matters as personal appearance (longer hair and beards were acceptable) and schedules. As long as you did your job, no one bothered to sweat the small stuff. SEALs, by and large, could be counted on to do their job and to train with a fervor that made them practically unimpeachable. Those that did not were shown the door.

Such flexibility extended to the dog program, where handlers were encouraged to bond with their dogs not just in training exercises and on deployment but in everyday life. There were two schools of thought about this. One school believed, and taught, that the relationship between a dog and his handler was almost sacred. At the very least, it was unique among military relationships. The handler and his team relied upon the dog to do work that could literally save their lives. And the dog relied upon the handler to guide him through that process as safely as possible. It was an intensely symbiotic partnership based on mutual respect and trust. And, yes, even love.

You didn't mess around with that stuff. It was fragile, and it was special. To promote the bond, and to encourage handlers to view their role as more than merely canine babysitters, handlers were given significant latitude in regard to how they developed those relationships. The dog was not just a tool; he was part of the handler's family. Technically speaking, the kennel was the dog's home, but if his handler wanted to take him back to his off-base apartment for the night, or for two nights, or three . . . well, that was okay. Everyone just sort of looked the other way. Cairo spent as much time at my house as he did on the base, and I have no doubt that he was a better working dog because of this. As with any relationship, the more time you spend with someone, the better you know him or her.

Cairo knew me well. And I knew him.

There was, however, another school of thought, one that reflected the more traditional and rigid way of thinking you sometimes come across in the military: rules are rules, and you don't break them. Ever. And if you do, there are consequences. Now, I understand this. You don't become a SEAL by being a maverick. You understand the importance of being part of a team and of embracing the team ethos, with all its rules and expectations. But within that framework, we were encouraged to make decisions—sometimes life-and-death decisions—and exercise sound judgment. We answered to our superior officers, but on each mission there were choices to be made, and it was understood that our experience and training would guide us in that process.

So if I wanted to take Cairo home with me because it made us both happier and encouraged a stronger union, well, who the hell cared?

As it turned out, people did care. And with good reason. Cairo was an amazing dog—a reliable and fearsome hunter when so directed, and a loving, playful companion when not on the navy clock—but he was probably something of an anomaly. The term *working dog* is deceptively benign. I was always just as likely to refer to every canine in the program, including Cairo, as an *attack dog*. It's not as delicate or benign a description, but it's accurate. It's the truth. Combat assault dogs are bred and trained to track and fight. As intelligent and reliable and well trained as they might be, they are still sometimes unpredictable, especially in an uncontrolled environment. You can't just take a dog like that, especially one still on active duty, and let him roam unrestrained among civilians. With few exceptions, it's too dangerous.

Cairo was the exception.

I would let Cairo hang out with buddies or girlfriends who came to my house to visit. Never had a problem. He seemed to understand instinctively the difference between work and play, friend and foe. Still, I was careful with him, especially in the early days. Unfortunately, there were some handlers who were less careful with their dogs, and some dogs, quite frankly, that should not have been allowed to leave the kennel. I understood the rule, and I didn't disagree with it, but I figured as long as there were no incidents related to Cairo, I could keep taking him home, and no one would complain.

I was wrong. By the time Cairo returned to Virginia, lodging regulations were being more strictly enforced. I don't know the details—whether there had been close calls with civilians, or whether there existed a feeling from someone at the kennel that handlers were exploiting the privilege. Regardless, things had changed. I had already been warned that even though Cairo was still "my dog," he'd have to spend virtually all his time at the kennel.

But this was his first day back. So . . . I didn't even think about the regulations.

"Hey, man. I'm taking him home," I said to the MA.

He just smiled. "Yeah, sure."

The MA understood and wouldn't have cared, anyway. It was the kennel manager who might have given me a hard time. But he wasn't around, so I gave Cairo a big hug and led him to my truck. He seemed strong and healthy, but as we walked through the gates and out into the parking lot, I noticed a slight hitch in his gait. It wasn't nearly as pronounced as it had been the last time I'd seen him, just a day or two after surgery, but it was there. The injury to his right foreleg had healed, but the wound and subsequent installation of hardware had left their mark. It didn't mean Cairo would not still be a great working dog, but he would be slightly slower and less agile. As for his battlefield temperament? That remained to be seen. Right now, as he jumped into the cab of my jacked-up Toyota Tundra and curled up against me, he seemed like the same sweet and affectionate dog he'd always been.

"Let's go home, buddy."

Like all working dogs, Cairo's diet and schedule were rigid. Two cups of dry kibble in the morning, two in the evening. Exercise and poop after each meal. If you find something that works with a dog, you don't mess with it, and while dogs, like humans, prefer good food, they're perfectly happy eating almost anything you put in front of them. Especially working dogs, with their extraordinary caloric output. But every so often, on special occasions, I'd give Cairo a treat.

That night, after we got home, I fired up the grill and cooked a couple of big steaks—one for me, one for Cairo. Nothing cheap or tough, either. Filet mignon. Prime beef. I cut it up into bite-sized pieces and hand-fed him so he wouldn't gobble it all at once and make himself sick. Then we sat down on the couch and watched movies together until we both fell asleep.

Sometime after midnight, I woke up and turned off the TV. I walked into the bedroom and slid under the covers, with Cairo trailing right behind me.

"Up, boy," I said, gently patting the bed. He didn't need a second invitation. As usual, Cairo snuggled up against me all night long, hogging the bed and giving me a nasty case of night sweats. But I didn't care.

My dog had come home.

# Chapter 15

Despite precautions and bite suits and a high level of expertise, accidents did happen to even the most experienced dog handlers. As I said, Cairo's first real bite had occurred not on deployment but during an early training exercise in Virginia, when he got a taste of my friend Angelo's lower leg.

Payback came more than a year later, when I got bit for the first time—and the perpetrator, appropriately enough, was Angelo's dog, a Malinois named Yari. I'd already been through one deployment with Cairo by that time; I'd seen what a combat assault dog could to a human being. Many times. But I'd never experienced a bite without the protection of a padded suit. It was, to say the least, enlightening.

It happened on a Friday afternoon, shortly after I'd gotten out of work for the day. I stopped by the kennel, and Angelo asked if I wanted to help him work on a scenario.

"Sure," I said. "Let's go." I had nothing else going, I loved my job, and it was always fun to work with Angelo.

We drove together to our training center, maybe twenty minutes away, and began setting up for the scenario—a combination of perimeter security, odor detection, and bite work. My job was to help one of the newer handlers get into his bite suit and prepare to serve as bait. It was an exterior scenario—Yari would exit a vehicle and run into some deep weeds or tall grass nearby, where the target would be hiding. Yari was a seasoned dog by this point, so it didn't take him long to find the handler and begin biting.

The guy began screaming immediately, which wasn't un-expected; it was part of the exercise, intended to give the dog an experience similar to what he would encounter on a mission. Real bites hurt, after all, and victims always scream. Still, I wanted to make sure everything was okay, so I began walking into the weeds. There, I saw the handler on his back, with Yari attached to his wrist. The guy had pulled his hand up inside the suit to stay protected, but Yari's bite was dangerously close to an unprotected area. It looked like he had probably caught Yari exactly as planned, but in the process had lost his balance, and now, as a relatively inexperienced handler, he was in trouble. In that situation, Yari might adjust his bite, meaning he would release for a second and then clamp down somewhere else—perhaps on the hand or even the face.

I stepped in and took hold of the handle on Yari's harness. Then I applied some gentle pressure against his back, This, again, is standard operating procedure, since it usually prompts the dog to just maintain his bite, rather than adjusting to a more vulnerable spot. Angelo would be rushing in soon enough, and he would call the dog off and the exercise would end safely. What I didn't realize was that Angelo, at that very moment, was giving Yari a hit with the e-collar—in effect, telling him to let go and re-turn. The combination of stimuli—the bite, the shock of e-collar, and my hand on his back—sent Yari into a frenzy. Suddenly, he released his grip, turned around and bit me on the knee.

"Ah . . . shit!"

The first thing that went through my mind was . . . *Well,*

*that really hurts.* The second thing was, *How am I going to get out of this?*

I still had Yari by the back of his harness, but now he had me by the knee.

"Yari," I said firmly. "Los!"

I knew Yari well, and he knew me. But as I looked in his eyes, I didn't see even a flicker of recognition. Yari was a combat assault dog, and right now he was in assault mode. It wasn't his fault—this is what he had been trained to do.

"Yari!" I said again. "Los!"

This time, he let go. But only for a moment. Before I even had a chance to react, Yari bit me in the biceps. As with my knee, the bite felt less like getting cut by something sharp than getting whacked with a baseball bat. That, I realized, is exactly what a puncture wound feels like.

At this point, I knew Yari wasn't going to quit, so I stood up, calmly and slowly, with him hanging from my arm. I lifted him by the harness so that he wouldn't rip my muscle or try to adjust his bite again, and then I began walking back toward Angelo and the rest of the team.

Slowly. Calmly.

Protocol in this situation dictates that you let everyone know exactly how serious the situation is by saying two simple words:

*Real bite.*

I didn't yell. I didn't try to run. I just shuffled along with Yari dangling from my arm, repeatedly saying, "Real bite . . . Real bite."

Angelo rushed right over and quickly got Yari to give up the fight. Then he drove me to the hospital. Along the way, both my arm and knee began throbbing. I was legitimately surprised by how much it hurt. Neither bite was that deep or that serious, but the pain was significant.

"Well, this is fair," I said to Angelo at one point. "My dog got you, and now your dog got me. I guess we're even."

Angelo just laughed. He continued to laugh in the emergency room, when one of the doctors explained that while both wounds were easily cleaned and appeared not to involve too much muscle damage, there was a possibility that the first bite might have punctured the bursa sac in my knee. And if that happened, surgery would be required. The surest way to determine whether the sac had been punctured was to insert a needle and fill the sac with fluid . . . and see if it leaked.

"Is this going to hurt much?" I asked the doctor with a laugh.

"It's not too bad," she said.

This was not true. It hurt like hell. And I say that as someone who has experienced a fair amount of pain and some big needle sticks. Fortunately, though, the bursa sac had not been ruptured. It was a clean bite, and I recovered quickly, but the whole experience gave me even more respect for the awesome power of a combat assault dog.

# Chapter 16

By the time we went on our next full deployment, in the fall of 2010, it was obvious that Cairo was once again ready for active duty.

For the better part of a year, we were based in Virginia, training every day for the next extended tour in Afghanistan. During this period, Cairo and I were mainly working partners. I was still Dad, but the restrictions around taking dogs home became even tighter, and so Cairo spent most of his nights at the kennel. There were plenty of training trips, though, where we worked on skydiving or backcountry hiking or other mock operations, and Cairo accompanied me on almost all those trips. As far as I could tell, there were no psychological ramifications related to his injury. He wasn't spooked by gunfire or explosions, didn't seem reluctant to enter a dark building, and obeyed every command he was given.

In other words, same old Cairo. Low maintenance, high energy. Friendly, tireless, loyal, and reliable. A fantastic dog.

On the next trip to Afghanistan—my third extended deployment there, Cairo's second—we were stationed at Jalalabad (J-Bad). By this time, the canine program was deeply established, as was our military presence in Afghanistan, so we had a pretty good setup, easily the best of any I experienced. We had two or three dogs throughout that deployment, and as handlers, we actually had our own little hut and training area, as well as a private kennel. This was convenient for us, and a bonus for some of the other guys who didn't necessarily like sharing their living quarters with dogs—even dogs that were as cool as Cairo.

My friend Angelo was there taking care of his dog, Yari. Angelo was one of those masters-at-arms I mentioned earlier, the kind of guy you trusted with your life on a mission, even though he wasn't a SEAL. We went on tons of operations together, and in addition to being adept at working with dogs, he was a hell of a fighter. Every time he was asked to step up and fight, well, he absolutely crushed it. We also had another trainer from back home, a former cop named Kevin who took care of a spare dog and got to see the kind of work we did on deployment. Kevin didn't go out on missions with us, but he did valuable work by helping out around the base, training and working the dogs. His experience at J-Bad also allowed him to return with knowledge about the kind of work we did in Special Operations; in turn, he could pass that information on to his bosses and help make any necessary adjustments to the canine training program.

Although the ever-changing rules of engagement in Afghanistan made our lives more difficult on this deployment—without getting into details, let's just say the term *bad guy* became a little bit harder to define—it was not a mission that resulted in any catastrophic losses or any high-profile victories. Which was fine. We did our job, day after day, night after night. Lots of ops, lots of targets eliminated. And everyone on our team came home in one piece. God knows that wasn't always the case. Just two months before our squadron arrived in Afghanistan, a helicopter crash in Zabul Province took the lives of nine American servicemen, including four Navy SEALs. It happened like that sometimes: multiple fatalities in a single incident. We all knew it could happen, and we were both motivated and repulsed by the possibility.

Personally, I really hated the idea of dying in a chopper crash, with no opportunity to fight my way out of it. I also knew that if I was going to die, a helicopter crash was the most likely scenario. Our chopper pilots, mostly guys from the U.S. Army 160th Special Operations Aviation Regiment (nickname: the Night Stalkers), were some of the most amazing guys I knew in the service. They were cold-blooded. And by that, I don't mean they were killers; I mean they had ice water in their veins. These guys handled a Black Hawk or a Chinook like they were driving a Maserati. Every one of them was a badass who could weave in and out of the tightest spaces, evade gunfire and RPGs, set a bird down on the side of a mountain in a dust storm . . . and they could do it without breaking a sweat. We relied on them to take us in, and we relied on them to get us back out. They never let us down. But the risks were great, and we all knew it. No matter how talented and fearless the TF-160th guys might have been, helicopters went down. It was a fact of life. And death.

Being a Navy SEAL is dangerous. That is no secret to anyone who signs up for the job, and especially not to anyone who has been through a few years of training and deployment. But the truth is, you're just as likely to die or get seriously hurt in a chopper crash or even during one of the endless stateside training exercises that make up so much of a SEAL's career as you are in a firefight. Every time we went off on a mission, we knew it was possible. We didn't talk about it, but it was always there in the back of our minds. And sometimes in the front, as well. In fact, the closest I came to serious injury on the J-Bad deployment was on a mission that, like so many others, involved a helicopter, a dog, and a rope.

The safest and least complicated way to get a dog on the ground during mission insert was to set the bird down and jump out, then hike in to the target. Sometimes this wasn't possible. There were occasions when parachuting was the best option, and other times when the pilot would lower the chopper to a safe distance above the insertion site and the team would exit.

Needless to say, fast-roping or rappelling out of a chopper, while holding a seventy-pound dog could be perilous. Cairo was generally even-tempered and not prone to freaking out about anything, but still . . . you never knew. In some ways, skydiving with a dog, safely packed away in a pouch, barely able to see anything, was less risky than fast-roping with a dog.

On this mission, our target was an isolated compound built into the side of a mountain. There was no place to land within several miles of the compound; rather than inflict upon us an exhausting hike of two or three hours, it was decided that we would get as close as possible, while still maintaining the element of surprise; we would do this by fast-roping out of the chopper.

Ordinarily, when fast-roping, I would just hook Cairo's harness to my belt with a carabiner and lower us both with my hands on a fixed rope. I also had the option of using a canine fast-rope device, which, while arguably safer, was much slower and more complicated. It really was an ingenious little tool, one that was a blast to use on training exercises. But I had only occasionally used it on missions simply because it took so much extra time and effort and because there was a chance, however slight, of things getting really fucked up on the ground. In a traditional fast-rope insertion, I just let go and got out of the way like everyone else. When using the canine fast-rope device, there was one additional step, and it was critical: I had to detach from the device . . . which was attached to the rope . . . which was attached to the helicopter.

Picture all of this happening at warp speed. Insertions are designed to be fast and efficient. Seconds after the last guy is off the bird, the pilot gets out of Dodge. He can't just hover fifty feet above the ground for thirty to sixty minutes while we complete our mission; he'd be a sitting duck for an RPG. Normally, this is not a problem. Last guy hits the ground, pulls the rope behind him, and the Black Hawk disappears, only to reappear at a prearranged extraction point sometime in the future. But when the last guy out of the chopper is a dog handler who has rarely used the canine fast-rope device on a mission . . . well, that could be a problem.

And on this night, it was.

The insertion began smoothly enough. All but two members of the team exited quickly and fast-roped to the ground. Then the final assaulter held Cairo while I attached us to the fast-rope device.

"Okay?" he shouted before exiting the chopper.

I nodded. "All good."

Cairo and I made a smooth and steady descent. As the ground reached up below us, I figured everything was okay; however, as soon as my boots touched down, I realized that the hillside was extraordinarily steep, probably forty-five degrees. Again, we had targeted compounds on difficult terrain in the past, but typically we would walk in from a distance. There was some margin for error, as well as time to adapt to the uneven terrain. This time, as soon as my boots touched down, I could tell that Cairo was uneasy. The rotor wash from the chopper sandblasted us nearly off our feet. Pelted by dust and debris, Cairo naturally recoiled and began pulling me downhill, away from the spray of the chopper blade.

Normally, this would not have been a big deal; it was a perfectly understandable response on Cairo's part. If I had fast-roped with my hands, no problem. Just get away from the bird and the rotor wash. Unfortunately, the helicopter was moving uphill, and we were still attached to the helicopter via the fast rope and the canine fast-rope device.

This was one of those occasions when time seemed to stand still. There was a flicker of recognition as Cairo tried to yank me downhill and the Chinook slowly began pulling us uphill, that we were in very deep shit. At first, it seemed almost impossible—unreal. And then the urgency began to sink in.

*Holy shit—we're going to get dragged right off this mountain.*

I thought about how it would feel to get yanked into the sky, and perhaps crash into a huge rock along the way. I thought about how I'd let him down. I thought about my teammates out there in the night, already walking toward the compound, and how they would accomplish their mission without a dog to take the heat off them. I was scared and angry and shocked . . . all at the same time.

And yet, it also seemed kind of funny.

*What a way to go. No one is going to believe this.*

Had we landed on level ground, without significant rotor wash, Cairo would have waited patiently for me to unhook him from the device. I could have done this in a matter of seconds. But now with the rope taut, I was faced with trying to pull myself back up the hill toward the slowly evacuating helicopter so that I could gain enough slack to unclip the carabiner. And to do that, I had to convince Cairo to march back into the rotor wash, which he wasn't willing to do. Reflexively, I scooped him up by the handle on his harness, tossed him a few feet in front of me, and then ran up after him. As soon as I had enough slack, I tried to detach the carabiner in a split second.

No chance.

I did this several times. Each time I tossed him ahead, Cairo would start to run back downhill. I'd have to retrieve him, pick him up again, and march back uphill toward the helicopter. The chopper pilot was in a terrible position, trying to hold the bird steady until we were released. We weren't communicating, so I didn't even know if he realized I was still down there, fighting for my life. And with each failed attempt at escape, I was growing increasingly fatigued.

After what seemed like an eternity, I finally got close enough to make one more attempt at detaching. This one was successful. Instantly, the Chinook peeled off into the night, while I fell to the ground, exhausted and beat to shit.

And the mission hadn't even started yet!

I rolled over onto my knees and tried to catch my breath. My arms and legs were burning. Cairo walked up and looked me over quizzically. He gave me a nudge with his head as if to say, "Let's go, Dad. Time to work."

I shook my head, stifled a little laugh. It's strange how a potential disaster can seem almost funny. Afterward.

"What are you looking at?" I said, giving Cairo a pat on the head. "That was your fault."

Not true, really. It was just . . . one of those things. We had the best pilots, the best soldiers, and the best dogs. Nevertheless, sometimes things went wrong. Sometimes things were beyond our control.

"You okay, Cheese?"

The voice coming over the radio was our troop chief. As it turned out, the entire team had been watching me wrestle with the helicopter. Amusement had turned quickly to concern, and then horror, and now relief. I'd gotten kicked in the nuts, but we still had a mission to accomplish.

"Yeah, I'll be fine," I said.

"Cairo?"

"He's good, too. Be there in a second."

Thankfully, the rest of the night went off without a hitch. We hiked through the mountains to the compound, dispatched a few bad guys, and we all went home. Safe and sound.

But that was the last time I ever used the fast-rope device.

I loved Cairo, and I loved being a dog handler, but incidents like that one certainly underscored the challenges of the job and helped me understand why even the most dog-friendly guys in Special Operations and in most of the military were reluctant to accept the assignment. Everyone in the squadron valued Cairo and the work he did for us—he was a brother—but the vast majority of them wanted no part of being responsible for a dog while on deployment. It was incredibly rewarding, important work, in my opinion, but there was no break from it. Where I went, Cairo went, usually attached quite literally to my hip. And the logistics of such a relationship were sometimes challenging, to say the least.

One mission grew out of intel, including live video footage, about a contingent of fifteen to twenty men marching through the desert at night. Admittedly, sometimes in Afghanistan— and Iraq, as well—it was hard to tell the good guys from the bad guys, or at least the benign guys from the bad guys. Generally speaking, a group of young men this large in number, moving as a group through the desert, with no women or children or animals in their company, was a sign of suspicious activity. If the group appeared to be unarmed, we might take a wait-and-see approach. In this case, however, it was clear that the patrol was weighed down with an assortment of AKs and RPGS and other weaponry. The video tracked the men as they made their way to a large house on the side of the hill and disappeared inside.

Watching the footage was part of our afternoon briefing. To

my eyes, and to the eyes of everyone else in the room, this was an easy one. An entire houseful of bad guys and weapons. Just blow the roof off that fucker.

Except, of course, we couldn't do that. The ever-changing rules of engagement forbade the demolishing of any structure without knowing, as clearly as possible, the identity of all inhabitants. By that, I don't mean we had to have names and ages, but we did have to be reasonably certain that destroying the building would result in no civilian casualties. And even when we were certain, the enemy would sometimes claim collateral damage in the aftermath of an explosive attack, simply as a political strategy.

Practically speaking, our hands were often tied. For the most part, we were resigned to the fact that most confrontations would have to be handled on an intimate level. It was at times frustrating, but we accepted it. We had been trained to fight under any and all conditions; moreover, none of us wanted to be responsible for taking the life of a woman or child or anyone who happened to be in the wrong place at the wrong time.

"This is the target," our team leader said. "These guys are not just out for a walk. This is a patrol; this is a training exercise."

The sheer number of people walking in and out of the house made this a more dangerous mission than usual. We had footage of fifteen to twenty men, but it was possible that twice that many, or more, were hidden in the house or in the area nearby. If we had to root them out on our own, without an air strike, there was likely to be a significant firefight involved. Again, we were totally prepared for this type of mission—we'd done it many times—but if you want to grade missions on a scale of one to ten in terms of danger, this one was well above the middle.

A few hours later, I found myself in the back of one of the ATVs, roaring through the desert with a Malinois sitting on my lap. With his tongue hanging out and his ears pinned back by the open air, Cairo seemed almost to be smiling.

"Get serious, buddy. We've got work to do."

On some level, Cairo knew what was coming. That's why he was happy and excited. It was time to fight.

By the time we got within range of the target, my lap was soaked with sweat and my lower back was sore, so I was happy to push Cairo out of the ATV and begin marching. Quietly, we advanced to a position only fifty meters from the front of the house. A sentry was posted outside, and when Cairo saw him, and doubtless got a whiff of him, he began tugging at his lead, straining to get away. He wanted nothing more than to be released and attack.

He wanted to bite!

But this was neither the time nor the place for that tactic. Cairo's role for the night had yet to be determined, but for now, I mainly needed him to remain quiet so that he wouldn't give away our position.

Outside the house, we set up a standard L-shaped formation—a time-honored battlefield strategy that allows a team to ambush an opponent from two sides, without any risk of cross fire and injury to its own men. The L-shaped formation presents a huge tactical advantage—presuming you can get the enemy to walk into the ambush. There are a few ways to accomplish this task, but the one that seemed to work best, and that was also the safest, was a simple flyover with the Black Hawk. Low and fast and loud. The sound of a big American chopper served as an effective kick at the hornet's nest, provoking someone—maybe everyone—to run outside, guns at the ready, to see what was happening. And when they appeared . . .

The crackle of automatic weapons instantly filled the air as several of the insurgents spilled out of the house and tried to scatter across the hillside. Some were killed instantly, but several ran off. Some returned fire; others did not. We knew they weren't merely fleeing. Their plan was to escape down the hill to the valley below, then regroup, perhaps with reinforcements, and renew the fight from a more advantageous position. To prevent that from happening, we gave chase. Eventually, the bad guys, knowing they could not outrun us, turned and fought. Over the course of the next half hour, we engaged in a heavy firefight that stretched from the target building to a position roughly a quarter mile away. Eventually, we dispatched every one of them.

Or, at least, everyone who had left the house.

Now it was cleanup time, which was sometimes the riskiest part of a mission. If we were sure the house was empty or occupied by only one or two remaining bad guys, we could have just called in an air strike, dropped a bomb, and called it a night. That was not an option. Instead, as was so often the case, we had to clear the building, room by room.

As we slowly approached the building, I kept Cairo close by my side. I was about to unhook him and send him inside when suddenly the front door flew open and a man ran out into the night, screaming at the top of his lungs and spraying AK fire wildly in every direction. Cairo strained at his lead.

"Easy, boy!"

In a heartbeat, the suicide gunner was down, hit by rounds from a half dozen SEALs, but not before coming perilously close to accomplishing his goal of taking someone with him. One of our guys had taken a round directly in his torso; fortunately, the bullet had been stopped by his side plate. He was bruised, but otherwise unharmed.

Now it was time to clear the building. I wanted to send Cairo in first, to see if anyone was still there, but something about the setting was unnerving. Cairo was accustomed to entering darkened buildings. This one was well illuminated, with several lights visible from outside. The front door was still open following the exit of the suicidal gunman. Just inside the door, in a seated position, leaning awkwardly against a wall, was the body of a man. He was clearly dead, but for some reason, Cairo wanted to attack him. This was not typically the case. Cairo usually ignored bodies and went after living, breathing targets, but something about the position of the man's body, combined with the lighting in the building, threw him off. He nipped and growled at the body.

"No!" I said, giving Cairo a little tap with the e-collar, but that got his attention only briefly. I tried to guide him through the doorway and into the building, but he was too focused on the body. Eventually, I decided to call him off, and we cleared the entire building ourselves. As it turned out, there was no one else inside. The dead guy must have been a straggler who took a bullet during the early stages of the firefight when we unloaded on the front of the building.

It was hard to find fault in anything Cairo had done. He was trained to bite and attack, and being denied that opportunity when confronted by what appeared to be a bad guy must have been frustrating. And my insistence that he enter the building despite the presence of a bad guy leaning against a wall just inside the doorway would surely have been confusing. It was, to Cairo, counterintuitive:

*Wait a minute! I'm not supposed to go in there until after I bite this guy. Right?*

Sometimes circumstances dictated a change in tactics. We all had to adapt and adjust on the fly. Even Cairo. Fortunately, he was a quick learner. Before long, we had cleared the entire building, packed up all our gear, and boarded a helicopter for the ride back to J-Bad. We had killed a bunch of heavily armed bad guys and sustained no casualties despite a hot and heavy firefight.

All in all, a pretty good night—better than most in the ever-evolving and seemingly endless war against terrorism.

# Chapter 17

Saying goodbye was hard, but I tried to think of it as a word that had no permanence. It was more like a transitional phase we were going through.

This was in early March 2011, after we returned from Afghanistan. I'd have a few weeks of vacation, but then I'd be reassigned, as would Cairo. This was not unexpected. I'd been a dog handler through two deployments. It was time for me to go back to being a "shooter," and it was time for Cairo to settle into a less hectic role.

He was close to six years old by this time and had served his country nobly through two long deployments and years of training. He had sustained serious injuries in the line of duty—injuries that no doubt still caused him some discomfort, even if you couldn't really tell by looking at him. I felt like he had earned the right to settle into a more peaceful life at home. I figured that home, eventually, would be with me, but I also knew it was too soon for that to happen. Dog handlers in the military, as with dog handlers in law enforcement, often are given right of first refusal when their dogs' service careers come to an end. Understandably, many dog handlers become quite attached to their dogs, and the dogs to them; certainly, this was the case with Cairo and me.

Cairo's skill and demeanor worked against him in that regard. He was a reliable and likable dog and still relatively young and physically fit. The navy determined, not unreasonably, that Cairo still had much to offer. He would not be retired. Instead, he would become a spare dog, which was sort of like a late-career phase for a working dog. Instead of being deployed regularly for long periods of time, a spare dog spent most of his days at the kennel in Virginia, or on training exercises, but he was always available for long-term or short-term deployment. Spare dogs were generally a bit older, but still sound and seasoned. They were low-key and even tempered, which made it easy to assign them to a new handler or unit. Simply put, they were adaptable, so they could be easily substituted if another dog was wounded or killed or otherwise deemed unfit for duty.

Selfishly, I hoped he would be retired soon so that I could take him home. Practically speaking, though, this wasn't the best idea. Since I was far from retirement age, and still in good health, I'd be traveling all the time and off on deployment for four to six months at a stretch. Someone else would have to look after Cairo while I was away. No, the spare dog gig was the right way to help Cairo ease into a less stressful life. He would spend more time at home and less time on deployment.

Unfortunately, that time would not be spent with me; I had to give him up. It was part of the job, and I understood the reasoning, but it hurt like hell to let him go. Softening the blow was the knowledge that he'd be in good hands, as the master-at-arms assigned to him was my good friend Angelo, who knew Cairo well and was one of the best dog handlers in the navy. Additionally, it was understood that when Cairo finally did retire—whether that was six months or six years down the road—I would have the option to adopt him.

I was still his handler.

I was his dad.

Over the course of the next month, I slowly distanced myself from Cairo. I'd stop by and see him once a week or so, if he wasn't away on a training exercise. I'd take him for a walk or play with him, but the visits almost made it harder to deal with the separation. When my team was assigned to a dive training trip in Florida at the end of March, I was eager to get out of town. Being a canine handler was such an all-encompassing job that withdrawal symptoms were probably unavoidable, especially for someone who loved dogs and had the good fortune to work with a dog like Cairo. But that very same immersive quality is the reason a SEAL typically does only one or two deployments as a dog handler: he needs a break, and someone else deserves the opportunity.

The Florida trip was a bit of a working vacation, a chance to sharpen water skills that might have dulled somewhat after multiple successive deployments to Iraq and Afghanistan, where dryland combat was the norm. Ocean training during the day was followed by relaxed evenings that included a few drinks and lots of good food. Nothing too crazy—just a way to unwind after a long winter deployment in the mountains of Afghanistan. We deserved it.

For two members of our squadron, however, the trip was cut short after only a few days; there were suddenly a pair of openings at the Military Freefall Jumpmaster Course in Arizona. I'm not sure about the selection process; I only know that I very quickly found myself in Arizona, at jumpmaster school, along with Nic Checque, one of my best friends. Like I said earlier, I wasn't the greatest skydiver and didn't really like it all that much, so I would have preferred to stay in beautiful South Florida. At the same time, getting certified as a free-fall jumpmaster could only help my career and make me a better SEAL. Anyway, it wasn't like I had a choice.

The jumpmaster course is a notoriously rigorous three-week program, during which students learn how not only to be better skydivers but also how to orchestrate a jump for an entire team. A skydiving insertion is technical and dangerous. Each individual must be highly trained and skilled; the exit itself is reliant on the experience and skill of the pilot, as well as the team member responsible for guiding everyone out of the aircraft at the appropriate time. It is a deeply choreographed maneuver; one mistake can be catastrophic for the entire team. Jumpmaster certification, therefore, is a big deal, and I was ready for the challenge.

But someone had other plans.

On the second day of school, I got a phone call from my assault team leader.

"Pack your gear, Cheese. We need you back in Virginia. Now."

"You've got to be kidding," I said. "I just got here."

"Yeah, I know. Something's come up. I can't tell you anything else. Just get home."

After nine years in the navy, I knew better than to pump him for more info. Shit happens. Plans change. You get an order, you follow it. Then you follow another one. In due time, more would be revealed. Hopefully, this would be something interesting.

"Okay," I said. "I'll leave tonight."

There was a pause.

"Hey, Cheese. One other thing."

"What's that?"

"Pick up Cairo when you get here."

I smiled and nodded.

"Got it."

In a class of two dozen candidates, Nic and I were the only SEALs, so he wasn't thrilled that I was leaving and he was staying behind, but he understood. Duty calls and all that. When he asked why I had been recalled to Virginia, I told Nic, quite honestly, "I have no idea. Guess I'll find out soon enough." In all honesty, I had trouble figuring out why I had been recalled and Nic hadn't. I can say without hesitation that Nic was a better operator than I was. He was a total badass. The only logical explanation was that, for some reason, Cairo was needed. And I had been Cairo's handler for a long time. We were a package deal.

I spent the next couple of hours packing my stuff and running around, trying to officially withdraw from jumpmaster school. This was much more challenging than you might imagine. The first person with whom I spoke seemed not just upset but incredulous.

"What do you mean you're leaving? No one leaves Jump-master."

"Well, sorry, sir. But something's come up."

"Something's come up?" he repeated, his tone dripping with sarcasm. "After two days?"

I nodded. "Yes, sir."

He shook his head disgustedly, then gave me the name of the person I would have to see to formally withdraw. I left one office, went to another, and was told to come back later. I knew what this meant; I was about to go down a rabbit hole of paperwork and protocol that could take hours, or even days, to complete. And I didn't have the time to spare.

"You know what?" I said to the last person who gave me the runaround. "Call my boss."

And with that, I was gone.

This wasn't as severe a breach as it might sound. I mean, I did tell . . . someone . . . that I was leaving. He just wasn't the right person. And I never put it in writing, which left the door wide open for Nic to have a little fun at my expense.

Nic and I had been close friends since BUD/S, and like a lot of SEAL friendships, ours was strengthened by a variety of factors, including shared discomfort, a commitment to the work we were doing, time spent together (his locker at the base in Virginia was right next to mine), and a frequently dark sense of humor. To put it bluntly, Nic and I had a long history of busting each other's balls. We picked at each other's apparent weaknesses (Nic didn't have many, as far as I could tell; the guy was confident, smart, and ridiculously good-looking) and pranked each other mercilessly. There was never any malice; it was just the way we were.

Well, my departure made it easy for Nic to leave a little scar on my reputation. The next day, after I left, Nic went to class as usual. During roll call, the instructor noticed that the number of SEALs in attendance had been reduced by half.

"Where's your friend?" he asked Nic.

Without missing a beat, Nic said, "He quit."

The entire class stared at Nic as he sat there in silence, offering up not another shred of explanation. Although the jumpmaster course is difficult and graduation prestigious, SEALs had always fared well. SEALs don't quit jumpmaster school. Hell, SEALs don't quit anything!

Right?

"Yes, sir. He quit," Nic repeated.

"Why?"

"I have no idea."

I guess I had it coming. I should have found a way to circumvent the process and make sure that it was understood that I hadn't quit; I had been recalled by my superiors for reasons that were not immediately made clear to me. Perfectly legitimate reason to leave, and one that was well beyond my control.

Instead, I disappeared. For Nic, this was an opportunity to pull the mother of all pranks, a giant kick to the very soul of a SEAL: his reputation for toughness and endurance and fortitude.

*Thanks a lot, Nic. Love you, too.*

In our long and ongoing battle of practical jokes, this one made Nic the undisputed winner. I actually kind of admired him for it. As I said the next time I saw Nic, "You got me good, you little fucker."

And I never did get even.


I flew overnight, arrived in Virginia the next morning, and drove straight to the kennel to pick up Cairo. I still had no clue as to why I had been recalled or why suddenly I had been reassigned to the role of dog handler after only about a month away from the job.

Nor did I care. You didn't have to be a genius to figure out that something unique was about to happen. This, obviously, was a mission that required the services of a reliable working dog, and Cairo was about as reliable as they came. And I was Cairo's handler.

It was hard to know why certain people were picked for certain assignments, especially those that appeared with very little advance notice. Sometimes people were unavailable; they had the right to turn down an assignment, especially if it conflicted with a serious personal matter or another professional obligation. Older guys, married, with kids and other responsibilities, were more likely to take a pass. That was okay. They'd earned the privilege, and everyone understood when it happened, although it didn't happen that often. I was still young and single. Being a SEAL was my life. If this was a plum assignment, I wanted in. Didn't matter what it was. And the fact that I would get to work again with Cairo only made it more appealing.

When I met him at the kennel that morning, Cairo bounced

around like a puppy. I let him stand and put his paws on my chest. I held his paws in my hands and then gave him a big hug and hooked him up to a lead.

"Time to go to work, pal."

Information came out in a trickle. I was accustomed to being told what I needed to know, when I needed to know it, but this was different. From the moment I was instructed to return to Virginia, I sensed an inordinate level of secrecy and caution. This continued when our squadron gathered in the team room at Dam Neck for the first official briefing.

There were approximately two dozen of us in the room when the master chief began his read-in (the sharing of details regarding a mission). This guy could break down an assignment quickly and flawlessly. If you had questions, he'd answer them without hesitation. Now, though, he seemed circumspect and anxious. He told us we were going to be part of an important and highly secretive mission. He didn't say where the mission would take place. He didn't tell us the objective of the mission or the reason behind it. He did say that our destination was some sort of military or terrorist operation that resembled the compounds we had all encountered many times in Afghanistan. He also said the insertion would be extremely challenging; because of its location and the need for a quick and quiet operation, we would be inserting directly above the target. Beyond that, he had nothing specific to offer. All questions, some of them quite basic and logical, were deflected.

"You'll know more at the appropriate time," he said.

He then told us that the members of the squadron selected for this assignment would be divided into four teams. Not surprisingly, Cairo and I were assigned to Team 4, which presumably would handle perimeter duties associated with the target. The first three teams would be assault teams. The person in charge of Team 4 was Rob O'Neill, a good friend of mine and one of the guys I admired most in the squadron. Rob was nearly a decade older than I was, with a ton of experience in high-profile deployments all over the world. I had enormous faith in his ability as a leader and as a fighter.

Actually, as I looked around the room, I realized what an awesome assemblage of talent and experience it was. Even though I didn't know the details of the mission, I had a feeling that it was something special, and I was proud and excited to be a part of it. I had a few moments like this during my SEAL career—times when I felt lucky simply to be working alongside guys like Rob and Nic . . . and many others who will remain nameless since I want to respect their privacy. I'm not trying to be falsely humble. I had a great career, took part in a lot of important missions, and I'm proud of the things I accomplished. I came from a little town in Texas and made it all the way through the funnel and wound up on SEAL Team ███████. It was a dream come true, and I worked my ass off to make it happen. That said, I know that my accomplishments and my career pale in comparison to those of many of the men with whom I served. That's one of the things about being a SEAL—if you ever fall into the trap of thinking you're hot shit, all you have to do is look at some of your teammates, and you'll quickly realize how much you still have to learn.

I was lucky. I came to the team in my early twenties and was immediately surrounded by generous and talented mentors. I decided right away that I would be a sponge, sucking up as much information as possible. If I were fortunate enough to last, maybe someday I'd be one of the mentors.

For the better part of a week, we hung out in Virginia, discussing the mission in vague terms—there was a target within a compound somewhere, and our assignment was to remove or eliminate the target. Where? When? We didn't know.

On Sunday, April 10, we packed our gear and drove to a

training facility in North Carolina. Again, we didn't know what
to expect when we got there. But, naturally, when you have a
week to pack your gear and discuss a mission shrouded in secrecy, there will be speculation. Given the clandestine nature of
the mission—and what appeared to be an unprecedented level
of confidentiality—it's probably not surprising to know that the
name of Osama bin Laden, the Al Queda leader who had mas-
terminded the attacks of September 11, 2001, came up once or
twice. *Maybe*, we thought, *this is it. Maybe we're finally going
after this motherfucker.*

For us and for the entire U.S. military, bin Laden was the
white whale. Get bin Laden, it was reasoned, and you put a deep
and lasting gash into his terrorist organization. It wouldn't end
the war—we all knew that—but his capture or death would
at least be a measure of revenge for the deaths of nearly three
thousand civilians who perished on 9/11. That was worth something. Simply put: bin Laden was the baddest of bad guys, and
for almost a decade, he had been out there somehow eluding
capture or execution, and we all wanted to take him down.

When you serve in Special Operations, though, you can't
get caught up in a single-minded pursuit. Every day brings a
new mission, a new objective. You treat each with professionalism and clarity and even a certain emotional detachment, and
then you move on. Regardless of what the objective of this mission might be, we would treat it no differently.

And yet . . . oh, how I hoped the rumors were true.

I was pretty pumped as I made the ninety-minute drive
with Cairo to North Carolina. There, in a facility that was as un-
assuming as it was top secret—maybe that was the point—we
were briefed by our commanding officer, Captain Perry "Pete"
Van Hooser. In addition to the two dozen members of our squadron, there were several people in attendance whom I did not recognize. Some I presumed were navy brass; others, I would find

out as the meeting went on, were U.S. intelligence officials. I'd sat through hundreds of mission briefings in my career, but this one was unique in terms of formality and attendance, and it didn't take long to figure out why that was the case.

Captain Pete thanked us all for our time and then quickly revealed the true nature of our mission.

"We're going after UBL," he said.

*UBL* referred to Usama bin Laden. While he was commonly referred to as *Osama* in Western media, intelligence agencies like the CIA and FBI preferred the Romanization of his name: *Usama*. Didn't matter to me. At the very sound of those initials, the hair on the back of my neck stood up. I revealed no emotion whatsoever; nor did anyone else in the room. The mood was sober, professional. There was a weight to the proceedings that I had not previously encountered.

The briefing went on for several hours and was accompanied by a wealth of information. Months, if not years of intelligence work had apparently pinpointed bin Laden's position to a large housing compound in Abbottabad, a city in eastern Pakistan. This was not shocking. While the war on terror had been staged mostly in Iraq and Afghanistan, it had long been thought that bin Laden might be hiding out somewhere else, in a country sympathetic to the Al Queda mission. Pakistan was a logical answer—and in fact, there had been other Special Operations missions into Pakistan stemming from reports that bin Laden might be hiding there. Still, it had been many years since the intelligence community had a solid lead on bin Laden's whereabouts, and it was astonishing to learn that he was not barricaded in an underground bunker or cave somewhere in the mountains but rather hiding in plain sight! Taking daily walks in a flowing white robe, circling the compound for hours at a time in a routine that earned him the nickname *the Pacer*.

There was no guarantee that the Pacer was in fact bin

Laden, but the intelligence officials at the briefing seemed confident. He was well over six feet tall and lean, with a long gray
beard. He looked very much like bin Laden. He behaved in the
manner of someone important, never taking part in the work
of others in the compound, which sprawled like nothing else in
the neighborhood. There were walls ranging from roughly ten
to twenty feet in height surrounding the compound, which was
comprised of a large three-story house, a small guesthouse,
and other smaller structures that were likely used for housing
animals.

The preparation that went into this briefing was impressive, to say the least, as was the intelligence accumulated. We
depended on great intelligence to get our job done, and this was
an example of what could be accomplished with a combination
of advanced technology and dogged determination. Here, right
in front of us, were high-resolution photographs of Osama bin
Laden's home. We knew where he was. All we had to do now
was remove him.

As the briefing progressed, we were told of other options
that had been discussed and discarded. The "softest" and most
diplomatic approach would have been to inform the Pakistani
government and try to convince them to either hand over bin
Laden or join U.S. forces on a multinational mission. Given the
fact that Pakistan had long been considered sympathetic to Al
Queda, this seemed like a terrible idea. An air strike might have
been effective, but the explosive power required to guarantee
success was so great that it would have leveled not just the
compound or even the accompanying neighborhood but most of
the city of Abbottabad.

Good luck selling that one to the White House . . . or most
of the world.

Nope, the only answer was a surgical strike. Send in a Special
Operations unit, breach the compound, and extract UBL—dead

or alive. It was a challenging, dangerous mission, one with a significant likelihood of casualties on the America side. It also was the mission of a lifetime. I couldn't believe we were getting this opportunity!

My enthusiasm did not wane even as the briefing dragged on and the risks were laid out in graphic fashion: one of our choppers being shot down by RPGs; heavy resistance within the compound; the high probability that the entire place was rigged with explosives and that even if we did manage to breach the compound and find our target, we'd all be blown to bits. That was fine with me. I mean, I didn't have a death wish or anything like that—no one wants to get shot or killed—but as long as we got bin Laden, I was okay with anything else that might happen.

In all candor, one of my first thoughts while listening to the briefing was, *Well, guess I won't be coming home from this one.*

My second thought was, *But as long we get this asshole, I'm good with it.*

The mission, we were told, had been given the name Operation Neptune Spear. The reason this name had been chosen was because Neptune's spear is a trident, and a trident is part of the U.S. Naval Special Warfare insignia. The trident, as every SEAL knows, is a three-pronged spear. Each prong of the trident represents a portion of the operational capacity of the SEALs: sea, air, land.

So Operation Neptune Spear it was.

Made sense to me.

We spent most of the next week in North Carolina, training intensely from sunup until deep into the night. There were long briefing sessions in which we went over details of the mission; more importantly, we physically rehearsed the entire mission, over and over, using a full-sized model of the compound that had been constructed on-site. When I first saw this thing, I was blown away. SEAL training often included rehearsal, but the sessions were almost always theoretical in nature. On deployment, we would get detailed information, but typically our first exposure to a target was the afternoon of the operation. Video and photos are nice, but the value of practicing an operation on a full-scale replica of a target cannot be overstated. It was reassuring to know that someone, maybe everyone—the navy, the CIA, the White House—understood the magnitude of this mission and would spare no expense in providing us with everything we needed to do the job right.

It should be noted, however, that the model allowed us to train on exterior tactics only: the approach, insertion, and setup, as well as—we hoped—a successful extraction. Intelligence could only speculate as to the interior layout of the buildings. But that was okay. We knew from experience that a floor plan was as likely to mess you up as it was to help. Even the best satellite or drone photos would not provide a foolproof interior layout, so the best you could do was guess, or use intuition based on previous experience with similar structures. If you studied and memorized a floor plan and then found something entirely different when you got inside, it could prove so disorienting that the mission was compromised. Better to just go with the flow.

In some ways, every mission, every insertion, was a combination of choreography and improvisation. I likened it to playing pickup basketball with a group of guys you know well. Read and react: "You go this way, I'll go that way." There was a basic outline for the mission, and everyone had a role that was understood not only by that person but by his teammates, as well. Within that basic framework of knowledge and trust, there was always a bit of freelancing. And while we had more intelligence than usual on this one, I had no doubt that once we were on the ground, something unexpected would happen and we would have to respond accordingly.

But I had faith in my teammates. I knew they would absolutely crush it just like they always did.

Cairo was deeply involved in most of the rehearsals and performed like the pro he was—with one notable exception. And, again, this was my fault.

We were rehearsing a breach of one of the compound gates, using live explosives. Since Cairo wasn't needed for the breach, I had left him in the parking lot, in the backseat of a navy-issued Chevy Suburban. When I say *backseat*, I mean loose in the vehicle. I had gotten used to doing this with Cairo over the years. If I went somewhere and left him in the car for a few minutes, I'd rarely bother putting him in his kennel; he could generally be trusted to chill out in the car until I returned. In fact, if there was some reason he wanted to get out, he was more likely to cause trouble when he was locked in his kennel.

We used to call him Houdini, a nickname earned after multiple Kennel escapes. This is going to sound like fiction, but I swear it's true; Cairo learned how to squeeze his foreleg through the front grate and use his paw to lift the latch on the kennel. If for some reason that didn't work, he would use his teeth and his legs to twist the front grate until eventually he created enough of a gap to squeeze through.

Anyway, on this particular night, Cairo was loose in the Suburban when the breaching and explosions began. I didn't think anything of it until we were through with the exercise and got back to the SUV. Inside, Cairo was bouncing around, panting and whining. He was also covered with tufts of white fabric that made it look like he'd been out in a snowstorm. In fact, he'd been creating a storm of a different type in the car, ripping the padded headrests off their foundations and shredding them to bits.

"Cairo!" I yelled as I opened the door.

He jumped into my arms and then fell to the ground and began running around like crazy. I quickly got him leashed up and took him for a short walk—at least he hadn't peed or pooped in the car. I wasn't really mad at Cairo. He was my responsibility, after all, and I had left him unattended. I should have known better. My bad, all the way.

"You know not to do that again, right?" Rob said to me.

I did, of course. Leaving Cairo in the car unattended while explosives rocked the surrounding area was unfair. I do not think he was frightened by the blasts. In fact, I'm pretty sure he was just excited and confused. See, to Cairo, explosions and gunfire were a signal to begin work. Dog training is based on a foundation of stimulus and reward. To Cairo, the sound of combat was a stimulus. The reward, which he had earned time and again, was the opportunity to fight and bite. To seek out a bad guy and engage. I can only imagine how confusing it would have been for him to hear those blasts and not be able to do anything about it. So, after that, I crated him at all times during any training exercise in which he was not an active participant.

Better safe than sorry.

We left North Carolina the following weekend and traveled straight to another training facility in the Southwest, this one designed to mimic not just the mission but the geography and climate in which it would take place. We trained at altitude in the desert. Over and over, we boarded helicopters, flew a distance approximate to that of flying from Jalalabad to Abbottabad, and fast-roped out of helicopters. Cairo made every exit with me.

By the end of the week, we had the insertion down cold. In all honesty, it was not that complicated a mission. We had performed similar ops a hundred or more times in the past. What made this unique, and uniquely lethal, was the fact that we were going after the highest-profile target in SEAL history; indeed, one of the highest-profile targets in military history. This significantly raised the ante in terms of both importance and risk. Fuck this one up, and the fallout would be felt for years, both from a military and a public relations standpoint.

And we'd probably all be killed.

Tactically, though, it was, on the surface, no more intricate or problematic than many other missions.

By the end of April, we had it down cold. We had rehearsed the insertion dozens of times—a luxury I personally had never been afforded prior to a mission—so we knew it by heart. Two Black Hawk helicopters would travel under cover of darkness from J-Bad to Abbottabad. My chopper included guys from two teams—one for perimeter security, and the other an assault team. The chopper would land outside the compound and drop off the perimeter team first. That included me, Cairo, Rob, an interpreter, a couple of snipers, and a gunner. Then our helicopter would hover over the main house, allowing the assault team to fast-rope to the roof. Eventually, the plan was modified slightly, with Rob joining the rooftop team to give us one more shooter on the main house.

My job was to help hold security outside the compound, perhaps against Al Queda forces, local law enforcement, or, more likely, from curious locals wondering what was going on in their neighborhood. We didn't know whether the locals knew that bin Laden was in their midst, but it was certainly possible. Regardless, we had to protect the perimeter of the compound so that the assault teams could do their work inside. Additionally, if the initial assault turned up nothing, or at least if bin Laden appeared to be missing, I would bring Cairo inside to do a more intensive search. It seemed reasonable to think that the Al Queda leader would have more than a few hiding places within the compound.

Meanwhile, the other helicopter would hover over the courtyard within or just above the compound walls, at a spot somewhere between the main house and the guesthouse. There, assault team members would fast-rope out of the helicopter while snipers provided much-needed security from the chopper. Needless to say, this helo faced the most dangerous task, as it would be open to attack for as long as it took the assault team to exit. If there existed within the compound a modestly trained and equipped security force, the helicopter would be an easy mark for an RPG.

Again, though, we weren't reinventing the wheel. If this sounds complicated and dangerous . . . well, yes, it was. But no more so than any number of missions we had successfully completed in the past. We had the advantage in terms of training, technology, intelligence, and weaponry. We had experience and the element of surprise—or, at least, we hoped we did. But there were things we didn't know, couldn't know, and those were the variables that pushed the mission into uncharted territory. It was not unreasonable to think that the most wanted terrorist in history would have some sort of heavily armed security force, even if our intelligence had indicated no such force existed at the compound. Also, there was a long history of terrorists going out with a bang when cornered. We expected to encounter suicide bombers within the compound; hell, we expected the entire place to be a suicide bomb. Finally, there was the possibility of interference not just from locals but from the Pakistani police or military, neither of which was likely to look favorably upon a U.S. military force flying unannounced beyond its borders. They could have accused us of attacking their country and retaliated accordingly. To say we would have been outnumbered would be an understatement.

And yet, as we neared the end of April and we received word that the White House was likely to approve the mission, I felt both confident and proud. When desert training ended and we all returned to Virginia, we were instructed to get our affairs in order. For me, that meant, among other things, making sure that my life insurance premiums were paid (the military offered us a good deal on a million-dollar policy) and that I had a current and fully binding will on record somewhere. Not that I had much to leave behind. I'm sure those last few days in April were especially tough on the married guys—saying goodbye to their wives and kids without being able to tell them why they seemed a little sadder than usual—but for me, it was just like going away on any other mission.

I did not call my mother before leaving. That was standard practice for me. For one thing, my mom did not hear very well, so phone calls were a challenge. Also, she worried too much as it was, and if I had called her this time, she would have suspected something was up. So I did what I usually did: I sent her a quick text and kept it short and simple.

I did call my father. That, too, was standard practice when I left on deployment. But this time felt different. Even though I'd been on my own for a long time and moved across the country, I still felt close to my dad. I wanted to say goodbye . . . just in case. It wasn't a long conversation—they never were with my father. I told him I was deploying unexpectedly—there was something important going on, and I was part of it. I also told him I might not make it back. He knew better than to ask for specifics.

"Be careful, okay?" he said.

"I will," I replied. "And, Dad?"

"Yes, boy?"

"I love you."

There was a long pause before he responded. I can only imagine what he was thinking.

"I love you, too."

Our first trip together. This is Cairo ready for a day of training in Ontario, California.

*(Photo by Will Chesney)*

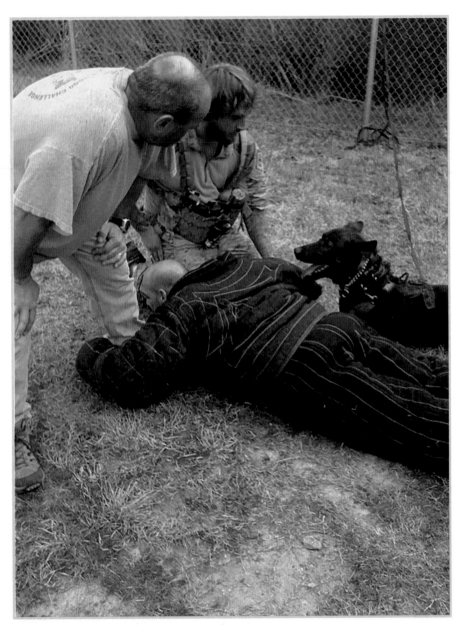

Working on "bite training" with Cairo and another handler and trainer early in my career as a dog handler. Note the bulky bite suit worn by the "target" just inches from Cairo's nose. Cairo was the best—he wouldn't move until instructed to do so.

*(Photo from the collection of Will Chesney)*

Training in California. This is Cairo in his kennel on the day he broke the door and busted out while I was in a classroom in Ontario. We were both new to the job!

(Photo by Will Chesney)

Bath day at the command. *(Photo by Will Chesney)*

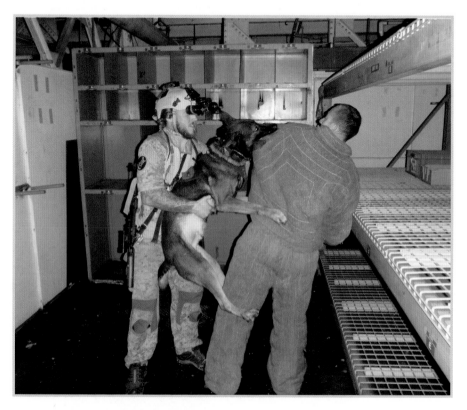

Getting in a little bite work with Cairo at a training facility.

Cairo wearing booties and "doggles," and chewing on his favorite ball, shortly before getting seriously wounded on deployment, in the summer of 2009.

*(Photo by Will Chesney)*

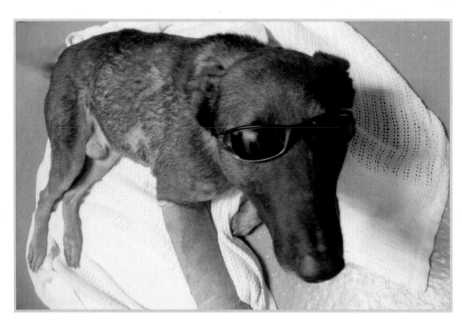

This is Cairo recuperating from gunshot wounds at Bagram, a day after life-saving surgery. He was a tough guy and a quick healer.

*(Photo by Will Chesney)*

Sitting with Cairo at the vet's office while he recuperated from gunshot wounds. Just trying to help him get comfortable.

*(Photo from the collection of Will Chesney)*

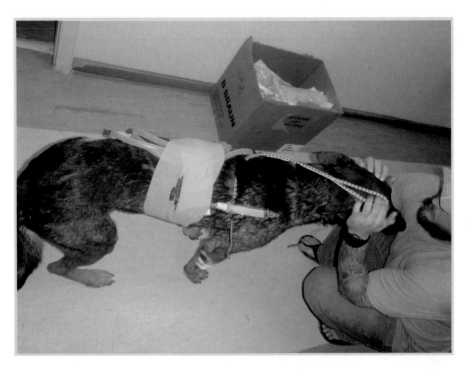

Not long after surgery for his gunshot wounds, Cairo was up and walking around outside. But we had to take frequent breaks.

*(Photo by Will Chesney)*

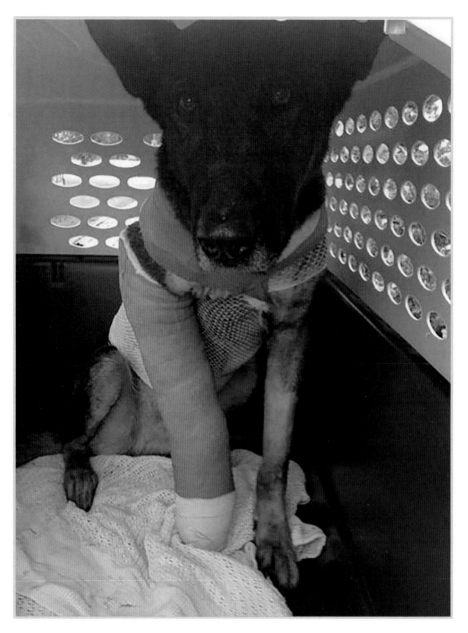

Cairo on his way to Lackland Air Force Base for rehabilitation after getting shot on deployment in Afghanistan.

*(Photo by Will Chesney)*

Getting in a little training with Cairo at the command in Virginia Beach.

*(Photo from the collection of Will Chesney)*

This is Cairo hanging out by my desk in the training office at Dam Neck after I became an instructor. The giant bone was a gift from a friend following the Bin Laden raid.

*(Photo by Will Chesney)*

Cairo with his friends, Sterling and Hagen, after a day at the beach in Virginia.

*(Photo by Natalie Kelley)*

After so many months of struggle, Cairo finally was retired. This is the day he came to live with Dad.

*(Photo by Natalie Kelley)*

That's me and Natalie taking Cairo for a ride in the sidecar. Wherever we went, people would naturally stare, but Cairo just loved being out in the open air.

*(Photo from the collection of Will Chesney)*

A day on the water with Natalie and the dogs. That's Cairo in the middle.

*(Photo from the collection of Will Chesney)*

Cairo, right, with his friend Hagen, on the way home from Florida, where Cairo had an unfortunate interaction with a bulldog (note bandages on his left foreleg). Lucky for the bulldog, Cairo did not even respond. He was such a friendly guy!

*(Photo by Will Chesney)*

# Chapter 18

*The claim is on you, the sights are on me*
*So what do you do that's guaranteed?*

In the back of a specially adapted MH-60 Black Hawk helicopter, I closed my eyes and let the roar of AC/DC's "Moneytalks" wash over me. Everyone had a routine—some guys slept on the way to an operation. Others tried to talk, although this was challenging given the noise in the aircraft. Some guys said nothing and merely rehearsed the mission in their heads.

Through a small iPod strapped to my shoulder, I listened to music—loud, heavy rock or country. Tonight it was AC/DC. As Brian Johnson screeched into my headphones, I leaned over and gave Cairo a pat on the head. The Black Hawk is much smaller than a Chinook, so we were packed pretty tightly. Cairo and I were both on the floor; he sat between my legs, as calm as always. I hooked a thumb through his harness—the same bloodstained vest he'd worn on every mission since getting shot the previous year—and rubbed his back. He arched his head and looked up at me eagerly.

There were roughly a dozen of us in the back of the chopper, along with a couple of badass Night Stalkers up front. Rob sat next to me on the flight in (although he had wisely planned well enough in advance to bring a small folding chair). We looked at each other a couple of times but didn't say anything. Approximately ninety minutes earlier, around 11:00 p.m. on the night of May 2, 2011, we had left J-Bad in two MH-60s. Now we were in Pakistani airspace and closing in on the city of Abbottabad. As always, a voice crackled over the radio to let us know we were ten minutes out. This was standard operating procedure, but like so many other things about Operation Neptune Spear, it didn't *feel* standard.

I turned off my music and envisioned the insertion for roughly the hundredth time. I checked my radio, my weapon, my night-vision goggles. I took a quick glance at the laminated card we each had, a map depicting the layout of the compound. I made sure Cairo was ready to go.

"Five minutes!"

The two helicopters had flown in tandem to this point, but as we approached the compound, the other chopper veered off toward the compound walls, and I lost sight of it.

"Two minutes!"

We made our approach to an area just outside the compound. The pilot set the Black Hawk down expertly, right on the *X*—the precise spot where we were supposed to begin the insertion. I jumped out with Cairo, the snipers and the interpreter, and immediately began working the perimeter. As we moved methodically toward the walls of the compound, I looked back over my shoulder and noticed the Black Hawk still on the ground. Seconds later, the rest of the assault team disembarked. I had no idea at this time what was happening, but it certainly didn't look good.

*Shit . . . we just landed and already something has gone wrong.*

Plans can change in a heartbeat. It can happen on any mission, and obviously it had happened now. For some reason, the assault team on our Black Hawk had redirected—instead of fast-roping to the roof of the main house inside the compound, they had decided to leave the helicopter now and breach from the outside wall. Fine. Unless someone told me otherwise, my job remained unchanged. I took Cairo off leash and began working him in a clockwise direction around the perimeter of the compound. As explosives went off behind me—the unmistakable sound of breachers at work, blowing doors and gates and accessing the compound by any means necessary—I walked alongside Cairo as he put his formidable nose to the ground in a thorough search for explosives.

As we rounded a corner, I looked up at the compound wall. In the distance, at the next corner, I could see something sticking up . . . almost resting on the top of the wall. It was the tail of a helicopter. But only the tail. The rest of the aircraft, I figured, must have been on the other side. It looked almost surreal. Not so much a crash but more like a landing that hadn't quite worked. In fact, it seemed so strange that my first thought was, *Hey, that helicopter looks just like one of ours!*

There was a reason for the similarity. It *was* one of ours!

What I did not know at the time—what none of us on the second Black Hawk realized—was that the first chopper had encountered severe and unexpected problems while hovering inside the walls of the compound, some twenty feet above the courtyard. While the helicopter tried to maintain a steady hover and the assaulters prepared to fast-rope down, the chopper began to shake violently. A combination of hot, dry air and the solid walls of the compound had created a turbulent air current that caused the chopper to basically get caught in its own rotor wash. Why hadn't this happened during any of our training exercises? Well, because the model of the compound that had been constructed in North Carolina was surrounded by walls that were indeed the correct height but not made of solid material. This allowed wind, including air whipped up by the rotor of a helicopter, to pass harmlessly through.

In Abbottabad, as it turned out, the compound's solid walls created a very different and far more challenging scenario. One with potentially catastrophic consequences.

Fortunately, the pilot recognized immediately what was happening; rather than fight the vortex—which would have proved disastrous—he orchestrated a perfectly executed "controlled crash." He turned the nose of the Black Hawk away from the walls and dropped it into the ground as gently as possible, leaving the tail on top of one of the walls. No one was hurt. Everyone jumped out, without a scratch, and the mission went on as planned.

The pilot of our chopper had witnessed the entire event from the cockpit. That's why he had decided not to elevate after dropping Cairo and me and the rest of the security team off. Instead, he told the assaulters that they would be unable to hover inside the compound. They had to exit the craft now and breach the outside walls.

All of this happened within a matter of just a few minutes and had almost no perceptible impact on the operation. We had rehearsed multiple scenarios, including one in which access to the compound was gained by breaching a gate or door or some other access point on the outside wall; that is what the assault team was doing while I worked the perimeter with Cairo. I could hear gunfire and more explosions. In my head, I tried to piece together what had happened. But I had complete trust in our guys, and so I stayed focused on my job—using Cairo to find explosives or insurgents hiding out beyond the compound walls.

Eventually, after two complete laps, it was determined that

the perimeter was fully secure. In a way, this was astonishing. If this really was the home of Osama bin Laden, how could there not be IEDs rimming the compound? Where were the bombs and snipers? It was almost too easy.

With several of our team holding security outside the compound, and, so far, no apparent encroachment from curious locals, I began to work my way inside. This was my role as a dog handler on many missions, and it was no different tonight. Once the outside was safe and secure, I was supposed to bring Cairo inside and use him to detect explosives and find anyone who might be hiding. Again, it seemed totally reasonable to expect both of these things.

By the time I got to the main house—and this was perhaps only ten to fifteen minutes after we had landed—the place was littered with debris and bodies, the obvious aftereffects of breaching and gunfire. We passed a couple of bodies on the first floor; Cairo naturally wanted to get in a quick bite, but it was obvious that both people were dead and thus posed no threat whatsoever, so I pulled him away and tried to keep him focused on his primary job: odor detection.

The floor was covered with broken glass, so I repeatedly scooped up Cairo and carried him over the shards before setting him down to inspect another room. Steadily and methodically, we worked our way through the first floor. There were, at this time, more than twenty SEALs inside the compound, the majority of them in the main house. I knew very little at this point. Although gunfire seemed to have ebbed, there remained a distinct possibility that it could erupt again at any moment. For all I knew, a dozen bad guys were hiding in the basement, or behind false walls, or almost anywhere. Trip wires could be hanging from the ceiling or strung across doorways. You couldn't let your guard down for a second. More than once, we had reached what we'd thought was the completion of an operation, with a structure apparently secured, only to be surprised by a gun-toting, suicidal insurgent leaping out from a hiding place.

We had lost more than a few people that way, so we never relaxed until we were back on the base.

The mission wasn't over . . . until it was over.

With Cairo by my side, I made my way to the second floor, trailing behind a growing train of shooters. I would guide Cairo wherever he was needed, as instructed. For the most part, I tried to keep his attention focused on explosive odor. The entire time I was in that building, I figured there was a good chance it would blow up. It just seemed impossible that the place hadn't been rigged with explosives—I mean, that's what I would have done if I were in their position—and our best hope was that Cairo could sniff out the danger before it had a chance to kill us. That's why I took him room to room on the first two floors. Even though we seemed to have gained control of the structure, I wanted to be sure that there were no surprises; utilizing Cairo's extraordinary odor detection ability was the best way to do that.

As I climbed the stairs to the third floor, I noticed a significant uptick in the level of activity. We had a bunch of guys on the third floor, but there was no fighting. I heard a lot of talking, a lot of commotion. One of the shooters came down the stairs while I was walking up.

"It's crazy up there, Cheese," he said. "You can go up if you want, but I don't think they need the dog. You should probably just stage the second floor unless they call you. It's over."

*It's over . . .*

That could only mean one thing: the intel had been correct, and bin Laden was in the house. And now he was dead. I felt a surge of excitement; I wanted to go upstairs to see for myself what was happening, but I wasn't going to disregard a teammate's suggestion just to satisfy my own curiosity. I trusted my guys completely. If one of them said that Cairo wasn't needed . . . then Cairo wasn't needed. His word was good enough for me. I retreated to the second floor, continued to lightly work Cairo, and hold my position in the event something happened, and our services were needed on the third floor.

As I exited a room and walked into a second-floor hallway, Rob came down the stairs from the third floor. We both walked into another room. Our eyes met. He nodded and sort of half smiled. It was a look I had rarely seen from Rob, who was typically all business during an operation.

"Dude," he said. "I think I just shot that motherfucker."

"What?" I said. "Seriously?"

Rob nodded. "Yeah. I just shot that fucker in the face."

He didn't use bin Laden's name, but I knew exactly who he meant. We both froze for a few seconds in the hallway. This information had already been conveyed to our ground force commander. Moments later, his voice came over the radio as he passed the information on to Admiral William McRaven, the SEAL in charge of Joint Special Operations Command.

"For God and country, Geronimo, Geronimo, Geronimo, EKIA."

We had a bunch of code words used to signify various stages of Operation Neptune Spear. *Geronimo* referred to Osama bin Laden; not necessarily that he had been killed but that he had been found and dealt with. The second half of the message, *EKIA*, represented the outcome of that confrontation: "Enemy killed in action." If the message was a little melodramatic, well, maybe the situation called for it.

"Fuck yeah!" I said, holding my hand high for Rob to smack. And right there, on the second floor of Osama bin Laden's house, we shared a high five.

Let me explain something: I had never high-fived anyone before, during, or after a mission. I had never seen any of my teammates celebrate in this manner. It was uncool, unprofessional . . . unacceptable. This was not a game. We were not cowboys; we were not vigilantes. We were part of an elite Special Operations unit that took great pride in dispatching its duty with proficiency and unblinking pragmatism.

We got in, we got out, we moved on to the next assignment.

A high five after a kill?

Come on, man. Who does that?

Well, on May 2, 2011, I did it. And while it might make me wince a little in retrospect, it did happen. And it absolutely felt like the correct response at the time. It was pure, unbridled joy.

Multiple books and lengthy magazine articles have chronicled in detail the drumbeat of Operation Neptune Spear, including some written by members of SEAL Team ▮▮▮▮▮▮. If you've read more than one of these accounts, you know that there is no consensus as to exactly what happened that night in Abbottabad. The entire operation lasted less than forty-five minutes, and in that time, not everything went smoothly, starting with the first helicopter being forced to ditch against a wall of the compound. The house and its surrounding neighborhood were mostly unlit, so night-vision goggles were needed throughout. There was tremendous pressure to complete the operation swiftly. And there was resistance.

I have neither the desire nor the qualifications to offer a definitive narrative of the mission, especially as it pertains to the climactic encounter on the third floor, where bin Laden was tracked by SEALs and killed, despite the attempted interference of two women (presumably his wives). I can tell you only what I witnessed firsthand and what I know to be certain based on evidence. I was outside the compound with Cairo looking for explosives as the assault team engaged and killed several hostiles, including one of bin Laden's couriers and his son Khalid. I was not witness to the final confrontation with bin Laden, during which more than one SEAL took aim and fired. As to which bullet killed him? I don't know. And I don't care.

Here is what I do know:

We got him.

The mission did not end with bin Laden's death. As a large group of operators gathered files, flash drives, compact discs, and other material from the third floor and threw everything into large plastic bags, I continued to work the first two floors, again using Cairo to carefully clear each room in the unlikely— but not unheard of—event that someone had survived unnoticed; or, far more likely, that the house was rigged to blow. We moved from the second floor to the first floor and slowly made our way outside into the courtyard, and finally back out to the perimeter. From there, off in the distance, I could see several small groups of people approaching the compound from the surrounding neighborhood. Not a huge mob, but enough of a presence to be of concern. This was a heavily populated city, and it wouldn't take long for us to be outnumbered if the locals were so inclined. A situation like that could turn ugly in a hurry.

Having Cairo out there was a big help. It might seem odd, but often a large and imposing attack dog will do more to dissuade curiosity seekers or insurgents than a handful of soldiers armed with automatic weapons.

We continued to work quickly. Several women and children who lived in the compound were brought outside and instructed to huddle together against one of the walls—at the opposite end of the compound from the downed Black Hawk—while we awaited extraction.

A couple of members of the team, including our explosive ordnance expert, then rigged the downed helicopter with timed charges so that we could blow it up. For both practical and public relations reasons, you never wanted to leave a piece of equipment behind after a mission, especially one as valuable as a Black Hawk helicopter. First of all, photos and video of a downed helo screamed *failure* to the world. More importantly, the bird was loaded with sophisticated technology, including surveillance equipment and weaponry. There was no way you could let that stuff fall into the wrong hands. If something happened to a helicopter and it was abandoned, then it had to be destroyed before you left.

This, despite protestations from the pilot of the downed chopper, who remained a badass to the very end.

"I can fly that thing," he said, even as it was being wired to blow.

"No, that's okay. Don't worry about. The Chinook is on its way."

"No, I'm serious," the pilot insisted, looking at the nose of the Black Hawk embedded in the ground. "I can lift it right out of here."

Like I said, the Night Stalkers were the best. You had to admire the guy. But we weren't taking any chances.

Four MH-47 Chinook helicopters—"flying school buses," we used to call them, because they were so big and unwieldy—had taken off from Jalalabad shortly after we had left. Two of the buses, loaded with a quick reaction force (QRF) comprised of a couple of dozen SEALs, had waited at the border, ready to jump in if disaster struck. The other Chinooks had crossed into Pakistani airspace and landed in a remote area, where they could be summoned if needed for help during extraction or with refueling.

We needed that help now.

The first Black Hawk was already on its way back to Abbottabad when we called in the Chinooks. A few members of the assault team went back to J-Bad in the Black Hawk, along with bin Laden's body, while the rest of us waited for one of the

Chinooks in a grassy area just outside the compound. The civilians were sent back inside the house and told to remain there.

As bad luck would have it, the Chinook drew near just as the charge on the rigged Black Hawk was about to blow. We were counting it down—"Thirty seconds"—when the Chinook came into view. There was an anxious moment when we realized that the Chinook was going to fly over the compound at almost the exact moment that the Black Hawk would explode. And yet, our team leader remained calm.

"Abort," he said into the radio. "Do a racetrack."

This was the team leader's way of letting the pilot know that something was wrong and that he needed to take a lap overhead (a "racetrack") before landing.

"Copy that," came the reply.

As the Black Hawk burst into flames, the Chinook completed a wide circle over the compound, then returned and flew dramatically through a giant mushroom cloud of smoke before settling into a safe landing nearby. It looked, and felt, like something out of a movie.

We climbed aboard quickly and huddled together, silently, as the Chinook lifted into the air and pulled away. I looked out the window and could see the flames and smoke rising above the compound. Cairo was at my feet, sitting calmly, but I reached down and scooped him up so that he could sit on my lap. Against the din of the Chinook's rotors, it was hard to hear much of anything. That was okay, because I didn't really feel like talking. Neither did anyone else. I think we all were shocked to be alive and weighed down by the magnitude of what we had just accomplished.

I pulled out my iPod and began scrolling through my music, stopping when I came to one of my favorite songs, "It's a Great Day to Be Alive," by Travis Tritt. I used to play this song all the time, but I stopped after Falco was killed in the line of duty. It had become too much of an emotional trigger, so I put it away; I literally had not cued up "It's a Great Day to Be Alive" since the night Falco was killed. But now, with Cairo settling into me, and my brothers all around me, it just felt like the right time.

I leaned back and closed my eyes . . . and sang along in my head.

> *Well, I might go get me a new tattoo*
> *Or take my old Harley for a three-day cruise.*

# Chapter 19

The flight back from Abbottabad to Jalalabad was in some ways the most dangerous part of the mission. We were in hostile airspace, lumbering along in a giant flying school bus—an easy target for any of the Pakistani fighter jets that might have been dispatched once word of the mission got out. But I don't remember feeling particularly worried. I hadn't expected to return from Operation Neptune Spear, and now that safety was within reach . . . well, maybe it just hadn't sunken in.

We landed first at J-Bad, around three o'clock in the morning. Admiral McRaven was there to greet us, along with some other navy brass and intelligence experts from the CIA and FBI. They pored over the materials we had brought back and conducted interviews with just about everyone involved in the raid as they attempted to construct, a coherent narrative. I know from experience that sometimes it can take days or weeks to cut through the fog of war—memory and stress and differing points of view combine to create a complicated story.

But this was the body of Osama bin Laden on the floor of an airplane hangar in Afghanistan, and the world would want to know what happened. At one point, Admiral McRaven stood over the body for a personal examination. There, just a few feet away from me, I could see bin Laden's blood-splattered face, practically split in half. McRaven walked around the body and gave it a good look. At first, I wasn't sure what he was doing. Turned out, he wanted to measure the corpse to see if it corresponded to what we knew about bin Laden—specifically, that he was a tall man, approximately six feet four inches in height. Unfortunately, no one had a tape measure, so McRaven asked a bystander, one of the taller guys in attendance, to stretch out on the floor next to the body. The dead man was slightly taller, but not by much.

McRaven nodded. DNA evaluation would soon officially confirm bin Laden's identity, but for now . . .

*Close enough!*

The next stop was Bagram, where there were more intelligence reps and navy officials, and more evaluation of evidence and gathering of reports. We all hung out together in the hangar, eating a big breakfast and telling jokes and generally celebrating the biggest operation of our lives—hell, maybe the biggest operation in the history of Special Operations. A large-screen TV had been brought into the building so that we could watch as the event was reported back in the States.

At 11:35 in the evening, local time, President Obama walked to a podium in the White House and addressed the world:

> *Good evening. Tonight, I can report to the American people and to the world that the United States has conducted an operation that killed Osama bin Laden, the leader of Al Queda, and a terrorist who's responsible for the murder of thousands of innocent men, women, and children.*
>
> *It was nearly ten years ago that a bright September*

*day was darkened by the worst attack on the American people in our history. The images of 9/11 are seared into our national memory—hijacked planes cutting through a cloudless September sky; the Twin Towers collapsing to the ground; black smoke billowing up from the Pentagon; the wreckage of Flight 93 in Shanksville, Pennsylvania, where the actions of heroic citizens saved even more heartbreak and destruction.*

*And yet we know that the worst images are those that were unseen to the world. The empty seat at the dinner table. Children who were forced to grow up without their mother or their father. Parents who would never know the feeling of their child's embrace. Nearly three thousand citizens taken from us, leaving a gaping hole in our hearts . . .*

*Then, last August, after years of painstaking work by our intelligence community, I was briefed on a possible lead to bin Laden. It was far from certain, and it took many months to run this thread to ground. I met repeatedly with my national security team as we developed more information about the possibility that we had located bin Laden hiding within a compound deep inside of Pakistan. And finally, last week, I determined that we had enough intelligence to take action, and authorized an operation to get Osama bin Laden and bring him to justice.*

*Today, at my direction, the United States launched a targeted operation against that compound in Abbottabad, Pakistan. A small team of Americans carried out the operation with extraordinary courage and capability. No Americans were harmed. They took care to avoid civilian casualties. After a firefight, they killed Osama bin Laden and took custody of his body.*

Damn straight we did!

On a night filled with extraordinary events, this was per-haps the strangest: to be sitting in an airplane hangar at Bagram, eating breakfast, watching the president of the United States announce to the world the outcome of a top-secret mission to take down Osama bin Laden . . . just a couple of hours after we had completed that mission . . . and (this is the best part) while bin Laden's body was just a few feet away from us.

Full disclosure: I was not the biggest fan of Obama. Noth-ing personal, but during his time in office, the tightening rules of engagement made our job harder and sometimes more dan-gerous. But he was still the president, and he did have the balls to pull the trigger on this mission. I took a bite out of a sand-wich and looked at the TV screen. I looked around the room, at the greatest group of guys I'd ever get to work with. And then I looked to my left at bin Laden's broken face.

Just a surreal moment.

Within thirty-six hours, we were back in Virginia, where, of course, we were treated like conquering heroes. Robert Gates, the secretary of defense, paid a visit just to shake everyone's hand in person. Everyone on the mission was awarded the Sil-ver Star for "gallantry in action against an enemy of the United States." It was a disappointment to me that Cairo did not re-ceive a Silver Star; he was every bit as important a part of the mission as anyone else. He risked just as much.

But at least he wasn't overlooked entirely. A few days later, we all were summoned to Fort Campbell, Kentucky, where the 160th Airborne is based. There, we met with President Obama and Vice President Joe Biden. The president delivered a short speech, a chance for him to "say on behalf of all Americans and people around the globe, job well done." He seemed legitimately moved and proud.

We were presented with a Presidential Unit Citation. In return, we presented to the president an American flag that had accompanied us on the mission and which we'd framed after returning home. The front of the frame had been inscribed with the words: *From the Joint Task Force Operation Neptune Spear, 01 May 2011: For God and country. Geronimo.*

Before the talk, the president had been briefed by our commander about some of the details of the mission, including the fact that Cairo had been an integral part of the of the raid. And that he was, in fact, with us right now.

Obama's reaction?

"I want to meet this dog."

Someone jokingly advised the president that if he wanted to say hello to Cairo, it might be wise to bring some treats, just to soften him up. He was, after all, a lethal attack dog. Both the president and vice president walked into a separate room, where I was waiting with Cairo.

"So this is the famous Cairo," President Obama said.

"Yes, sir," I replied.

Obama nodded and said some nice things about Cairo and me and everyone on the team, and then we shook hands and took some pictures. Both Biden and Obama gave Cairo a gentle little pat on the back. Good dog that he was, he didn't even flinch. As usual, he seemed to be having a pretty good time.

Of course, Cairo was wearing his muzzle the entire time. I wasn't about to take a chance in a situation like that. Can you imagine if Cairo took a nip at the president? Now that would have been a lousy footnote to the biggest mission in SEAL history: me standing next to the president of the United States, asking, "Am I fired?"

# Chapter 20

The first night home, I took Cairo to my house for a celebratory steak dinner. More filet mignon—one slab for me, one for him. He spent the night at my place, hogging the bed, sleeping like a baby. The next day, when I brought him back to the kennel, I received a rather stern rebuke. The rule regarding working dogs remained in place: they were not allowed to go home with their handlers under any circumstances. I knew this. I also did not care.

"Come on, man," I said. "It's a special circumstance."

"No, Will, really. You can't do this anymore."

"But we just killed bin Laden!"

"Understood. Great job. You still can't take him home."

"Seriously?"

"Yeah, seriously."

I wouldn't say I got in trouble for that one, but it was certainly made clear to me that next time . . . well, there had better not be a next time. Hey, look, I get it. I understood the policy, and I knew it was coming from a place of logic and practicality. I'd been on enough deployments and had worked with dogs long enough to see what they could to a human being under the right—or wrong—circumstances.

So after that night, I didn't push my luck. I was supposed to be separating from Cairo, anyway. I tried to get on with my life, which mainly meant getting on with work. As much as I missed Cairo, I was excited about the opportunity to do something different.

I made a point of staying in touch with him, visiting the kennel roughly once a week as long as neither one of us was away on a training trip, and he always seemed happy to see me. We'd play fetch for a little while, I'd take him for a walk— sometimes I'd just grab him and leave and we'd hang out for a few hours. Then we'd go our separate ways. I didn't press anyone about taking him home, in part because the new master chief in charge of the kennel was, to put it mildly, a difficult personality. My best guess is that they had assigned him the kennel job because he had trouble getting along with people; maybe, they figured, he'd do better with animals. And it wasn't like there was a lot of competition for the job.

The kennel manager and I did not get along, but since I was no longer a handler, we didn't have to spend much time together, and I tried to keep a respectful distance even when I stopped by to play with Cairo. One day, a couple of months after the bin Laden mission, I came home from a training trip and drove over to the kennel. Cairo bounced into my arms, tried to dance with me as always, and generally seemed happy and healthy. I knew Cairo was getting plenty of high-quality training and care in case he was ever needed on deployment. So far, that hadn't happened.

As I gave Cairo a hug and ran my hands along his back and legs, I felt a lump. And then another lump. And a third.

"Whoa, boy? What's going on there?" I said as I rolled one of the lumps between my fingers. I'm no veterinarian, but I'd been around dogs long enough to know the lumps were not necessarily cause for concern. In all likelihood, they were merely benign cysts . . . fatty deposits. Dogs get those all the time. Then again, maybe it was a sign of something more serious, so I called the vet and got permission to bring Cairo in for an examination. The doc looked him over and determined the lumps to be nothing more than fluid-filled cysts. They would cause no long-term debilitation, and they were not a precursor to cancer; however, they did have to be drained. He lanced the cysts, cleaned up the wounds, and applied bandages. Cairo took all of this with his usual good spirits.

"He'll be fine," the doc said afterward. "Just take him home with you tonight and keep an eye on him."

*Uh-oh . . .*

It made sense. Like humans, dogs have a tendency to find surgical wounds sensitive and irritating. Unlike humans, dogs do not understand that they should not mess with their wounds, regardless of how minimal they might be. At the kennel, Cairo would be one of a dozen dogs. It would be easy for him to start scratching or biting his wounds without anyone noticing. Surely, the kennel manager would agree with the doc's assessment.

Then again, maybe not.

"No," the manager said. "He does not leave the kennel."

As I said, the kennel manager was also a SEAL master chief, so he outranked me. It wasn't like I could argue with him. Instead, I called my master chief and explained what the doctor had said: that it was not advisable for Cairo to return to the kennel that night. I asked him to call the kennel manager. The two of them could thrash it out—master chief to master chief.

The master chief in charge of the kennel was not persuaded. Maybe it was because he didn't like me; maybe he felt like his authority was being threatened; or maybe he was just a dick.

Regardless, despite knowing that the doc felt it was preferable for Cairo to be at home with me, being closely watched, the kennel manager made his decision.

*"Bring him back."*

I did as I was instructed. Cairo got through the night just fine and healed quickly, but that pretty much soured my relationship with the kennel manager for good. I'd still stop by once a week when I was in town. Sometimes, especially on holidays, I'd sneak in some food for Cairo. I talked with Angelo all the time and knew my dog was in good hands.

Meanwhile, my training was going well. As much as I missed Cairo, I'll admit that it was kind of liberating to not be tethered to a dog all day, every day. I was in a good frame of mind, sharpening my skills as an assaulter, and looking forward to the next deployment.

And then the Extortion went down.

It happened very early on the morning of August 6, 2011. A U.S. Army Chinook bearing the code name *Extortion 17* had just entered Afghanistan's Tangi Valley. There were thirty-eight personnel aboard the Extortion, including a SEAL contingent of seventeen men and one military working dog, thirteen additional U.S. soldiers, seven members of an Afghan fighting troop, and one interpreter. The Extortion 17 had been called in as an Initial Reaction Force (IRF) in support of a strike force that had flown into the valley aboard a sister Chinook known as *Extortion 16*.

The strike force, comprised mainly of fighters from the 75th Ranger Regiment, had been inserted into the central portion of the Tangi on a mission to track down a Taliban leader named Qari Tahir. In the aftermath of a firefight, the Extortion 17 IRF was dispatched to support the mission. As the Chinook descended to an altitude of fewer than three hundred feet over the valley floor, the fighters prepared to land and exit. Under the cover of night, they did not see a pair of insurgents hiding in the tall grass below, each of them armed with rocket-propelled grenade launchers.

To anyone who has experienced combat duty in Afghanistan or Iraq, RPGs are the stuff of nightmares. It may look like a comical mismatch—a guy in a man dress crouched in the weeds, with a six-foot tube resting on his shoulder, taking aim at a massive Chinook hovering a hundred feet or more in the sky overhead. But it is not a mismatch. While most RPGs do not find their mark, a few invariably do. And the results are often devastating.

So it was with Extortion 17 as an RPG tore into the Chinook's rotor blade, creating an explosion that killed everyone on board.

The Extortion disaster was the deadliest incident in the history of U.S. Special Operations, which meant that it was also the deadliest incident in SEAL history. It was also the largest number of American casualties created by a single event in the long history of the Afghanistan conflict.

It's no overstatement to say that the Extortion disaster rocked Naval Special Warfare. We all knew the risk of serving in combat, and we'd all lost close friends. It comes with the territory. But to lose so many good people—so many brothers—in a single night . . . to a single RPG . . .

It was overwhelming.

Everyone handles grief in their own way. If you're a soldier—and I suppose this is especially true of anyone who has served in Special Operations—you just swallow it back and get on with life; you pretend it doesn't affect you, because that's what is expected. I went to a bunch of funerals after the Extortion went down, cried with some of my teammates . . . and then went back to work. I'd lost friends before; this was no different. The wounds would heal.

But a strange thing happened. They didn't heal. Not right

away. They festered and kept me up at night. I'd sit alone in the living room, watching TV for hours on end. I'd find myself waking in the dark at 3:00 a.m., sweating, panicky, unable to fall back to sleep. To counter the insomnia and sleep deprivation, I turned to a tried-and-true formula: alcohol. A little at first, and then a lot.

I would never try to imply that I'd been squeaky clean when it came to social drinking. The truth is, SEALs, when not on deployment or in the middle of a heavy training trip, can party hard. I liked going out with the guys, having a good time, building camaraderie. It was part of the brotherhood, and I won't deny it or make excuses for it. I enjoyed it. We all did.

But I'm not talking about that kind of drinking. I'm talking about coming home from work and immediately cracking open a beer, all by yourself. And then another one. And another. And then eventually the evening grows late and you switch to something harder, and the hours go on and on, and eventually you wake up the next morning, on the couch or in a chair, with your head pounding and your stomach churning.

Every day.

The fact that a significant number of American military personnel—particularly those who see combat duty—suffer from post-traumatic stress, combined with or exacerbated by traumatic brain injuries, is no longer much of a secret. Nor is their tendency to self-medicate. As long as you're still wearing the uniform, options are limited. If you fail a drug test, your career can end quickly. (An exception is Ambien, the use of which is so accepted in the treatment of jet lag and insomnia that it can and does lead to abuse.) But no one tests for alcohol; drinking is just part of the culture. It's not a problem . . . until it is.

That's how I dealt with the Extortion disaster. That's how I dealt with grief. It was like a slow burn rather than an explosion. Eventually, the damage was noticeable. For one thing, my hair began falling out. Not like a few strands but giant clumps like I was going through chemo. I had thick hair in some places, bald patches in others. This was not a hereditary thing; it was much weirder and more sinister. Next, my fingernails began cracking and falling out. Not just the tips, either—entire nails. I didn't know what was going on. I had always been in such great physical shape and so happy-go-lucky and confident. Now?

I was falling apart.

My deteriorating appearance, combined with a sudden inability to do my job as well I had done it in the past, led to an intervention of sorts. I'd been late for work a few times, and I reeked of booze early in the morning and was obviously hungover. There is a line you don't cross in Special Operations, and that line is the one separating those who can do their jobs, under any circumstances, from those who cannot. I was getting dangerously close to that line. Thankfully, I was lucky to have some good friends who stepped in and called me on my bullshit from a place of love and concern.

"Cheese, this isn't like you," one of them said one day. "You need to get some help."

I didn't put up much resistance. I loved these guys; the look of disappointment I would see on their faces—*Come on, man; get your shit together*—was almost too much to bear. I knew I had problems, and if I didn't address those problems, I was going to lose my career, my health . . . everything.

I agreed to enter an outpatient program to address not just my drinking but the reasons behind it. Honestly, it wasn't all that complicated to me—*Just stop drinking yourself to sleep every night, you idiot!*—but obviously my own approach wasn't working out very well. So I worked the program, cleaned up my act, and thirty days later went back to my team. Physically, I felt better, although it took a while for my hair and fingernails to grown back. The hair loss, they said, was stress-induced alopecia.

The fingernails? I don't know what they call that, but it also was triggered by stress.

Returning to active duty wasn't exactly going to cut down on the stress in my life, but it did make me happy. I needed to get back to work with my teammates, and now that I had stopped drinking and gotten my head on straight, I was looking forward to the next deployment. *Just get back out there*, I figured, *and everything will be fine.* Kill a few bad guys and all will be right with the world, or at least my little corner of it.

# Chapter 21

When I returned to Afghanistan for my next deployment, in the spring of 2012, dogs remained an integral part of my working life. Unfortunately, none of those dogs was Cairo.

As penance for my drinking issues, I was assigned to a team that was responsible for training new members of the Afghan Special Operations. I don't want to sound bitter or ungrateful here. The fact is, I had screwed up, and I had no one to blame but myself. By the time we deployed, I was in great physical shape again. My mood was good, and I was eager to get back to work, but the powers that be decided I had to prove myself worthy, and part of that process included a stint assisting with the Afghan special forces.

In general, I didn't have a lot of respect for the Afghan military. Their fighters didn't much like to fight, and their training was, to put it mildly, substandard. There were exceptions, but I think the prevailing opinion among U.S. soldiers, especially in combat, was that the Afghan military was, at best, not much help, and at worst, a liability. But the long-term goal was for the country to wage its own battle against the Taliban, and that wasn't going to happen without a lot of help and support from the United States military. This extended to Special Operations, which is where I came in. I was part of a group of instructors that also included another SEAL, a handful of Army Rangers, and a few private contractors. I don't know if any of us were particularly happy to be there—we all would have preferred to be in the thick of the fight—and I didn't ask their stories. Objectively speaking, it was an important job; someone had to do it.

I just didn't want to be that someone.

But if there was one thing I learned while coming up through the ranks of Naval Special Warfare, it was this: there are no shortcuts. It was perfectly reasonable that I had been held accountable for my actions. The fastest route to resuming my role as an active operator was to do a professional job on this assignment, and that's what I did.

As with most unpleasant things, the anticipation was worse than the reality. For one thing, everyone in the Afghan special forces was at least a real soldier, with advanced training and skills and a legitimate desire to join the conflict. This was not true of the Afghan military as a whole. It would have been easy to take an elitist or condescending attitude about the whole thing, but that wasn't going to help anyone. I'd gotten this far in my Naval career in part by telling myself, repeatedly, "Just do your damn job."

This was no different.

A month or two went by painlessly enough, and pretty soon, I rejoined my squadron on deployment at Forward Operating Base Shank, located in Logar Province in eastern Afghanistan. It felt good to be back with my teammates, going out on ops, hunting down bad guys, doing the kind of work I had been trained to do. If there was any letdown following Operation Neptune Spear, I didn't notice it. I mean, the rules of engagement continued to change and constrict, but there was no perceptible diminishing of professionalism or enthusiasm among the guys on the ground. I still loved my job, and I was grateful to have been given a second chance. And I liked the freedom that came with being an assaulter as opposed to a dog handler.

If I needed a "Cairo fix," I didn't have to go far. He'd been deployed to Logar, as well, to be utilized as a spare dog on-site, available for short- or long-term duty on a moment's notice. I stopped by to see him and Angelo once a week or so, and Cairo was always affectionate and playful. I do think he missed me, but we each had a job to do, and for now, those jobs did not overlap.

In mid-June, we got word of a high-value target hiding out in a desert compound. Nothing strange about that. It was a mission that in many ways was no different from a hundred other ops . . . or a thousand. Same afternoon briefing, same nighttime helicopter ride, same landing in the middle of nowhere, same hike into the target.

Including support personnel, we had close to thirty people out there in the desert as the compound came into view. There was an unusual amount of radio chatter that night, including a conversation indicating the enemy knew we were on our way. Now, sometimes they would say this kind of stuff strictly as a deflective device—to make us think they were prepared when actually that wasn't the case. It didn't really matter; we weren't going to call off an op just because the bad guys knew we were coming. We might shift our tactics somewhat, but it wasn't about to scare us off. Sometimes we'd share misleading or inaccurate information just to misdirect them.

We hiked for a couple of miles before the compound came into view. It was a smallish compound, just two modest buildings, each two stories in height. Pretty much a standard Afghan desert setup. Using terrain for cover, we followed a rough, barely visible path to a distance of maybe one hundred meters from the compound. My team took cover in a shallow ditch while waiting for orders. As always, we were patient, careful. Once it was time to move, we did so with expediency and commitment.

After a few minutes, the team leader ordered me and another guy, Tommy, toward the second building.

"Cheese, I want you guys on the roof to hold security. Okay?"

"Got it."

We rushed to the building and held our positions, then began creeping slowly along its length. Suddenly, shots rang out from above us. The crackle of automatic gunfire.

*Pop-pop-pop!*

I figured the gunfire was most likely coming from a second-story window. Someone had seen us approaching. Immediately, Tommy, who was a few feet away from me and had a better angle, returned fire. I held tight to the outside wall so that I wouldn't throw him off in any way. This was standard combat protocol. As soon as he stopped firing, I sprinted back and out into the surrounding terrain to get a better look. Soon enough, another operator, Curt, joined me, along with an explosives ordnance disposal (EOD) specialist named Richard. The three of us stayed there for a minute, fanned out in a row, maybe ten or fifteen feet separating each of us. I kept my rifle trained on the window, just waiting for someone to pop up, if only for a fleeting moment.

"Come on, fuck face . . . show yourself."

The next thing I heard was the sound of breaking glass. Like a window shattering, but in a very specific way. When someone sprays gunfire through a window, it basically disintegrates. This was more like someone throwing a rock through a window. I knew instantly what it meant, because I'd heard it before. A thought ran through my head just before everything went momentarily dark.

*Grenade . . .*

I don't know how much time passed—probably no more than ten or fifteen seconds. There was a crushing pain in my lower back, as if someone had walloped me with a baseball bat, and then a momentary loss of awareness, followed by a concussive haze. Next thing I knew, I was on my knees, holding my rifle, surveying the field for damage. I looked up at the window but saw nothing. As I started to move, I felt a blistering pain in my lower back. And I could hear Richard moaning. As my vision cleared, I could see that he was in rough shape. He'd been blown several meters away, and his uniform had been badly charred. I looked around and saw Curt, who appeared to be uninjured, but I couldn't tell for sure.

In my memory, I stood up and squeezed off a few rounds, put some fire right through the same window where the grenade had passed. But memory is an unreliable thing when you've just been blown up. As I watched the grainy drone surveillance video a few days later, what I saw was a guy rocked by a grenade: standing, but not responding. My gun remained low and at my side. In my hands, but unused.

This much I can confirm: the scene was somewhat chaotic after the blast. I stumbled back out into the field and began looking for . . . well, I'm not sure what I was looking for. We quickly had guys all around the compound and on the roof of the building as we moved into full assault mode. I could hear shots being fired as I lurched out into the field, and I remember thinking, *You're kind of unprotected here, dude. What are you doing?*

Good question. No answer.

Eventually, I made my way toward some guys who were holding security on the perimeter.

"You okay, Cheese?" one of them asked.

"Uh . . . not sure. I think I got hit."

Soon enough, a corpsman was on the scene, pushing me to

the ground and pulling at my uniform and looking for wounds. This guy was awesome. His name was Anthony. He was a SEAL who hadn't yet gone through the Training Team but talked of it all the time. A few years later, he finally got his chance. Tragically, he drowned while training on his own for one of the underwater tests.

Anthony was one hell of a corpsman, incredibly calm and focused under pressure. I don't care who you are—a civilian or a SEAL—when you get shot or blown up, there is an overwhelming sense of disorientation, not to mention pain. I had no idea what was wrong with me, and I wasn't sure I wanted to know.

"Drop your pants!" Anthony calmly instructed.

"Huh?"

He pushed me to the ground.

"On your knees. Let's go!"

I did as I was told. I felt kind of silly out there in the open, naked ass sticking up in the air, but he was the corpsman, and I trusted him completely. I could feel his hands examining my lower back and butt, both of which were intensely sore.

"You got shrapnel in your ass, Cheese, but you'll be okay. No arterial bleed or anything like that. You're going to need some work, but you'll live."

As Anthony cleaned my wounds and stuffed some gauze into the holes, I felt something trickling down my face and into my mouth. The metallic taste told me what it was.

"Hey, man," I said. "Think I'm bleeding at this end, too."

Anthony quickly moved from stern to stem. The blood on my face freaked me out a bit, because I knew I'd suffered a concussion—my ears were ringing, and I had a pulsating headache—and thought maybe I'd picked up an open head wound, as well. This was my first combat injury, and what they say is true: it's a complete mind fuck.

"Yeah, you've got some shrapnel up here, too," Anthony said, making it sound as benign as a bee sting. "We'll get you cleaned up. You'll be okay."

I started to get woozy and worried I was going to pass out in the middle of a mission. But as it turned out, the mission was basically over. Curt, as it turned out, had also taken shrapnel from the grenade blast, so we now had three guys down and weren't even in the building yet. When the resistance is that strong—when the bad guys start chucking grenades at us and a few of them find their mark, we change tack. In this case, that meant calling in a bird to evacuate the wounded and another to bomb the building.

"Everybody get down," I could hear one of the team leaders say after we had moved a safe distance away. "We're going to drop the building with Hellfires."

I remember seeing the Apache helicopter overhead, armed with AGM-114 missiles—Hellfires—and thinking, *Fuck that, I'm not getting down. I've been on the ground all night*. I stood up, crouched over, my back aching and my head pounding, and listened as the bombs exploded in the distance.

The first stop was Logar. The docs and nurses triaged us quickly, determined my wounds to be the least in need of immediate attention (which was correct), and wheeled the other two guys in ahead of me. Richard was charred on the legs, back, and side from shrapnel, and he seemed to be woozy. Curt had a small hole in his chest, which looked nasty but was actually a pretty quick fix. As is often the case, though, the worst damage wasn't immediately visible. This was true of me, as well. I was wheeled into the medical tent on a gurney, stripped of my clothes, and given a thorough assessment. There was shrapnel in my buttocks, lower back, leg, arm, and face. They told me I'd be fine, put me asleep, and went about the business of cleaning me up.

It was astounding to see and experience the damage that could be done by a single grenade lobbed through a closed window from close range. In a matter of seconds, it had cut down three members of one of the most elite fighting units on the planet. A grenade is an impressively effective little tool, spraying white-hot metal in all directions when it explodes. Even the tiniest of fragments can burn through clothing and body armor and embed deep within the victim's tissue. And there's no way to get it all out. The docs removed what they could while I was under anesthesia, but the smaller fragments they left behind, knowing full well that I'd be squeezing them out like pimples for months to come—in the shower or on the toilet seat. Eventually, my body would eject just about all the foreign matter; anything left behind was probably harmless.

Over the course of the next few days, Richard and I were shipped to a larger base hospital in Germany for further evaluation and recovery. Curt appeared to recover quickly and remained on active duty, but he soon developed complications and saw his deployment come to an end.

The concern at that time was basic wound care. Keep everything neat and clean, avoid infection, get back to work. I had a dozen or more wounds; the smallest were like bug bites; the largest, on my ass cheeks, were the size of quarters, deep and painful. I spent nearly two weeks lying flat on my stomach, with drains inserted in my buttocks to keep the toxins running in the right direction. If that sounds awful, well, it really wasn't. The hospital staff was attentive and compassionate; they appreciated our service and wanted to give us the best possible treatment. I was uncomfortable, for sure, but the pain meds did their job, and I got to hang out with my fellow wounded buddy as we commiserated and told stupid jokes and rested up for what we thought would be an imminent return to duty.

We were wrong.

For all three of us, that grenade signaled the end of our deployment and the beginning of a long struggle with rehabilitation and recovery. I sure as hell had no idea what I was in for. When you hear the word *shrapnel*, you don't realize what it means—the weeks and months of shuffling around like an old man, attached to tubes and machines that suction off fluids and prevent infection; the medication; the nagging sense that something isn't quite right, even as your injuries appear to be healing.

From Germany, I was transferred to Walter Reed National Military Medical Center in Bethesda, Maryland. Amazing place. Great doctors, nurses, technicians, and rehabilitation staff. I didn't come across a single person at Walter Reed who seemed anything less than 100 percent committed to their job, and respectful and appreciative of anyone who was injured in the line of duty. My next stop, at a hospital in Virginia, was less impressive overall, but I did have one great nurse who made the experience tolerable by helping me to understand exactly what was happening at all times and by generally just being a pleasant and compassionate person, which is really the most important thing when you've been recovering from battlefield injuries for more than a month.

Eventually, I went home. The navy flew in my father to spend some time with me, which was a big help, because there were still a lot of things I couldn't do for myself like making sure my wounds were completely clean. With persistence and daily rehab, I started to improve. I kicked the pain meds without any trouble. Given the issues I'd already had with alcohol, I was a little worried about the weaning process, but it went smoothly enough, and before long, I started to feel like my old self again. I was twenty-eight years old and figured I had at least a few good years left as an operator.

I was mistaken.

# Chapter 22

The migraines started a few months after I got home, just as I was beginning to feel strong and healthy from a physical standpoint. I couldn't figure out what was happening or why it was happening. The wounds had mostly healed, the soreness in my back and buttocks had diminished to the point where I was ready to start training again, and suddenly, out of the blue, came crippling headaches like nothing I had experienced before.

Migraines are another of those maladies that are unfairly dismissed as a mere inconvenience, as opposed to the soul-crushing experience they can be. This, I think, is because a lot of people will get a bad headache once in a while and describe it as a "migraine." I might have been guilty of that in the past; maybe not. I don't really recall. I do know that the headaches I began experiencing in the fall of 2012 were uniquely debilitating and painful. They would come on without warning, at any time of the day, usually starting as a soreness in the back of my neck before creeping inexorably upward, crawling across the back of my skull and toward the frontal lobe, until it felt as though my entire head was in a vise grip.

I couldn't think straight.

I couldn't see straight.

All I could do was retreat to the couch or the bedroom—sometimes with a stop at the bathroom to vomit—and sleep away the day. It was like having the worst hangover in the world, when you've done nothing to merit the punishment.

In the beginning, the migraines were random and infrequent, maybe once every week or two. Then they began making more frequent visits: twice a week, three times a week . . . four or even five times a week. Great, yawning stretches of time during which I could barely function. And other stretches where I felt okay, although not quite myself. It wasn't long before I was shuttled off to a job that was physically less demanding, working as an instructor for guys on the Training Team. In theory, this would allow me to have more time to commit to the many doctors' appointments that clogged my schedule. But even the instructor's job was frequently more than I could handle, especially when combined with training trips. I was lucky to have great bosses, guys who had known me for a long time and who knew that something was seriously wrong. Hell, I'd always been one of the most reliable guys in the squadron. I wasn't a superstar or anything, but I wasn't a malcontent or a slacker, either. I didn't complain. I didn't get hurt or sick or injured. I just plugged away, day after day.

Now?

I was a mess.

There were days when I'd be stumbling around, one eye closed to guard against the withering effects of sunlight, trying to do my job, and my boss would look at me like I was dying.

"Go home, Cheese. Take care of yourself."

"I'm sorry, man. I don't know what's wrong."

He would nod compassionately and send me on my way. And for the rest of the day, I'd curl up in a ball while miniature blacksmiths pounded away inside my skull.

Migraines are difficult to properly diagnose and treat, as they can be triggered by a variety of factors, both physiological and psychological. I was convinced at first that my headaches were primarily a delayed consequence of the grenade blast in Afghanistan. And maybe they were. But I also understood the power of post-traumatic stress, the havoc it can wreak on your body as well as your mind, and the danger of pushing it all down inside to someplace where you think it can't touch you. Except eventually it all boils up to the surface again. It's a vicious cycle: stress and emotional upheaval will cause a physical symptom like a headache. The headaches then become chronic, and the chronic pain causes deepening depression. And it won't stop until you figure out a way to deal with all the shit in your life. A traumatic brain injury adds another layer of complication— indeed, in some cases it may even be the very first layer— making the puzzle even more challenging.

A decorated SEAL is not supposed to suffer from depression, because mental health issues are a sign of weakness, right? But that's just bullshit. The truth is, I'm not the only guy who has struggled with these issues—maybe because of the stress associated with the job, or maybe because of injuries that lead to self-medication, or because of undiagnosed traumatic brain injury. In my case, I think it was a combination of factors, although I still believe that TBI was the dominant factor. I've done a lot of research and worked with many doctors and therapists. There is enough evidence out there to support the notion that years of combat duty—with close exposure to thousands of concussive blasts, each door being breached, each Hellfire dropped, serving as stealth concussion, with a price to be paid later—has a cumulative and degenerative effect on the human brain. And the odds of developing symptoms increase if you experience an obvious head injury. I don't know if I have chronic traumatic encephalopathy (CTE), and I suppose no one will

ever know until they do an autopsy after I'm gone, but I do believe that something happened to my brain when that grenade
went off, and it changed me.

I'd spent most of my life acting like nothing bothered me. In
fact, almost nothing did bother me. Now I lost my temper easily.
I had no patience. And my memory! I couldn't remember a phone
number five seconds after it was given to me. I'd forget instruc-
tions or miss appointments. Names I'd known well suddenly became elusive. I had trouble with the simplest of mental tasks. I
can imagine all of this is scary enough when you're eighty years
old and shuffling toward dementia, but at twenty-eight?

I was confused. I was angry.

Let's be honest: I was terrified.

There was a lot of shit I'd either left unprocessed or was
still trying to process. Like the fact that the raid on which I'd
been injured had turned into a public relations nightmare, with
the Afghan government claiming that the compound we had
bombed had been the site of a wedding, and that civilians, including women and children, were killed in the assault. I wasn't
part of the cleanup effort following the raid, but I did speak to
some of the guys who were involved, and they said there was
no indication that any women or children were killed. As for
a wedding? Well, it was one o'clock in the morning. And who
throws grenades out the window during a wedding?

Regardless, some blame was accepted; a formal letter of
apology was issued by an American general. When I heard that,
I remember thinking, *Huh? We're apologizing for killing a
bunch of bad guys? How come no one apologized to me or my
buddies? We all got blown up.*

We did receive Purple Hearts, which was nice, although a
Purple Heart is not something any serviceperson actively seeks
for obvious reasons. I also received a commendation from the
same American general, thanking me for my service. I found it

more amusing than anything else, especially since it had been addressed to Petty Officer Chesney, but the word *officer* had been scratched out. You could literally see where it had been removed! So instead, the letter was addressed to "Petty Chesney," which was kind of funny. I'm sure it was just a stamped signature and someone acting on the general's behalf must have known I was an enlisted man but was unfamiliar with the term *petty officer*. An army oversight, no doubt.

At the time, I didn't think any of this was a big deal, but maybe it bothered me more than I realized. Maybe it was one of many factors contributing to an overall decline in mental and physical well-being. I just know that I felt like my life was spinning out of control.

There were other contributing incidents, like the death of Nic Checque, my closest friend on the team. Nic was the one who had pranked me when I'd bolted from jumpmaster school before Operation Neptune Spear, but our friendship went way beyond that kind of good-natured nonsense. We went through BUD/S together, were drafted by the same squadron together, and went on countless missions together. Nic was the closest thing I had to a brother.

He was a hell of a fighter, too, honorable and courageous and skilled. Nic had been transferred to a different squadron to help fill vacancies after the Extortion 17 disaster. On December 8, 2012, Nic was part of a secret mission to rescue an American physician from a heavily guarded compound in eastern Afghanistan. As the first man through the door of a one-room hut where the hostage was being held, Nic was fatally wounded by a Taliban guard, but his actions allowed other team members to complete the mission and bring the American hostage home alive.

For his bravery, Nic posthumously was promoted to the rank of chief; he also received the Navy Cross, the navy's second-highest award for valor. One of Nic's teammates, Ed Byers, received the Medal of Honor.

I was home in Virginia when I got the news. It was terrible, but strangely familiar. By now, I was growing accustomed to hearing about the passing of my teammates. I'd been to enough funerals and hugged enough teary-eyed parents and wives and girlfriends. But this was different. Nic wasn't just another SEAL. He was my best friend.

By the spring of 2013, I was in rough shape. In addition to the headaches and other symptoms, my hair had fallen out again after Nic's passing. It had been nearly a year since I'd been injured, and I had slowly come to the realization that I'd likely experienced my last deployment. Although I continued to work on the base, primarily as an instructor, a lot of my time was devoted to chasing a diagnosis for my ongoing physical and mental health issues. Frankly, I didn't care about the diagnosis; I just wanted some relief. But the treatment, such as it was, sometimes seemed worse than the illness it was designed to mitigate.

As was the case with the care and rehabilitation I received following my injury in Afghanistan, I was given access to a number of earnest and talented physicians and therapists and nurses. I also saw a few who seemed disinterested and bored. They could never seem to reach a consensus about what was happening to me. Was it physical? Mental? Both? I can't fault their effort or their willingness to throw a ton of shit at the wall, hoping something would stick. I had never been a new age kind of guy, but some of the alternative therapies—acupuncture, meditation, stress-relief breathing—seemed to offer temporary but noticeable relief.

Most pharmaceutical therapies were, at best, ineffective. Hey, I was a complicated case, and I don't want to suggest that medication can't help, or hasn't helped, a lot of people who have a similar constellation of symptoms. But for me, the endless pushing of pills became dispiriting, exhausting, debilitating. I tried every type of migraine medication you can imagine. A few helped, at least for a little while. Most did not. They all had terrible side effects. Some would knock me out; others would make me jittery or anxious or sick to my stomach. Virtually all of them induced a sense of brain fog that made it hard to function. It sucked. But I guess, for a lot of people, it beats the skull-crushing pain of a migraine.

Even worse were the psychiatric meds prescribed to alleviate the symptoms of PTSD: the anxiety and depression and moodiness. I *hated* those! Made me feel like I was someone else. Not better, not happier, not in less pain. Just . . . different.

I would never suggest I was mistreated in any way. To their credit, every hospital and treatment team approached my case from an interdisciplinary angle; they never suggested the symptoms were "all in my head" (even though they were, if you know what I mean). They did their best. It just didn't help very much.

You know what did help? Stopping by the kennel to play with Cairo. I know that probably sounds crazy, but it's the absolute truth. Cairo was eight years old by this point, and while he had clearly lost a step (or two), he remained one of the smartest and most reliable dogs in the program. Some dogs lose interest or experience a change in temperament, or they suffer so badly from the effects of old age or injury that they can't do the job any longer. Despite nearly getting killed in the line of duty and serving his country for more than five years, this had not happened to Cairo. By this point in his life, he required little maintenance to keep up to date on his training. He had been around the block so many times, and seen so much, that you could plug him into almost any scenario and get outstanding results.

For that reason, Cairo's retirement was continually pushed

back. But it wasn't the only reason. I heard from more than one person that Cairo might never be allowed to leave the base because of the fame that had come with taking part in Operation Neptune Spear. Now, on the one hand, I sort of understood this. Naval Special Warfare is a highly secretive organization; there is a code of silence and selflessness that comes with serving as a Navy SEAL. The bin Laden mission was the most notable operation in the history of Naval Special Warfare, and the last thing anyone wanted was for the famous Cairo to be paraded around as some sort of spectacle—you know, appearing on talk shows or whatever.

On the other hand . . . who cares? It's not like Cairo was going to give up any intel about the mission.

I think the navy was just concerned about too much attention being placed on Cairo, which in turn would lead to questions about the mission and the organization in general, as opposed to letting it retreat into the shadows to eventually take its rightful place in history. The easiest way to deal with this concern was to let Cairo work as long as possible and then live out his final days at the kennel, which would not have been as horrible as it probably sounds. As the elder statesman of the kennel, he was not required to work as much as the primary dogs, but he was well cared for. He was such a good-hearted dog that even guys who were not handlers loved spending time with him, so he never lacked for companionship.

Still, I couldn't help but think that he had earned a better life—an opportunity to chill at home with Dad, eating steak a couple of times a week, running loose in the yard or at the beach, watching television, sleeping wherever the hell he wanted to sleep. Cairo had served his country honorably. He had saved my life and the lives of others. I didn't know how many years he had left—Malinois generally have a life expectancy of twelve to fifteen years, but obviously Cairo had experienced far more stress than a typical dog. Regardless, it seemed only right that he get a chance to have a few happy and relaxing years. Hell, thoroughbred horses win a few big races and are rewarded with years, if not decades, of sex and food and sleep. Not a bad retirement. Cairo had been an integral part of the biggest mission in SEAL history. Didn't he deserve . . . something?

I felt like he needed me, and I sure as hell needed him. As it became increasingly apparent that neither one of us was ever again going to set foot in a combat zone, I found myself drawn to Cairo even more than I had been in the past. I'd stop by the kennel two or three times a week, sometimes every day, just to give him a few treats or talk with him, to scratch his belly and play fetch. Sometimes I'd bring him to the office and let him hang out with me. He wasn't technically my dog—he was still a spare dog, eligible for work—but since most of his time was devoted to lounging around the kennel or doing light training, no one said anything about my frequent visits. Eventually, we all knew he'd be coming home with me. It was only a matter of time. Or so I hoped. In the meantime, I settled for visitation rights. I didn't get to take him home at night, but sometimes I would pick him up and drive to the beach, where there was room to run and play. He seemed to like that. I did, too.

Although I was still stuck in a cycle of medication and hospital visits and migraines and depression—all while trying to hold down my job as an instructor—spending time with Cairo proved to be the best therapy anyone could have ordered. It's very difficult to convey what he meant to me. I had a Doberman named Sterling at home who was a gentle and loveable fellow, and I was in the process of adopting a Malinois puppy. But Cairo was special. We'd been through some extraordinary times together; and like any handler, I did not think of him merely as a dog. There were times at home when I would find myself sifting through memorabilia, photos of old buddies, some long departed, and I'd break down crying. That wasn't me. I'd never been that way. I'd think back to BUD/S, and how I was the guy who never let anything bother him. I was the guy laughing at the insanity of it all while other guys were crying and quitting.

And now?

Other guys had left the navy and were doing their jobs, raising families, going to school, starting businesses—multitasking like crazy—and I was having trouble functioning. I'd look at some of these guys—my friends!—and think, *That guy was me. We were the same. Why can't I get my shit together?*

Something was very wrong . . . and I just couldn't put my finger on it.

But Cairo helped. Sometimes, after a crying jag or a panic attack or a migraine, I'd stop by the kennel to see him, and instantly a sense of calm would overtake me. And it seemed like the same thing would happen to Cairo.

"Yeah, buddy. Dad is here. I'll get you home—promise. Just be patient."

Whenever someone leaves his job as an operator and takes a different role within Naval Special Warfare, he can naturally begin to lose touch with his teammates. Life goes on, as they say. I was stuck in Virginia, working as an instructor, spinning from one doctor's office or hospital to another, while most of my buddies were still on the treadmill of training and deployment. I missed them, and I missed my old job, but there was nothing I could do about it. There was no way I could go on deployment while suffering from chronic migraines; I might have gotten someone killed.

Life didn't suck completely, thanks mainly to a young woman named Natalie Kelley. She was working as a server at a coffee shop in town. She was friendly and pretty, with a persistent smile and a disarming manner. I liked her right away, but

I'm not exactly the aggressive or confident type when it comes to meeting women, so things moved kind of slowly at first. Natalie's roommate dated one of my friends at the time, so we got to know each other, and I think people put in a good word for me, since Natalie was a bit wary of dating navy guys. She'd moved to Virginia from Orlando and had heard a lot of stories from friends and acquaintances who had lived in the area for a while. But I got lucky. She thought my shyness was cute, rather than creepy, and eventually she approached me.

"Hey, Will. Would you want to go out sometime?"

"You mean, like, on a date or something?"

She laughed.

"Yeah . . . or something."

I shrugged, smiled. "Sure. That would be great."

Natalie came along at a point when I was about as low as I could be, and she didn't run the other way. Instead, Natalie became my partner; together, we navigated the turbulent waters of mental health care and rehabilitation and eventually medical retirement from the navy. She understood my attachment to Cairo (even though she did not know of his background or that he had any role on the bin Laden mission; only that he had been my dog), and not only fell in love with him but helped me bring him home. I had a lot of good days when Natalie and I first got together, but I had a lot of bad days, too. And she hung in there for me.

In the late fall of 2013, I got word that Cairo was soon going to be retired. It seemed overdue. He'd served long enough. Cairo was eight and a half years old, and his most recent deployment had been cut short because he was suffering from debilitating periodontal disease. No dog is perfect, and while Cairo came close, his one genetic weakness, revealed only after he'd been on the job for a while, was bad teeth. By the time he was retired, seven of his original teeth had been pulled or broken, and he suffered from chronic halitosis—or, should I say, everyone around him suffered.

As a side note; it's long been rumored that combat assault dogs are sometimes fitted with titanium teeth, either to replace teeth that have fallen out, or even prophylactically. The truth is, any crown or implant will be weaker and less effective than the original tooth, so the idea of ripping out a dog's perfectly healthy teeth and outfitting him with a new grill is just ridiculous, even though it would surely give the dog a truly badass appearance. As for replacing bad teeth with titanium implants, well, I heard that it happened with some dogs, but I never saw it with any of the dogs in our unit. It sure didn't happen with Cairo. He finished his career with a few broken teeth and several holes where teeth used to be.

Rather than waiting for the wheels of military bureaucracy to finish grinding, I made it clear that I still wanted to take Cairo home as soon as he was officially retired.

"He's my dog," I explained. "Always will be. He belongs with me."

I didn't expect any pushback. Now that I was stationed in Virginia and no longer subject to deployments, what logical reason could there be to deny my request? It was still possible that Cairo might not be released from the kennel at all, given his fame and stature, but I'd heard that was unlikely. The navy actually did want Cairo to have a good home. And what better home than mine? It all seemed so obvious . . . so logical.

But I didn't get a response right away. Instead, I kept visiting Cairo, with greater frequency and for longer periods of time. The more time I spent with him, the more I wanted to take him home. It was the right thing to do—for both of us. I figured I would just have to play the waiting game and that eventually everything would be resolved.

It wasn't quite that simple.

One afternoon while I was visiting the kennel, I found out that I wasn't the only member of the Cairo fan club.

"You have some competition," I was told.

"What are you talking about?"

"There are a couple of other guys who want to take him home."

I did not respond well to this news. Cairo was a terrific dog, and I could see him having a strong impact on anyone who worked with him on deployment—or even at the kennel, for that matter. But I was Cairo's first handler and had been through two long deployments with him, as well as years of training. He had saved my life by nearly sacrificing his. I had held him in my arms as he nearly bled to death on the battlefield. We were profoundly connected.

I needed him now, and he needed me. It was as simple as that.

Except, of course, that it wasn't.

I formally applied to be Cairo's permanent caretaker. This was a process that, true to all things in the military, involved reams of paperwork. I put together my application and then I sat around and waited. As the weeks and months went by, I became frustrated. I was still dealing with chronic pain and migraines. I was unhappy with work and missed my friends. I felt like Cairo would ease some of that pain. I visited him several times a week. After a while, I started to get these crazy thoughts. I'd sit there at the kennel and talk to Cairo, and the stuff that came out was . . . well, not exactly rational.

"You know what, buddy? I'm just gonna take you out of here. Screw 'em. We'll run off somewhere and hide. Just me and you."

This was pure fantasy, but it became, for a while, one of the persistent thoughts in my head. I'm not just taking about a daydream, either. I made *plans*.

Needless to say, this would not have worked out well for anyone. Not for me, not for the navy, and not for Cairo. And I never would have gone through with it. But it's an indication of my emotional state at the time that I even thought about it.

A few months after I submitted the paperwork, there was movement. The guys who ran the dog program were charged with conducting interviews of each person who had applied to adopt Cairo (there were three of us, I believe). The interview wasn't exactly rigorous, a lot of basic questions to ensure that Cairo would be cared for in a safe and appropriate manner.

**Q:** Where will he sleep?
**A:** With me.

**Q:** What will he eat?
**A:** Mostly steak, but whatever he wants.

**Q:** What are you going to do with him?
**A:** Well, pretty much everything. It's not like I got a lot else going on.

**Q:** Why do you want him?
**A:** Because I love him. He's my dog.

There were other questions, none of which were hard for me to answer. They opted not to do a home visit, but I figured that didn't mean much because some of them were friends of mine and had been to my house in the past, anyway. Frankly, I didn't know whether they would look favorably on the fact that Natalie and I already had two dogs living with us. I hoped that it was a good sign. I had friends who worked at the kennel; most of them knew me and liked me. But I'm sure there were also a couple of guys who did not like me. Assigning Cairo a permanent home in his old age should not have been a popularity contest, but that's life, I guess. I just hoped that I had enough votes in my favor.

The interview lasted about thirty to forty-five minutes and was conducted by someone I considered to be a friend. But he did not tip his hand at all. Instead, he was polite but formal, which was fine. He had a job to do. I respected his position. I also felt like he had my back. When it was over, we stood and shook hands.

"How long before you make a decision?" I asked.

He smiled, shook his head. "You know the navy, Will. Things don't move quickly."

I laughed. "Copy that."

A few days went by. Nothing. A week. Two weeks. A month.

Almost every day, I stopped by the kennel to see Cairo and to hand-feed him or play with him. He was approaching nine years old, and although he still looked lean and fit, he did seem to be slowing down a bit. He wasn't quite as eager to run around or play. His mood was fine; he just seemed to be a little more laid-back. I presumed he was just starting to feel his age. It was no surprise. Once in a while, I'd chat up my friends at the kennel, ask them if they had heard anything about the adoption process. The answer was always the same.

"Nothing yet. Sorry."

I tried not to make a pest of myself. For one thing, I didn't want my nagging to have a negative impact on the process. Second, this was life in the military—everything moved at a glacial pace. Chances are, whatever decision was being made, it was happening at a level (or two) above my buddies at the kennel. I'm sure everyone wanted what was best for Cairo, but there were political factors in play, and the possibility that common sense and compassion might not win out caused me some sleepless nights. A dozen years earlier, when I'd first enlisted, almost everything rolled off my back. That's how I made it through BUD/S. But whether I wanted to admit it or not, I had changed, and not necessarily for the better. Multiple deployments, injuries, brain trauma, migraines, PTSD, depression—all of these had conspired to create a guy who was more anxious and short-tempered and generally less happy than the kid who had graduated as a member of BUD/S Class 246. I hated to admit any of this, but it was the inescapable truth.

There was no way I would ever get my old job back, but I wanted my life back. I wanted my personality back. Cairo was a part of that deal.

Finally, one afternoon in April 2014, I got a phone call at work. It was my friend from the kennel, the same guy who had conducted the interview.

"Hey, Cheese . . . the orders came through."

"For Cairo?"

He laughed. "Yeah, why else would I be calling?"

I paused for a moment to let it sink in. I have never been the most emotional guy, but at that moment, holding the phone, I could barely catch my breath.

"He's mine?"

"Sure looks that way. You just have to come by and finish the paperwork."

"On my way," I said. Then I dropped the office phone, grabbed my cell, and typed out a quick text to Natalie. My hands were shaking as I fumbled over the keypad.

*He's coming home!*

I checked out of work early, drove straight to the kennel, and began filling out the required forms. Not surprisingly, there was a lot of paperwork. You can't requisition a new stapler in the navy without filling out a book. Adopting the most famous military working dog in history? Well, that takes some time.

Not that I cared. I ran through every page as efficiently as possible, signed all the forms, promised to do everything that was required (no breeding, no giving him away, no parading him around as some sort of trophy . . . and a dozen other stipulations that weren't even on my radar). Among the most interesting of these was an agreement to change Cairo's name. That's right. Apparently, the navy was so concerned about Cairo's fame, and the attention he might receive in the public realm, that the paperwork accompanying his release referred to him by a pseudonym:

Carlos.

I sympathized with the navy's sensitivity in this regard, and obviously I was no stranger to the SEAL's commitment to secrecy and faceless, nameless service. Still . . . Cairo's name had already been made public; he had met the president, for God's sake! The idea of changing his name now seemed like overkill. But I went along for the ride. I would have agreed to almost anything to get him home. The fact is, my buddies and I did refer to him as both *Carlos* and *Cairo* for a while, but after a few months, Carlos slipped away, and only Cairo remained.

Once the paperwork was completed, I walked out of the office and into the kennel, where Cairo sat quietly in his cage. As usual, he stood up and began wagging his tail. He let out a soft "Woof!" which was just his way of saying hello. Cairo was accustomed to my visits by now, so he knew the drill. He'd be let out for a while and we'd play together, maybe go for a walk or have something to eat.

I took a seat on the ground as he trotted into my arms. Then I hooked up his harness and led him to the parking lot. As we walked out of the kennel for the last time, I couldn't help but smile.

"No more metal box for you."

I threw open the door to my truck. Cairo jumped into the passenger side of the cab and curled up contentedly. I turned the key. As the engine rumbled, I reached over and gave him a scratch behind the ears.

"One stop on the way home."

Cairo pushed his head against my hand and growled warmly.

"Steak for dinner," I said. "Hope you don't mind."

# Chapter 23

*I have a picture from Cairo's first day home. We had to reintroduce him to me, because I hadn't met him in the house, only outside the house. Plus, we had two other dogs, and we wanted to make sure they all played well together. But it was no problem at all. Cairo was great. He just walked around, sniffing out the place, exploring. Will had gone over a couple of things with me, like, "If he picks up a toy, don't grab it from him." It all made sense—he's an attack dog. But Cairo? I just never saw that. From the moment he came home, I felt like there wasn't anything to worry about. Yeah, he was intimidating looking, but he was like a big teddy bear. I never saw him be aggressive, not even at the beginning. And Will was so happy about him being home. I mean, it was like all was right in the world. I can't imagine it going in the opposite direction, and how that would have been.*

*Will was still in rough shape at that point. He was spending so much time in hospitals and doctors' offices, hanging out in waiting rooms. They had him on lots of medication because he was depressed and in so much pain. I don't think they were just checking boxes; I think they were doing the best they could to help him, and they didn't know what else to do. But they ended up prescribing so much medicine, because they think it will make you feel better, and it doesn't make you feel better. Or at least in Will's case it didn't. So he was going through a really difficult time, and then finally this good thing happens— Cairo comes home! It was huge. I honestly don't know what it would have been like if Cairo had not gotten retired, or if he had gotten retired but not come home with us. It would have been so detrimental to Will's mental state and getting out of the pain he was in.*

*—Natalie Kelley*

It was something of a shock to discover that I wasn't the only one in the house apparently suffering from PTSD.

The signs were subtle, at first, like the way Cairo preferred not to be left alone. He was totally comfortable that first night and for the next couple of days because I took him everywhere with me. Then I started to notice that if I walked from the kitchen to the living room, Cairo would get up and follow. If I went outside, he would stand at the door and scratch the screen. Then he would whine or bark until I let him out. Once he was with me, everything was fine. He'd trail alongside, happy and content.

But the real kicker came maybe a week after we got him home, when a big spring storm rolled through the area. I was sitting in the living room when I noticed Cairo panting. Then he started pacing nervously around the room, his tongue hanging out, drool falling from his muzzle.

"What's the matter?" I said.

Cairo walked over to me and jumped up on the couch. He

pushed his head into my hands but refused to lie down. Instead, he stood on the sofa for a moment, trembling and panting, and then jumped right back down and resumed pacing.

"What's wrong with him?" Natalie asked.

"I have no idea. I've never seen him do anything like this before."

Cairo walked to one of the windows and stared outside. Then he went to the door. I stood up and followed him, thinking he'd heard something in the backyard. I couldn't imagine what that might be. It wasn't like we got a lot of wild animals in our neighborhood, and even if there had been a coyote or some other visitor, the Cairo I knew would merely have been excited.

Not terrified.

I looked out the window. The late-afternoon sky was growing dark in a way that signals the unmistakable approach of rough weather. Suddenly, off in the distance, there was a rumble of thunder. It didn't last long, and it wasn't very loud. Nonetheless, it provoked in Cairo an immediate response: he hid under the dining room table, shaking and cowering.

"Holy shit," I said to Natalie. "He's afraid of the thunderstorm."

She felt terrible for him, but as someone who had only been exposed to ordinary dogs—most of whom aren't particularly fond of thunder or other loud noises—she didn't see this as odd behavior.

"Has he always been like this?" she asked innocently.

I shook my head in disbelief. "Uhhh . . . no."

That was an understatement. Cairo was an utterly fearless dog who would run into a gunfight in a dark room full of assholes and not think twice about it. He would sit calmly in the back of a Black Hawk or Chinook as it was buffeted by wind or danced out of the way of RPG fire. He'd been shot at nearly point-blank range and still not given up the fight. He'd held his ground as grenades shook the earth around him.

Nothing bothered Cairo.

Nothing.

But I suppose there was a price to pay for all that he endured. A lot of the shit I experienced didn't faze me in the least—until I didn't have to deal with it anymore; until I came home and had to live in the "normal" world, after a decade of training and fighting and living with one purpose; and trying to figure out a new purpose amid the constant noise in my head and the persistent, inexplicable physical pain that went along with it.

That shit will fuck you up.

It fucked me up. And obviously it had affected Cairo, as well.

"Come here, boy," I said, coaxing him out from under the table. "Everything will be okay."

For the most part, it was. We learned to deal with the thunderstorms (which, after all, make frequent visits in the coastal mid-Atlantic region). Although he often would end up sleeping in our bed, we gave Cairo his own room and his own bed. If a storm happened to roll through in the middle of the night, while he was sleeping, Cairo invariably would wake in a puddle of his own urine. We'd have to sit with him and calm him down until the storm passed. Then we'd toss his bedding into the laundry and give him a different place to sleep. There was no point in correcting any of this behavior. He wasn't trying to be disrespectful or troublesome.

He was just scared out of his wits by something that presented no real threat to his safety, something that had never frightened him in the past. If that's not PTSD, then I don't know what is.

Getting Cairo home was one of the happiest days of my

life—and I hope his, as well—but there was a period of transition for both of us. Like many recent retirees, Cairo struggled with boredom and restlessness. It took a while for him to feel completely safe and comfortable at home. As a handler, I had been Cairo's teammate, but I was also his boss. I was Dad, and like any dad, I tried to balance affection with discipline. Cairo knew I loved him, but he also understood our respective roles, especially on deployment. Now that he was no longer working, and—like me—suffering some emotional and physical fallout from his years of service, I found myself reluctant to be hard on him.

Any dog will take advantage of that situation if you let him; the smarter and more strong-willed the animal is, the more likely you are to suddenly find yourself in a turf war.

For the first few weeks that Cairo was home, I let him do pretty much whatever he wanted. I was so grateful to have him around, and he was happy to no longer be living in a cage. One day, on the way home from work, I stopped to pick up a tuna sandwich. When I got home, Cairo was wandering harmlessly around the house. I gave him a hug, then set the sandwich on the ottoman in the living room before going into the kitchen to grab something to drink. I'm not sure what I was thinking. I guess I had grown accustomed to living with two other dogs that had been trained to leave food alone unless they were expressly given permission to touch it.

Anyway, when I walked back into the living room, there was Cairo, lying on the floor, with the sandwich between his front paws. Tuna fish and mayonnaise covered his snout.

"Cairo," I said. "Come on, man."

I didn't scold him. After all, this was mostly my fault. I'd left the damn sandwich out in plain view, easily accessible, and Cairo naturally crushed it. He had been living in a kennel, where gifts such as this simply never presented themselves. Also, while I was upset about him stealing my lunch, I had to admit it was an impressive bit of thievery. In a matter of just a couple of minutes, Cairo had managed to remove about two feet of plastic wrap from the sandwich; most dogs would have devoured the whole thing and either spit out the plastic or pooped it out later. Not Cairo. He had somehow removed the wrapping. Moreover, rather than eating the sandwich quickly, he had licked out the tuna and cheese from the middle. When I caught him in the act (or right after the act), he looked up at me impishly as if to say, "What's the big deal, Dad? I left you the best part."

After a month or so, we got into a nice rhythm. Cairo was no longer a working dog, so there was no need to do any hard-core training. But the truth is, he loved working, so I had to keep him busy and incorporate some of the more interesting and fun aspects of his old life into his new life. No more gunfire or explosions, no more bite work, but plenty of fetch and running on the beach or in open fields. Unfortunately, the slight hitch in his step by now had progressed to a limp that was frequently noticeable after a few minutes of retrieving balls. No surprise. He was a nearly ten-year-old dog with a metal plate in his leg and thousands of miles on the engine. Even without the injury, Cairo surely would have experienced the effects of arthritis, just like any other aging veteran of Special Operations. The job beats you up. But his drive to work and run remained strong. Cairo would never quit a game of fetch. He would push right through the obvious pain. It was up to me to keep him from getting too banged up.

Life was pretty good for most of that summer. Cairo spent a lot of time just lazing around the house, being loved not just by me and Natalie but by everyone who came over to visit. In anticipation of Cairo coming home, I had bought a Ural Patrol motorcycle with a sidecar. I liked to ride bikes in nice weather and thought it might be cool to share the experience with Cairo. Turns out, he loved it! We used to get some great looks from people as we rode around town together, Cairo sitting in that sidecar, wearing a helmet and doggles, mouth open, trying to catch the wind. He liked going out on my boat, as well. Cairo had never been much of a water dog. By that I mean, he wasn't a swimmer. Didn't even like getting wet in the rain. For some reason, though, he enjoyed sitting on my boat as it rocked in the waves, and we spent endless hours doing exactly that.

With few dietary restrictions and a more relaxed exercise regimen, Cairo naturally began to lose a little bit of his leanness. I wouldn't exactly say we fattened him up, but if you had seen him on deployment, in his prime, you would have noticed the difference. He no longer had the look of a world-class athlete; instead, he looked . . . healthy. Content. He was leading a life of leisure, just as he deserved.

Still, there were issues even on the best days, primarily because of his PTSD. For example, Cairo suffered occasionally from separation anxiety, a condition that manifested itself in a number of ways. The fact that he liked to follow me around was no big deal. More challenging was the destruction Cairo would sometimes cause when we left him home alone. He started with the blinds in the living room. Every time I drove away, I'd see Cairo's head appear in one of the front windows. Sometimes he'd just sit there and wait. Other times, I'd return to find the blinds pulled from their rods or chewed into pieces. While this behavior was frustrating (and expensive!), I knew it was not malicious. The blinds gave Cairo the feeling of being boxed in. When I left the house, he wanted to know where I was and when I'd return. In his mind, a better view would provide some of the answers. It was simply a matter of insecurity, and it made my heart sink, for Cairo had once been a dog seemingly impervious to stress of any kind.

For a while, we tried confining him to a spare bedroom when we left, but that didn't work at all. He would just destroy the entire room. The next step, unfortunately, was to confine him to a kennel when we were out of the house, but that lasted only a few days before he figured out how to escape, just as he had in the past. Eventually, I used a sheet of plexiglass to rig the kennel in such a way that it was almost escape-proof.

*Almost . . .*

Meaning, sometimes he got out; sometimes he didn't.

I guess you could say Cairo won the war if not every battle, since we ultimately decided that it was best to leave him alone as little as possible. Sometimes I took him to work, although that was frowned upon for some very practical reasons; maybe it's not a great idea to bring an attack dog to the office. A lot of the time, I was home, anyway. Natalie and I worked different schedules, and we tried as much as possible to limit Cairo's periods of solitude. We weren't completely successful, but we did the best we could. For the most part, wherever we went, Cairo tagged along.

Cairo and I didn't always get along in retired life. Even though he was a sweet, bighearted dog, we had our disagreements. Retired or not, he was still a combat assault dog, and I had to keep that in mind—not just when Cairo was around other people but whenever I was tempted to let him get away with expressing dominance or ignoring rules and regulations. Cairo knew how to take advantage of every little thing that you gave him; over time, all the freebies led to a degree of arrogance and disrespect. He was never hostile or angry, just increasingly unwilling to do what he was told. I had to take responsibility for this because, after all, I was his handler. I knew better. You can't let an alpha dog like Cairo—a perfectly bred and trained fighting machine—act like he's in charge. Even as an old-timer, he'd be more than a handful.

Cairo's reluctance to do what he was told was particularly evident when I was out of the house. He was affectionate with Natalie but did not always do as he was told. This happened with other people, as well. Part of this stemmed from the fact that everyone was naturally attracted to Cairo. He was handsome and friendly, with an almost majestic appearance. The combination of being physically intimidating and personally charming allowed him to get away with a lot. Sometimes, with Cairo (and any working dog), you had to go beyond a simple verbal correction. Most people were reluctant to do that with Cairo; hell, I was reluctant. But once in a while, I did it, anyway. If he didn't do what he was told, I'd put him in his kennel for a few minutes, just to get the point across.

But we always made up in the end. I loved Cairo, and he loved me. Nothing would ever change that.

One of the most surprising things about Cairo was how well he adapted to sharing a home with other dogs. The Belgian Malinois as a breed is known to be prickly around unfamiliar dogs; a trained assault dog can be aggressive and territorial. But we never had a problem with Cairo. From the moment we brought him home, he coexisted peacefully with our Doberman, Sterling, and with Hagen, a female Malinois who was still in the puppy stage, which meant she was excitable and energetic; to Cairo, she was endlessly annoying, forcing play sessions that didn't interest Cairo in the least. This was like a toddler insisting on wrestling with her grandfather, and frankly, Cairo often wasn't up to it. But he never protested. Instead, he'd just lie on the floor while Hagen bounced around, pawing at him, jumping on his back, even nipping at his neck. The first few times this happened, I pulled Hagen away—ostensibly for her own good. After a while, I didn't even bother to intervene; I just let them play. Sometimes Cairo would halfheartedly roll around for a few minutes, but not once did he display any aggression toward Hagen. Somehow, he knew that it was all just fun and games.

One time we drove to Florida to visit Natalie's family. They had a bulldog that was generally well behaved and friendly, especially with humans, but he didn't like sharing his toys with other dogs. At one point, the dogs were outside playing when Cairo tried to run down a ball. The bulldog didn't like that. As Cairo went after the ball, the bulldog went after Cairo.

I was in the shower when all this went down, but Natalie filled me in soon enough. Apparently, the bulldog leaped at Cairo with a growl and clamped its jaws down around Cairo's leg. For a few seconds, she envisioned the absolute worst. Cairo was old and somewhat softened by age and other circumstances. Still, there was no doubt that if so inclined, he could have ripped the bulldog to pieces. And just about any other dog, for that matter. It was sort of like that scene in *Gran Torino*, when crusty old badass Walt Kowalski (played by Clint Eastwood, who was nearly eighty years old at the time) confronts a trio of knuckleheads on an abandoned Detroit street corner as they harass a young woman (Walt's neighbor).

"Ever notice how you come across somebody once in a while you shouldn't have fucked with?" Walt says as he steps out of his pickup truck and spits on the ground. "That's me."

Incredibly, Cairo barely even responded to the attack. He shook the bulldog off, dropped the ball, and meekly walked away. He didn't yelp, didn't bark, didn't even growl. It was like he barely even noticed, or simply couldn't be bothered to respond.

*Well, this isn't worth my time.*

The dogs retreated to opposite sides of the yard for a while and then went about their business. When I came outside, Natalie told me what happened. I figured they both had been lucky. A few minutes later, though, I noticed that Cairo was limping— and it wasn't the usual little hitch that I knew so well.

"Come here, buddy," I said, clapping my hands. Cairo jogged over slowly and stood in front of me. I ran my hands over his leg and felt something wet. Sure enough, Cairo was bleeding. I pulled his fur back to get a better look. The wound was maybe two inches long and deep and ragged enough to be problematic.

"Gotta get him to the vet," I said. "He might need a few stitches."

Natalie and her mom both felt terrible about what happened, even though it wasn't anyone's fault. The truly remarkable thing is that Cairo had barely even reacted to having his leg filleted. To say he had mellowed with age would be an understatement. He was a gentle old soul now—a lover, not a fighter.

Retirement agreed with Cairo, and I have to admit that I sort of envied him. By this point, I had come to terms with the approaching end of my own navy career. Some guys evolve naturally from operator to instructor or even commander. Not me. I had been drawn to the SEALs because I wanted to be in the heat; I wanted to test myself under the most rigorous conditions. I was, or at least had been, a fighter. If that was taken away from me, then my career was over. I had no interest in a more sedentary form of service. I have great respect for the instructors in BUD/S or the Training Team. They're a bit sadistic and twisted, but they clearly serve a vital role in Naval Special Warfare. Without them, there would be no SEALs.

It's just that I had no desire to spend the next ten years filling that role. And anyway, I was neither physically nor emotionally suited to the job. The headaches and back pain, and the sudden, crippling bouts of anxiety that would come on in waves—all of these conspired to make me less than reliable. Having Cairo around helped improve my mood, but the truth was, I had lost my passion for the job. It was time to move on. Unfortunately, separating from the navy—and especially from Special Operations— is not the simplest thing. If you've got twenty years under your belt and you're in decent physical and emotional shape, then you simply retire and collect your pension.

I was only thirty years old, with twelve years of service. I'd given everything I had to my country and my brothers. But like Cairo, I was now damaged goods. In my current state, I had nothing left to offer. I just wanted to get better and then figure out what to do with the rest of my life. In order for that to happen, I had to apply for a medical retirement from the navy, a process that can be maddeningly slow, complicated, and frustrating.

I have no real complaints about anyone with whom I worked. Both as a SEAL operator and as an instructor or desk jockey, I was fortunate to serve alongside some incredible men and to learn from generous and talented mentors. When my health began to deteriorate, I was lucky to have the support and understanding of bosses who knew that I was struggling and in pain. Everyone seemed to want to help; it's just that no one really knew how.

That's the challenge faced by so many veterans: how to cope with chronic pain and depression, with the mysterious and debilitating effects of injury and its consequences, denoted by any of a host of acronyms (TBI, PTSD, CTE). It's not that support isn't available; it's that you don't know which lifeline to grab.

For me, having Cairo home seemed more beneficial than almost any other type of therapy or treatment I tried during this period. Unfortunately, we were separated again after just a few months, when the navy strongly suggested that I undergo treatment for substance abuse. As before, there had been a lot of concern on the part of my friends and coworkers and superior officers. And once again, I felt like it would have been incredibly ungrateful of me to disregard their concern, which was obviously a sign of love and support. And from a practical standpoint, I got the sense that denying I had a problem and refusing treatment might have negatively impacted my application for medical retirement. Which, let's be honest, was fair enough.

The truth is, my drinking had escalated steadily since I'd gotten back from deployment. I won't make excuses for it. A lot of guys in the military self-medicate to ease the symptoms of chronic pain and PTSD. I was one of them. If I hadn't sought a medical retirement, I'm not sure anyone would have confronted me—certainly not as quickly. Regardless, I was forced to look in the mirror once again, and while I did not consider myself an alcoholic or an addict—my drinking was situational and triggered by chronic pain—it was hard to deny that I had a problem. So off I went to rehab again, and this time it wasn't just an outpatient program. I spent thirty days in a residential treatment program in Williamsburg, Virginia, surrounded by psychiatrists and therapists and doctors and a bunch of patients whose lives had been totally wrecked by addiction to alcohol or drugs.

Although I was sympathetic to their stories and to their pain, I can't say that I felt a kinship with them. Maybe that was the point: to get help before I sank any further. Most of the other clients had been battling their addiction, unsuccessfully, for many years. I was a relative newcomer and still felt like I could stop drinking at any time.

"Then why don't you?" one of the therapists said to me repeatedly.

"Okay," I answered. "I will."

Thirty days later, I was out and clean. I still felt like shit, but I'd keep working to get better. I would do it for myself. I would do it for the friends who cared enough to tell me I had a problem.

And I would do it for Cairo.

# Chapter 24

Dogs throw up. A lot. That's not exactly news to anyone who has ever owned a dog for even the briefest of time. Dogs are messy. They poop and pee and puke. Sometimes in the house. In fact, I've known a lot of people over the years who have given up dogs because they didn't want to deal with some of the sights and smells that are part of the bargain.

I always thought it was a small price to pay. And anyway, you get used to it after a while.

With even a modicum of training, most dogs will quickly adapt to a schedule that makes it easy to accommodate pooping and peeing. Get up in the morning, eat breakfast, go for a walk. Clean out the system. Not much different from their owners, really. Vomiting is not part of the program, but it doesn't usually signify anything serious. Dogs routinely eat all kinds of disgusting stuff they are not supposed to eat—garbage, roadkill, mushrooms, dirt, even other dogs' poop. Just about any of these things will induce vomiting as surely as a spoonful of ipecac syrup. But in most cases, it's an isolated incident and the dog feels better almost immediately.

Cairo had been raised in a bubble, carefully trained and

sensibly fed (the occasional steak dinner notwithstanding); he had never been much of a scrounger when it came to food. In short, he was a healthy dog, so when he began throwing up with some regularity in the late fall of 2014, I took notice. The first time it happened, I found Cairo in the kitchen, standing over a small puddle of yellowish liquid. At first, I thought perhaps he'd peed on the floor, which would have been strange enough. But it was too small a puddle, and the look on Cairo's face, along with his demeanor, reflected not so much embarrassment or mischief as it did queasiness.

"What's up, pal? You okay?"

Upon closer inspection, I could see that Cairo had thrown up a small amount of bile. This struck me as odd, since it had never happened before, but I shrugged it off and cleaned up the mess, and then took Cairo for a walk. He was a little woozy and needed a nap afterward, but otherwise okay. By that night, he was back to his old friendly, happy self. I chalked it up to heartburn (or whatever it is that dogs get that feels like heartburn) and forgot all about it.

Until a couple of days later, when it happened again.

And a week after that, when he threw up his dinner less than an hour after eating.

"Something's wrong," I said to Natalie. "This isn't like him."

Since Cairo was a retired military working day who had spent his entire career with the SEALs, I figured I could just take him to one of the veterinarians at the base. They were happy to help, but a cursory examination turned up nothing dramatic.

"He's getting old," the doc said. "It's perfectly normal. I wouldn't worry about it."

Cleaning up after Cairo became a common, although not frequent, part of our routine. Most of the time, he seemed just fine. A bit less energetic, maybe, but not sick.

In December, Natalie and I began making plans for a holiday

trip. I had always wanted to visit the National September 11 Memorial and Museum (a.k.a. the 9/11 Memorial) in New York City, and this seemed like a good time to do it. Although I still suffered from migraines and back pain, and my mood varied greatly from day to day, it's fair to say that I had improved somewhat. I wasn't drinking or taking psychiatric medications, and my medical retirement was moving forward. I certainly didn't feel like my old self, but I did feel . . . *better.*

I wasn't sure how I'd be affected by the 9/11 Memorial. You might think that everyone in Special Operations would have visited at some point, as the 9/11 Memorial and what it signifies is so directly related to the counterterrorism work to which we were devoted. But that isn't true. For me, it seemed like there was never enough time; when I was a SEAL, I used my vacations to get away from the stress of work. I didn't need to be reminded of the horror and tragedy of 9/11; I knew precisely what had happened. I lived with the fallout every day. I devoted my life to ensuring that nothing like it ever happened again.

But now that I was no longer deploying, and I had larger blocks of time that needed to be filled, I felt a gnawing sense of curiosity; maybe even obligation. Neither Natalie nor I had ever been to New York City, so we decided to knock a couple of things off the bucket list: not only would we visit the 9/11 Memorial, but we would celebrate New Year's Eve in Times Square, watching the ball drop and counting down the seconds as the clock approached midnight. To make things even more interesting, we decided to take Cairo and Hagen with us. Sterling we left with a friend (sorry, but three dogs in New York City was more than even I was willing to bite off).

We loaded up Natalie's Mazda CX-7 and left Virginia on December 29. A seven-hour ride felt more like twelve hours because Cairo vomited twice along the way. Cairo had traveled all over the world—by car, plane, helicopter, and boat—and

rarely suffered from motion sickness, so his sudden and persistent nausea was distressing, but it wasn't exactly a shock.
In addition to his ongoing gastrointestinal issues, Cairo had
exhibited some unusual behavior in the days leading up to
the trip. For one thing, he had no interest in playing; he simply
wanted to lie around the house and sleep. More disturbing was
the fact that I had caught him eating dog poop in the backyard.
I don't know whether it was his own poop, or if it belonged to
Sterling or Hagen. Not that it matters. I'd known Cairo since he
was three years old, and I had never seen him do this. Not once.
I was so surprised that I didn't even yell at him when it happened. I just sort of walked over and pulled him away.

"What are you doing, boy? That stuff will make you sick."

It sure did. The first time Cairo vomited, we were crossing
into Delaware on I-95. Fortunately, as seasoned dog owners and
travelers, we always carried a few towels in the car, so when
Cairo began grunting and retching, Natalie grabbed one and
turned around just in time to give him a target. The second time
was somewhere on the New Jersey Turnpike. Same thing. I felt
sorry for Natalie, but she didn't complain. She was just worried
about Cairo.

Despite all the adventures I had experienced in the previous decade, I still got excited as we crossed the George Wash-
ington Bridge and entered Manhattan. I'd seen a good chunk
of the world, but I remained a country boy at heart, and there
is nothing like New York City to make a country boy feel wide-
eyed. The sheer scope of the city is remarkable—so many
people and skyscrapers and cars and buses, all crammed into
one little patch of land; it's a wonder the place works at all.

The week between Christmas and New Year's is among the
busiest of the year in New York, so we just tried to relax and
not get all stressed out about the traffic or the crowds. It was
all part of the experience. By the time we pulled up to our hotel

(we splurged and made a reservation at the Ritz-Carlton on Central Park South so that we could walk the dogs easily and still be fairly close to Times Square), Cairo was lethargic and beat up from car sickness and the long ride. Hagen, who was barely a year old, bounced excitedly around the car.

I'd been traveling with big, imposing dogs long enough to know the protocol for arriving in a new city, especially at a hotel with valet parking. A lot of hotels do not accept dogs, but since Cairo was a retired service dog, and Hagen, technically, was a working dog in training, we were usually allowed to take them with us wherever we went. Still, it wasn't wise to pull up in front of a place like the Ritz, in the middle of Manhattan, with thousands of people nearby, and let two big Malinois hop out of the car.

I pulled into the valet lane, put the Mazda in park, and asked Natalie to wait with the dogs. Then I got out and explained the situation to the valet.

"We have a couple of big dogs here," I said. "They're friendly and well trained, and we'll have them leashed. The hotel knows we're coming."

The valet smiled warily and peeked into the window of the car.

"Ummmm . . . no problem, sir."

We emptied the car, checked in, and went up to our room. As we walked into the lobby, some people stopped and stared; actually, most people stared. It takes a lot to get someone's attention in Manhattan, but Cairo and Hagen were both beautiful dogs, tall and strong and impressive. Several people approached and asked if they could get a closer look, or maybe even pet the dogs. They were both muzzled, so we said sure. Even people who were clearly afraid of dogs—or at least these two dogs— stared in wonder. I guess, to them, it was like looking at a lion in the zoo; even if your response is primarily one of fear and intimidation, you can't help but admire the animal as a physical specimen.

The hotel was beautiful, and so was the view from our room. Rather than take the dogs out for a walk right away, we decided to leave them in the hotel room in their kennels while we walked around the neighborhood. This was partly just to get some exercise after a long day of driving but also so that we could assess the size of crowds and what we'd be dealing with if we took either of the dogs out for any length of time.

Over the next couple of days, we took Hagen almost everywhere. She was so easygoing and friendly, and she loved interacting with people, especially in the park. She was a puppy who had not been trained to bite or attack and therefore could largely be trusted around crowds. We had only one minor incident with her on that trip, when someone accidentally stepped on her foot as we walked along Central Park South. Like any dog, Hagen could be unpredictable when hurt, but on this occasion, she barely registered anything more than mild surprise. Still, it taught us to be particularly sensitive to our surroundings. New York is a beautiful and vibrant city, but it's a challenge for anyone visiting with a large dog—or two large dogs.

Sadly, Cairo didn't get to see much of it. He was pretty sick for the first couple of days, and so we took him outside only long enough to go to the bathroom. Although he stopped throwing up by the second day, he lacked energy and just didn't seem like himself. We didn't want to test his temperament with strangers when he wasn't feeling well, and he seemed content to hang out in the hotel room, anyway.

By the morning of December 31, the crowds had begun to swell to such an extent that the idea of taking Cairo or Hagen to Times Square was laughable. Frankly, we weren't even that excited about walking down there ourselves. The very thought of it made me feel claustrophobic. We changed hotels and moved to a Courtyard Marriott in midtown where we'd have a direct view of the Times Square New Year's party from our room on an upper floor. We ordered takeout for dinner, and the four of us curled up together on a king-sized bed and watched the festivities on the nice flat-screen television in our room. When the ball dropped, we pressed our faces against the window and watched it in real time, counting down the seconds as 2014 gave way to 2015.

It was a nice night.

Two days later, on January 2, we drove to lower Manhattan and visited the 9/11 Memorial. I wanted to take Cairo; part of the reason the trip was so special was because I thought it would be cool to walk through the memorial with Cairo by my side— not because I wanted to show him off or anything but simply to share the experience with him. I know he would not have understood, but for me, Cairo's presence would have heightened the impact. It just seemed . . . *appropriate*.

Unfortunately, while Cairo had rallied somewhat—he was able to hold down his food—he remained lethargic and disinterested. He wasn't a problem. When we left the hotel room, he just slept. But I'd done enough research on the 9/11 Memorial to know that it was likely to be extremely crowded, and I didn't think it would be fair to put Cairo through an experience like that if he was sick.

We did take Hagen, and she responded admirably. It was nice to have her with us, but it would have been even better with Cairo. No offense to Hagen, but Cairo, like me, was an outgrowth of 9/11. The tragedy of that day, and the response to it, ultimately had led to our coming together. We were partners ten years later, tethered together on the ground in Pakistan, when the man responsible for the atrocity of 9/11—for the killing of thousands of civilians—was finally brought to justice.

I needed to see the memorial, to experience it firsthand. And I wanted Cairo to be there with me. He just wasn't up to it.

Even without Cairo, seeing the memorial was a profoundly moving experience. I suppose that's true for anyone who visits—certainly there was an air of respect and solemnity around the memorial that was unlike anything I had ever experienced—but it's compounded, I'm sure, by emotional proximity to the event itself, or to events that have arisen in its wake. I can't imagine what it's like to walk through the 9/11 Memorial if you lost a loved one on that day. It was hard enough for me just to see the names on the wall and to think of the way some of those people died—forced to make a choice between jumping from the ninetieth floor of a building or burning to death within its walls. I thought of the first responders who rushed to the site and selflessly gave their lives.

And I thought of the brothers I had lost over the years, men who had died while fighting an endless and often thankless war sparked by 9/11.

I remember feeling so overwhelmed that I couldn't speak. I remember feeling like I wanted to cry, but not being able to shed a tear. I remember feeling a profound and almost incomprehensible mix of sadness and pride as I stood in front of a display case devoted to Operation Neptune Spear and the killing of Osama bin Laden: a brick from the compound where bin Laden was found; a long-sleeved camouflage jersey worn by a SEAL on the night of the raid (the owner was unidentified, but I knew it belonged to Rob O'Neill). I remember holding Natalie's hand without saying a word. I remember being grateful for the anonymity that the moment demanded, for being able to experience it without anyone knowing who I was.

And I remember reaching down and giving Hagen a hug, and wishing that Cairo were by her side.

# Chapter 25

Through the windshield of my Toyota Tundra, I watched as the mountains of Tennessee and Arkansas gave way to the flatland of Oklahoma and the Texas Panhandle. Cairo sat on the seat next to me, a comfortable copilot, as usual. We'd seen a lot of the country together over the years, much of it from the cab of a truck, where you can relax and let the road unspool at its own leisurely pace.

Our destination was a small town not far from Grand Junction, Colorado, where one of my best friends, Jack, lived. He was a retired SEAL. We'd known each other a long time and had gone through BUD/S together, and Jack had invited me to stay at his place while I worked at a security internship nearby. By this point, it had become clear that I would be separating from the navy, most likely via the medical retirement route. But the process remained slow and daunting, dominated by endless paperwork and interviews and treatment and therapy.

It was an enormously frustrating time. I tried to see it from the navy's point of view: before granting a medical retirement, all avenues of rehabilitation and recovery had to be exhausted to avoid any precedent of exploiting the process. But I knew my career was over. I had been wounded in the spring of 2012. It was now late February 2015. Nearly three years had passed, and while there had been some sputtering progress toward recovery, I frequently walked around like a zombie, plagued by headaches and back pain and memory loss and by bouts of sadness and depression that came and went in waves. In my more selfish and self-pitying moments, which I hate to even acknowledge, I got angry.

*I gave twelve years to the navy. I'm proud of my service, and I wouldn't trade it for anything, consequences notwithstanding. Please . . . let me move on.*

If the navy appeared to show little compassion or understanding, well, the same cannot be said of many of the navy personnel with whom I worked. I had a lot of friends and bosses who patiently rode out my bad days and gave me all the help and support they could muster. But life goes on. Most of my closest friends and teammates were either still in the grinding cycle of training and deployment or they had retired; a few, of course, had died.

Meanwhile, I was in what felt like a permanent holding pattern.

Some relief came in the form of outside opportunities like the internship in Colorado, which would be followed immediately by another internship in Iowa, this one involving a dog-training program. Both of these represented a chance to explore other opportunities in the post-military world, and I was fortunate to have supervisors who wholeheartedly endorsed the idea. There was, however, the issue of what to do with Cairo. I would be on the road for roughly a month, and I felt bad about leaving Natalie at home with three dogs. While Cairo was not his old self, he had rallied somewhat since our trip to New York, so I decided to take him with me.

Frankly, I didn't know what else to do. Like me, Cairo seemed to have good days and bad days. He could go for a walk or play fetch and seem perfectly fine in the morning. Then in the afternoon, he might retreat into sickness or exhaustion. Not every day, mind you, but often enough that it remained worrisome. I regularly brought him in to see the base veterinarian but kept getting the same message: he's old, and he's been through a lot. This was indisputable and logical. Malinois often live a dozen years or more, especially if they come from good stock, are well cared for, and get lucky. Cairo, obviously, was impeccably bred, but he had endured significant trauma and stress. It made sense that he was feeling the effects of that now, but the symptoms didn't necessarily signal anything worse than premature aging.

I wasn't so sure, and as a result, I made myself something of a nuisance, bringing Cairo in to see the vet a couple of times a month, or even weekly. This was a problem not merely because they didn't think there was anything wrong with Cairo but also because he was no longer a working dog. He had been retired, which meant he was ineligible for unlimited free care by navy docs. That might seem unfair, given Cairo's stellar résumé and the wounds he'd absorbed for his country and his fellow soldiers, but that's the way it was.

"Will, you're going to have to find an outside vet," I was told. "You can't keep bringing him here."

Cairo tolerated the cross-country trip reasonably well. We made it from Virginia to Colorado in three days, and I think he vomited only once. But it wasn't long after we arrived that Cairo started to go downhill. He seemed tireder than usual, disinclined to interact with my friend Jack, and even somewhat ambivalent toward me. For the first few days, all he did was sleep. I thought perhaps he was having trouble adjusting to the altitude of the Rockies, but when he began throwing up—not just once in a while but once or twice a day—I grew more concerned. Cairo was losing weight and seemed even sicker than he had been before we went to New York.

"I'm worried about him," I said to Jack. "I think he needs to see someone."

Jack agreed. "Let me make a call."

I was lucky. Jack had dogs, as well, and was friends with a local civilian vet. Jack explained the symptoms, and the doc said to bring him right in.

The vet took some x-rays, which revealed issues with Cairo's stomach and digestive system. But the results were inconclusive. To find out what was really going on, he needed to cut Cairo open. It was scary, but necessary.

"There's obviously something very wrong," the doc said. "But I can't give you any definitive answers without surgery."

Whatever was bothering Cairo, it was obviously a big problem. The vet told me he would do the work free of charge after he found out that Cairo was a retired working dog. He had no idea that this was the famous Cairo, but he refused to take payment and did the entire procedure and follow-up appointments out of the kindness of his heart. The gratitude I have for such a person . . . well, I cannot put it into words. People like that are hard to find.

After the surgery, the vet came right out to explain what he had found. It was complicated, and not encouraging. Cairo was so bloated that his spleen had been displaced. In effect, it had flipped over his stomach and gotten lodged in between the stomach wall and other vital organs. Dogs have a rudimentary digestive system that usually causes no problems, but when something malfunctions, the results can be catastrophic. The very description of Cairo's malady made me queasy; it also made me feel so sorry for him, imagining what he had gone through for the last several months and how uncomfortable he must have been.

Fortunately, Cairo made it out of the surgery without any complications. The doc said he was able to put everything back in its proper place. The prognosis was as good as it could be given Cairo's age and history. The best thing for him now, the doc said, was plenty of rest.

For the next two weeks, I slept with Cairo in Jack's basement. Whenever I wasn't working, I was right by his side. Jack had to leave town for a while to work, but he and his wife and kids were kind enough to let me stay while Jack was away. They took care of me and Cairo while he was recovering. Although he lacked much of an appetite—which isn't unusual after gastric surgery—he seemed to be doing okay. Eventually, I loaded up the truck and headed east to Des Moines, Iowa, for my second internship. While I enjoyed the work, my heart wasn't really into it; neither was my head. I worried about Cairo. He seemed to do better for a few days, maybe a week, then began deteriorating again. The vet had warned me to look for bloating in Cairo's midsection—an indication that he was retaining water and that his digestive system was once again acting up. One morning, he threw up. Afterward, I ran my hands along his belly.

Nothing out of the ordinary. In fact, he seemed to be the opposite of bloated. I could feel his ribs sticking out.

"What's the matter?" I said as Cairo lowered his head into my chest and tried to snuggle.

With only a few days left in March, I called Natalie and told her I would be hitting the road shortly. The internship was not over, but Cairo was clearly not doing well, and I wanted to get him home.

We made it to Virginia in two days, driving roughly ten hours a day. Cairo did not appear to be in great distress, but neither was he the copilot I had come to know and love. As we cruised across I-64 through Illinois, Indiana, and Ohio before dipping south into West Virginia, I kept looking over at Cairo. I'd scratch him behind the ears, pat him on the head. Sometimes he'd look up at me or roll over as if to ask for more; for the most part, though, he just slept.

I thought that being in his own home would do Cairo some good and he would start eating more and naturally recuperate. This was not the case. We got him home, and within a couple of days, he had stopped eating completely. We decided to take him to a vet whom command had been using on and off for a long time. He was a great doctor and had done some work for us in the past. When we arrived at the vet hospital, though, a receptionist told us the doctor was going to be busy in surgery all day.

"Would you mind seeing one of the other doctors?"

I looked at Natalie. She shrugged. What choice did we have? Cairo was obviously very sick—his weight had dipped to fifty-five pounds, and he had trouble holding his head up; his eyes were sunken and hollow—and we did not have an appointment. This was an emergency.

"Of course," I said. "No problem. Thanks for squeezing us in."

The doctor was friendly and seemingly thorough in her examination, but in the end decided that maybe the best thing was to simply give Cairo an injection of an antiemetics to stop the vomiting, and then let him go home and recuperate. He'd been through a debilitating surgical procedure and been on the road for a month. It wasn't surprising that he was sick. The recovery would take time, she said. We agreed to take him home and pamper him and to bring him back in a few days if there was no improvement. But just as we were getting ready to leave, the other doctor walked into the waiting room, fresh out of surgery.

We shook hands, made small talk for a few minutes, and then he bent down and began examining Cairo. He had known

Cairo for a long time, and I could tell by the look on his face that he was concerned.

"You know," he said. "Let's get some x-rays . . . and start him on some fluids."

The scans this time revealed a large mass in Cairo's stomach, but there was no way to determine the nature of the mass without opening him up. Heavily invasive surgery.

Again.

It seemed so cruel. Cairo hadn't even come close to recovering from the previous surgery. I worried that he wasn't strong enough to go through it again. But what choice did we have?

"Okay," I told the doc. "Do what you have to do."

He agreed that Cairo was too weak to endure another surgical procedure right away. My job, he said, was to take Cairo home and help him get stronger; soon enough, he'd be ready for surgery.

In preparation for the procedure, Natalie and I blended Cairo's food and fed him through a syringe. We gave him intravenous fluids and lots of medication. We nursed him and slept with him and told him how much we loved him. Sometimes Hagen or Sterling would try to get him to play, but Cairo had no interest; for the most part, they were nice enough to leave him alone. After a few days, Cairo showed minor improvement. He still had no interest in eating on his own, but by pushing fluids and force-feeding, we were able to put a few pounds on him. When I brought him to the vet on the morning of his surgery, he seemed to be in decent spirits. There was even a slight bounce in his step as we walked up to the door. I remember feeling bad for him, because he had no idea what was coming. At the same time, I clung to a thread of optimism.

"We're going to get you all fixed up, Cairo. Don't worry."

I gave him a hug, handed the leash to one of the three cheerful young women who worked the front counter, and walked away without looking back.

For the next several hours, I did everything I could to try to make the time pass without worrying. It was impossible. In the early afternoon, I got a phone call saying he had made it through surgery and was ready to be picked up. The doctor would go over what he found when we got there.

Natalie and I hopped into my truck and drove as fast as we could to the vet hospital. When they brought Cairo out, he was still woozy from the surgery but seemingly okay. I was just happy he was alive. As we waited in an examining room, the doctor came in to talk with us. I could tell by his demeanor—serious, thoughtful—that the news was not good. In addition to the mass that had shown up on the x-ray, the surgery revealed that Cairo's stomach wall was "about ten times thicker than normal." The doctor had taken tissue samples from the stomach wall and from the adjacent mass. The biopsy results would be available in a few days.

Interestingly, he never once used the word *cancer*, but just by the way everyone was acting—the doctor, nurses, even the receptionists—I could tell the prognosis was poor.

"What do we do now?" I asked.

"Same as before," he said. "Take him home. Feed him, give him fluids, try to make him comfortable."

He urged us to have faith, to not jump to any conclusions, and while I appreciated the effort, I did not find it to be a convincing speech.

Cairo came home on March 31, 2015. My birthday. He was in rough shape, but very much alive. *Maybe*, I thought, *he'll be okay.* After all, this wasn't his first rodeo. Cairo had been sick before. He'd been shot. He was no ordinary dog. He could survive anything.

We celebrated my thirty-first birthday that night. Just me and Natalie and the dogs. A quiet evening at home. As much as possible, we tried to include Cairo, but he wasn't in a partying mood. None of us were, really. That night, Cairo slept in his fa-vorite dog bed. I slept on the floor next to him and tried to make sure he was comfortable. Every so often, he would roll over and groan, but for the most part, he just slept. In the middle of the night, I heard a sound and woke to find Cairo half crouching, his legs quivering. I moved my head just in time to avoid being sprayed with diarrhea.

Even after he was done, the cramping went on for several minutes. I kept a hand on his back until the spasms passed. Finally, he slumped to the floor.

"I'm sorry, pal," was all I could offer. Natalie and I cleaned up the room, and then we all went back to bed.

Three days passed in a haze of sickness and mess. Cairo had no interest in eating, and whatever we pushed into him via syringe or IV came rushing back out almost immediately. The nausea and diarrhea were incessant and exhausting. Once, on the third day, he threw up violently, and the material he expelled looked and smelled not like vomit but feces. It was disgusting and shocking; more importantly, it seemed enormously painful to Cairo. I'd seen a lot in my day, but I'd never seen anything like that. All I could think was, his digestive system was so messed up that it was basically working in reverse, which, as it turned out, wasn't far from the truth.

It finally got to the point where we couldn't take it any-more, so we brought him back to the vet. They wanted to weigh him when we arrived, but Cairo could barely stand on the scale. I had to hold him in place. He was a virtual bag of bones by that point, his weight having dropped to slightly more than fifty pounds. At his peak, he had weighed between seventy and seventy-five pounds, so he'd lost nearly a third of his mass. The doctor who had operated on Cairo was tied up in surgery when we arrived, so we saw his associate again.

She was compassionate and soft-spoken as she looked him over and delivered the news. The biopsy was positive. Cairo had cancer. Advanced.

"Is there any chance he could recover?" I asked.

She shook her head sadly.

"I'm sorry. No."

I looked at Natalie. She was sitting with Cairo on the floor, rubbing his back and trying not to cry.

*Okay . . . Enough.*

It was time to let him go. We had reached the point where we were keeping Cairo alive not for him but for us. We were being selfish. He had experienced an unreasonable amount of pain, and it was only going to get worse.

The doctor agreed with our decision—actually, it was 100 percent my decision; it would not have been fair to solicit Natalie's opinion. We both knew that. Cairo had risked his life for me, many times over. I could never repay him. But I could end his suffering. That was my responsibility, and mine alone. It was heartbreaking, but it was the right thing to do.

"We provide services for this kind of situation," the doctor explained. "Whatever you need."

I leaned down and gave Cairo a warm rub on the back.

"Thank you," I said. "But we'll take care of it. I want to take him home."

I scooped Cairo up, carried him outside, and loaded him into the truck. Natalie and I drove him home, the miles unfurling in silence. I carried him into the house and gently placed him on his bed. I gave him a shot of Tramadol to help him feel more comfortable. Then I made a phone call to one of the navy vet technicians and asked him for a favor. A short time later, he arrived and began laying out the tools and medication he would need to euthanize Cairo. Natalie and I both lay down on the floor next to him and stroked his head. I took his paw in my hand.

"Everything is going to be okay, buddy."

It was over quickly and painlessly. On April 2, 2015, at 3:20 in the afternoon, Cairo slipped peacefully away, surrounded by his family, with Daddy holding his hand.

"I love you," I said through tears. It didn't matter that he couldn't hear me. My head was pressed against his. He could feel me. He knew I was there.

Afterward, the vet tech made a call for us. There was, he said, a woman who lived not far away who ran a small crematorium business out of her rural home. Her clients were mostly people like us, who had lost beloved family pets. She would help us with Cairo's remains. As Natalie and I drove up to her house, with Cairo in the backseat, wrapped in his favorite blanket, a sweet, sad song poured out of the radio. It was Adele's cover of "Make You Feel My Love," written by Bob Dylan.

*I'd go hungry, I'd go black and blue . . .*
*To make you feel my love*

The woman who owned the business welcomed us into her home, offered her condolences, and then asked to see Cairo. She explained her service, discussed the fee structure, and promised to take good care of him.

A couple of days later, we returned to her house to pick up Cairo's remains. In a large coffee can, with paw prints and his name written on the side, were Cairo's ashes. In another can was the hardware that had been implanted during surgery after he was wounded in Afghanistan—a handful of screws and a metal plate—along with whatever else had been inserted during other surgeries. Basically, anything that hadn't disintegrated in the crematorium. There was also a plaster impression of his paw print, and a small, tight bundle of Cairo's hair intended for Natalie.

"This is for you," the woman said with a smile as she pushed it across the counter.

We gathered everything together in a box and thanked her for her kindness and professionalism. She knew that I was a navy guy, but I don't think she knew I was a SEAL or that Cairo was a working dog; she certainly didn't know of his accomplishments. If she had asked, I would have told her: Cairo lived a great life. He was a heroic working dog and a faithful companion; I can honestly say I could not have asked for a better dog. Or a better friend. He never knew what he had accomplished or the lives he saved, but he knew that he made people happy.

And that was the most important thing to him.

# Epilogue

One thing I've learned is that you can't rush recovery. Whether you're talking about the head or the heart, healing takes time. Grief recedes like the tide, leaving memories that make you smile or laugh. Life is for the living, after all, and you can only walk around in a daze for so long.

On July 31, 2015, nearly four months after Cairo passed away, my medical retirement finally came through. After so many months of waiting—after the endless rounds of applications and evaluations and interviews and testing—it was strangely anticlimactic.

Honestly, it felt like a long time since I'd been a Navy SEAL. I say that with no malice or regret. The simple truth is, I enlisted in the navy as a boy fresh out of high school and chased the dream of becoming a SEAL with everything I had. I did it because I wanted to serve my country at the highest possible level, on the front lines of a battle against a global enemy of freedom. Was that naïve or simplistic? Maybe a little. The world is a whole lot more complicated than I realized when I left Texas, having never known what it was like to kill someone or to watch one of my friends die. But I believed in the work that we did, and I remain proud of my contributions. I am grateful for having been given the opportunity to be part of such an amazing organization and to have served alongside men I can honestly say are the best of the best.

But three years had passed since I'd held the job I'd signed up for, and there was no way I would ever again be healthy or young enough to go back to it. It's strange to feel like an old man at thirty-one years of age, but that's the way it was for me. Ultimately, the navy agreed.

My career came to an end quietly and gradually, with three years of limited service—none of it involving jumping out of planes or hunting down bad guys or blowing things up. I was wounded. I'd suffered a traumatic brain injury. It happens. As a result, I didn't go out the way I would have liked, but that's often the case with guys in Special Operations. I tried not to feel sorry for myself. It could have been a whole lot worse. More than ninety members of the Naval Special Warfare community have been killed in action or during training exercises since 9/11. Hundreds more have been seriously wounded and struggle today with scars far more damaging than mine.

In all ways, I was lucky, and I had to remind myself of that fact—even on the very worst days.

After my retirement was official, I took a security job in Alabama. That was a mistake. It was much too soon. The headaches worsened, and the brain fog rolled in like a burgeoning storm. After six months, I left the job and filled the next year traveling with Natalie and the dogs. We spent time with her family in Florida and my family in Texas. We visited friends in various places around the country. Eventually, we bought a little house on a lake in East Texas and settled into a comfortable routine.

Through friends in the navy, I connected with some terrific folks at the Brain Treatment Foundation in Dallas, an organization devoted to providing support and guidance to combat veterans suffering from traumatic brain injuries and post-traumatic stress. A lot of vets struggle with symptoms related to their service, and often they feel like they have to suffer in silence. Alone. I felt that way a lot of the time. But there is help, and I was fortunate to find it. I'd like to help others find it, as well.

Through the Brain Treatment Foundation, I was referred to the Brain Treatment Center in Carlsbad, California, which is affiliated with the USC Neurorestoration Center. There I was exposed to therapies—transcranial magnetic stimulation, neurofeedback, brain stimulation—that were unlike anything I had tried in the past. Over time, I began to heal. The headaches and back spasms receded. Freed from chronic pain, I weaned myself off most medication, and my mood naturally lifted. Was this a result of alternative treatment or merely the passing of time? I don't know. Perhaps some combination of the two.

I still get headaches sometimes, and there are days when I think about the friends I have lost, and the cloud rolls in. But it passes. I don't stay in the dark for long. My memory is better than it has been in years. I feel . . . better. Almost whole again.

Natalie and I have added two more dogs to the family: another Malinois and a Dutch shepherd. They're cute as hell, and they keep us busy. Sometimes one of the Malinois will cross one paw over the other and tilt its head a certain way, and the resemblance to Cairo is uncanny.

And it makes me smile.

Occasionally, I have to travel for work—I take freelance security assignments, and I'm working with the Brain Treatment Foundation to encourage more veterans to seek help and support. Sometimes I'll take one or more of the dogs on the road with me. But even when they stay at home, I am rarely alone. That coffee can with the paw print? The one that contains Cairo's ashes? I usually carry it in my backpack when I'm on the road. I drive almost everywhere. Doesn't matter if the trip is two hundred miles or two thousand miles—I'd rather sit behind the wheel and roll down the windows and crank the music. Once in a while, though, I am forced to fly; it hasn't happened often, but there have been a couple of times when I have taken Cairo with me, which has caused some interesting reactions at airport security.

> **TSA screener (holding up coffee can, looking at paw prints):** What's this?
> **Me:** That's my dog, sir. He was my best friend.
> TSA screener (gently placing can back on table): Oh . . . I'm sorry.
> **Me:** That's okay. He goes everywhere with me.
> TSA screener (nodding sympathetically): I understand.

He doesn't really understand, of course. But then, how could he? I never tell anyone that the can contains the ashes of not just any dog but one of the most amazing dogs who ever lived. That's something I've always sort of kept to myself.

Lately, though, I've thought that it would be nice if more people knew about Cairo and had a chance to hear his story, and maybe connect with him in some way. I've been thinking about donating some of my personal memorabilia to the 9/11 Memorial, including reminders of my time with Cairo. I still have the bloodstained harness he wore the night he saved my life—and that he later wore during operation Neptune Spear. It would be hard to part with that, but it would be a fitting tribute to Cairo if others had a chance to see it.

Maybe I'll donate his ashes, as well, or at least a portion of his ashes. I'd like to keep some for myself, tucked safely in a coffee can in my backpack, so that Cairo is never far away, and so that he will always know . . .

*I love you, buddy.*